AQA Drama and Theatre Studies

A2

Exclusively endorsed by AQA

KT-178-704

21487467

Su Fielder
Pat Friday

 Nelson Thornes

Text © Su Fielder and Pat Friday 2008
Original illustrations © Nelson Thornes Ltd 2008

The right of Su Fielder and Pat Friday to be identified as authors of this work has been asserted by them in accordance with the Copyright, Designs and Patents Act 1988.

All rights reserved. No part of this publication may be reproduced or transmitted in any form or by any means, electronic or mechanical, including photocopy, recording or any information storage and retrieval system, without permission in writing from the publisher or under licence from the Copyright Licensing Agency Limited, of Saffron House, 6–10 Kirby Street, London, EC1N 8TS.

Any person who commits any unauthorised act in relation to this publication may be liable to criminal prosecution and civil claims for damages.

Published in 2008 by:
Nelson Thornes Ltd
Delta Place
27 Bath Road
CHELTENHAM
GL53 7TH
United Kingdom

08 09 10 11 12 / 10 9 8 7 6 5 4 3 2 1

A catalogue record for this book is available from the British Library

ISBN 978 0 7487 8290 1

Cover photograph by Corbis
Illustrations by Angela Knowles and Pantek Arts Ltd, Maidstone
Page make-up by Pantek Arts Ltd, Maidstone

Printed and bound in China

The authors and publishers wish to thank the following for permission to use copyright material:

p2: © Donald Cooper/Photostage; p4: © Donald Cooper/Photostage; p6: © Donald Cooper/Photostage; p7(both): © Danny Lehman/Corbis; p10: © Donald Cooper/Photostage; p11: © Donald Cooper/Photostage; p16: © Donald Cooper/Photostage; p20" © Donald Cooper/Photostage; p24: © Donald Cooper/Photostage; p27: © Donald Cooper/Photostage; p31: © UWM Libraries, Archives Department, Mark Avery Photography Records, UWM Manuscript Collection 155; p35: Tom Lawlor © Gate Theatre/ArenaPAL; p36: © Donald Cooper/Photostage; p37: © Ivan Kyncl/ArenaPAL; p38: © Donald Cooper/Photostage; p44: © Donald Cooper/Photostage; p47: © Donald Cooper/Photostage; p49: © Donald Cooper/Photostage; p50: © UWM Libraries, Archives Department, Mark Avery Photography Records, UWM Manuscript Collection 155; p51: © Donald Cooper/Photostage; p64: © Richard H. Smith; p65: Richard H. Smith; p72: © Donald Cooper/Photostage; p72: © Donald Cooper/Photostage; p78: © University of South Carolina – Department of Theatre and Dance; p85: © Roger Morton; p86: © Bettmann/Corbis; p86: © Roger Morton; p87: © Roger Morton; p92: © Donald Cooper/Photostage; p95: Mary Evans Picture Library; p98: © Catherine Ashmore, Coram Boy, The National Theatre; p110: © Ian Cole; p112: © Donald Cooper/Photostage; p116: © Forced Entertainment/Hugo Glendinning; p137: © Ed Dimsdale; p141: The students of Rugby School; p149: © Lebrecht Music & Arts/Corbis.

Penguin Group for extracts from Molière, 'Tartuffe' in *The Misanthrope and other Plays* by Molière, translated with an introduction by John Wood (1959). Copyright © John Wood 1959; The Wiley Agency UK Ltd on behalf of the Estate of the author for extracts from Arthur Miller, *A View from the Bridge*. Copyright © 1952 Arthur Miller.

Every effort has been made to contact the copyright holders and we apologise if any have been overlooked. Should copyright have been unwittingly infringed in this book, the owners should contact the publishers, who will make the corrections at reprint.

Contents

AQA introduction

Nelson Thornes and AQA

Nelson Thornes has worked in collaboration with AQA to ensure that this book offers you the best support for your AS or A Level course and helps you to prepare for your exams. The partnership means that you can be confident that the range of learning, teaching and assessment practice materials has been checked by the senior examining team at AQA before formal approval, and is closely matched to the requirements of your specification.

Blended learning

Printed and electronic resources are blended: this means that links between topics and activities between the book and the electronic resources help you to work in the way that best suits you, and enable extra support to be provided online. For example, you can test yourself online and feedback from the test will direct you back to the relevant parts of the book.

Electronic resources are available in a simple-to-use online platform called Nelson Thornes *learning space*. If your school or college has a licence to use the service, you will be given a password through which you can access the materials through any internet connection.

Icons in this book indicate where there is material online related to that topic. The following icons are used:

💡 Learning activity

These resources include a variety of interactive and non-interactive activities to support your learning.

✅ Progress tracking

These resources include a variety of tests that you can use to check your knowledge on particular topics (Test yourself) and a range of resources that enable you to analyse and understand examination questions (On your marks…).

🔎 Research support

These resources include WebQuests, in which you are assigned a task and provided with a range of web links to use as source material for research.

📑 Study skills

These resources support you in developing skills that are key for your course, for example planning essays.

🔍 Analysis tool

These resources help you to analyse key texts and images by providing questions and prompts to focus your response.

When you see an icon, go to Nelson Thornes *learning space* at www.nelsonthornes.com/aqagce, enter your access details and select your course. The materials are arranged in the same order as the topics in the book, so you can easily find the resources you need.

How to use this book

This book covers the specification for your course and is arranged in a sequence approved by AQA. The introduction contains information on what to expect in the Drama and Theatre Studies course, as well as how you will be assessed. Unit 3 is divided into 2 sections: Section A supports section A of the examination, focussing on the interpretation of the pre-twentieth century plays from a performance perspective. Section B supports section B of the exam, focussing on each of the twentieth century plays in turn and considering aspects of presentation. Unit 4 supports the practical presentation of a devised drama, focussing on specific theatre skills, theatrical styles and the supporting notes.

Definitions of any words that appear in bold can be found in the glossary at the back of this book.

Learning objectives

At the beginning of each section you will find a list of learning objectives that contain targets linked to the requirements of the specification.

The features in this book include:

Key terms

Terms that you will need to be able to define and understand. These words are coloured blue in the text book and their definition will also appear in the glossary at the back of this book.

Who's who

The names of key drama practitioners. The short biographies given are intended to enhance your understanding of drama and theatre studies and encourage further research.

Think

A short reflective activity. Thinking about the issues brought up in this feature will help you develop an interesting range of ideas that you can write about in your exam and coursework.

Theatre trivia

Fun facts about the theatre to add variety to your study.

Links

Links to other areas in the text book which are relevant to what you are reading.

Background information

Interesting facts to extend and support your background knowledge.

Activity

Activities which develop skills, knowledge and understanding that will prepare you for assessment in your drama and theatre studies course.

Further reading

Suggestions for other texts that will help you in your study and preparation for assessment in Drama and Theatre Studies.

AQA Examiner's tip

Hints from AQA examiners to help you with your study and to prepare for your exam.

AQA Examination-style questions

Questions in the style that you can expect in your exam.

AQA examination questions are reproduced by permission of the Assessment and Qualifications Alliance.

Introduction to Drama and Theatre Studies A2

In this introductory chapter you will learn about:

- how A2 builds on your experience of Drama and Theatre Studies at AS

- the similarities and differences between the AS and A2 courses

- how your work is assessed.

Drama and theatre studies, at A2 Level, is a course that builds on, deepens and extends the knowledge, understanding and skills that you acquired during your AS course.

The written unit, Unit 3, allows you to study two plays, each chosen from a range of six options. You are expected to choose one play that was written pre-20th century and one that was written in the 20th or 21st century.

The practical unit, Unit 4, allows you to devise your own drama within a theatrical style of your choice.

This book will help you to step up from AS Level work to the more challenging demands of A2 Level work. However, you should still draw on the guidance offered in the AS coursebook as you consider your new set texts from the points of view of director, designer and performer. There will be references back to specific chapters in your AS coursebook, so do ensure you have a copy on hand.

Similarities between the AS and A2 courses

- At A2, you will continue to study set plays in order to discover how meaning can be communicated to an audience through the collaboration of a director, designers and performers.

- At A2, you will still go on theatre visits as preparation for presenting your own practical work.

- At A2, you will still work in groups to create theatre for an audience, realising clear dramatic intentions.

Differences between the AS and A2 courses

- At A2, you are expected to formulate your own 'creative overview' of each of your two set texts and to be able to demonstrate, in your examination answers, that you understand the whole play and the playwright's intentions throughout.

- At A2, you will visit the theatre to support your research into a particular style of theatre which you will explore in your practical work; you will not have to write about live productions in an examination.

- At A2, your practical examination is not of a published play but of your own devised drama which you will create collaboratively in your groups; you will be drawing upon all your shared drama experiences to achieve a piece of theatre, performed in your chosen style, for an audience.

How will my work be assessed and examined?

As in your AS year, you will take one written paper, Unit 3, at the end of the A2 course. This examination assesses your knowledge, understanding and creative interpretation of your chosen set plays.

You will take one practical test, Unit 4, in the spring or summer term, in which your ability to devise drama in a specific style, chosen by your group and developed collaboratively, will be assessed in performance.

AQA Examiner's tip

You may choose any recognisable theatrical style for your devised work. The specification offers the following as examples: comedy/tragedy/melodrama/farce; commedia; naturalism/realism/expressionism/symbolism; epic theatre; political theatre/feminist theatre; Theatre of Cruelty; creative adaptation (of well-known stories or poems, not plays); docu-theatre; verbatim theatre; physical theatre.

▨ The units at a glance

Unit 3: Prescribed plays – written examination

A2 Unit 3 is assessed by a written paper divided into two sections: A and B. Section A will offer you a choice of two questions on your chosen pre-20th-century set play. Section B contains a single compulsory question on your selected 20th/21st century text.

You will need to be aware of the social, cultural and historical context of your selected plays in both sections of the unit.

Section A

For Section A, you will study one of the following plays:

▨ *The Revenger's Tragedy*, by Thomas Middleton/Cyril Tourneur (1607)
▨ *Tartuffe*, by Molière (1664)
▨ *The Recruiting Officer*, by George Farquhar (1706)
▨ *The Servant of Two Masters*, by Carlo Goldoni (1746)
▨ *Lady Windermere's Fan*, by Oscar Wilde (1892)
▨ *The Seagull*, by Anton Chekhov (1896).

As at AS Level, exam questions will ask you to adopt the point of view of a director, an actor or a designer. However, unlike AS Level, the questions will not refer to specific sections of the play.

So, if you have been asked to write about how you would perform a particular character, for example, you will have to select your own examples from the play to support your ideas for performance. Your selection of appropriate moments from the play will be an important aspect of demonstrating your understanding of the character's role and purpose.

Whether you are answering a question from the point of view of a director, a designer or a performer, you will need to select examples from the play that suggest you have a creative overview of it. You will also need to demonstrate your understanding of the playwright's intentions in creating specific characters or presenting specific scenes in a particular way to contribute to the meaning of the play as a whole.

This is a more sophisticated task than the one you were asked to fulfil in Unit 1, Section B, at AS Level.

As you did at AS Level, you will need to consider the following production and performance elements in your study of your set text in Section A:

▨ choice and use of staging form/performance space
▨ the actor/audience relationship
▨ casting and appearance of characters
▨ physical qualities/age/build/height/facial features
▨ movement/posture/gesture/facial expression
▨ vocal qualities – volume/pitch/accent/pace/timing/intonation/phrasing/emotional range
▨ visual qualities – costume/make-up/mask/use of props
▨ character motivation and interaction
▨ development of pace and pitch/climax
▨ stage directions and practical demands of the text
▨ patterns of stage movement

- creation of mood and atmosphere
- design fundamentals – scale/shape/colour/texture
- use of scenic devices – revolves/trucks/projections
- use of lighting – direction/colour/intensity/special effects
- use of sound – direction/amplification/music and/or sound effects, both live and recorded
- other technical elements – pyrotechnics/smoke machines/flying.

Section B

For Section B, you will study one of the following 20th century or contemporary plays:

- *Blood Wedding*, by Federico García Lorca (1933), translated by Gwynne Edwards, published by Methuen Drama
- *The Good Person of Szechwan*, by Bertolt Brecht (1943), translated by John Willett, published by Methuen Drama
- *A View from the Bridge*, by Arthur Miller (1955)
- *The Trial*, by Steven Berkoff (1981)
- *Our Country's Good*, by Timberlake Wertenbaker (1988)
- *Coram Boy*, adapted by Helen Edmundson from the novel by Jamila Gavin (2005).

The way in which the 20th century/contemporary set text is examined is different from AS Level. Section B represents an aspect of **synoptic assessment**, drawing upon your experiences of drama and theatre as acquired throughout the course. In Section B, you will need to offer suggestions for a complete stage realisation of an extract from your set text, which will be printed on the exam paper. The extract will be about 70 lines long – that is roughly between two and three pages of your play text.

There will be a single compulsory question asking you for your interpretation of the extract. The question will be:

> As a director, discuss how you would stage the following extract in order to bring out your interpretation of it for an audience.
>
> Your answer should include suggestions for the direction of your cast and for the design of the piece. You will need to justify how your suggestions are appropriate to the style of the play and to your creative overview of it.
>
> You should also supply sketches and/or diagrams and refer to relevant research to support your ideas.

Aspects of the presentation of the extract to be considered may include some of the following:

- choice and configuration of stage space
- actor/audience relationship
- direction of actors, both physically and vocally
- interaction, delivery of dialogue, motivation, subtext
- use of space; groupings, movement, use of levels
- the stage setting and design
- creation of period, style and atmosphere
- costume design
- make-up and/or mask design
- creation of pace, tension, comedy, pathos, mood (as appropriate)
- application of technical elements and special effects.

Key term

Synoptic assessment: the type of examination that tests your knowledge and understanding of the connections between different aspects of your course. For example, in Unit 3, Section B, you will draw on your theatrical knowledge and experience, acquired throughout the course, in order to answer the question.

Unit 4: Presentation of devised drama – practical examination

For this unit you will be working in groups to present a piece of devised drama in a theatrical style of your choice. Your group should contain between two and eight students offering acting as their chosen skill and may include, in addition, a director, a set designer, a costume designer and one or two technical designers. These guidelines are exactly the same as those issued for your AS practical work. The performance of the devised piece (which may treat any subject matter, theme or topic) should last between 15 and 40 minutes, depending upon the size of your group.

Your teacher will guide you in your choice of theatrical style. You will need to undertake research into that style and to provide evidence of your research in your supporting notes. These notes should follow the same format and length as those you produced to support your practical work at AS Level. Further details about the devising process will be found in Chapter 22.

1 Context, period and genre

In this section you will learn about:

- the context, period and genre of your set play

- different styles of pre-20th-century theatre.

AQA Examiner's tip

Read the material about *all* of the set plays, not just the one you have chosen to study. This will broaden your knowledge of theatre and also deepen your appreciation of the range of theatrical styles as you begin your devising work for Unit 4.

Who's who

Thomas Middleton (1570–1627): produced comedies and tragedies which offered a keen insight into early 17th-century society. He is admired especially for his perceptive presentation of women. He collaborated with William Rowley (1585–1637) in writing *The Changeling* (1622) and possibly with Cyril Tourneur in writing *The Revenger's Tragedy*.

Cyril Tourneur (1575–1626): associated with the authorship or joint authorship of a number of Jacobean plays.

Key term

Revenge tragedy: Elizabethan/ Jacobean popular drama in which the main character seeks bloody revenge for the murder of a close friend or relative. In some plays, the revenge action ends up destroying both the revenger and his or her victim(s).

Chapter 12 of your AS coursebook focused on the importance of understanding the context, **period** and **genre** of the play(s) that you were studying. At A2 Level, it is equally important to have a full understanding of these aspects of your selected play.

All the plays covered in this section were written before the 20th century. One of your primary tasks, whichever play you are studying, will be to understand how context, period and genre affect the production style of the play.

As you think about your own interpretation of your chosen text you will need to find out as much as you can about the period in which the play was written and about the composition of its original audiences. All of these plays are classic texts that have stood the test of time. They have been interpreted and re-interpreted in many different ways since they were first produced.

The Revenger's Tragedy, 1607

Although the authorship of *The Revenger's Tragedy* is disputed, it has become acceptable to acknowledge the likely collaboration between two **Jacobean** playwrights: **Thomas Middleton** and **Cyril Tourneur**. Its title suggests that it is written in the style of **Revenge tragedy.**

Period and production context

The play was written early in the 17th century but it harks back to even earlier forms of drama. Seneca was the Roman dramatist (4BC–AD65) who provided a model for some Jacobean playwrights. His plays were written to be read aloud rather than performed. He wrote, amongst other things, dramas that contained bloody, sensational scenes, introducing ghosts, tyrants and witches, strewing the 'stage' with horrific images of murdered men and women.

Seneca's style was imitated by Thomas Kyd (1558–94). Kyd's own version of the Senecan bloodbath, *The Spanish Tragedy*, was the prototype for many Jacobean tragedies, including *The Revenger's Tragedy*.

There are also elements of medieval forms of drama where characters are presented as personified abstractions of various vices and virtues. For example, in *The Revenger's Tragedy*, **Lussorioso's** name means 'lecherous', and **Supervacuo's** name means 'vain and superfluous'. **Castiza's** name signifies her chastity and **Gratiana's** name suggests her grace.

A final influence upon the style of the play is that of the dramatic **satire** which was popular at the turn of the century. In this play, satire contributes to an almost comical, grotesquely farcical style as deaths pile up and murders are committed in an increasingly outrageous manner.

■ Theatre trivia

John Webster's play *The White Devil* contains several bizarre but inventive murders:

- Duke Brachiano murders his wife by poisoning the portrait of himself that she habitually kisses at bedtime.

- He then has his lover's husband strangled during exercise over a vaulting horse.

- His dead wife's brother then ensures that Brachiano also suffers a painful death by sprinkling the helmet of his armour with a corrosive poison that eats into his head!

■ Activity

Watch the film *The Revenger's Tragedy*, starring Christopher Eccleston as **Vindice** and Eddie Izzard as **Lussurioso**. The film's director, Alex Cox, transposed the setting to the 21st century (2011) and set it against the urban landscape of inner-city Liverpool.

Context to the play's action

In common with many plays of the time, Middleton/Tourneur set the action of the play within the court of an Italian Duke rather than suggesting that the British monarchy itself was a hotbed of intrigue and sin. The king and his court were great patrons of the theatre, so the authors would not have risked causing offence by such a direct correlation.

However, *The Revenger's Tragedy* was undoubtedly written as a response to the corruption of the court of James I, where the corrosive effect of concentrating wealth and authority into the hands of a few privileged noblemen was highly evident. On one day alone, King James created 40 new noble titles for his favourite courtiers.

These favourites wielded tremendous power and indulged their sensual appetites at the expense of those less fortunate than themselves. However, their status was often transitory. The play is full of references to ruined gentlemen and discarded ladies who, finding themselves out of favour at court, were left destitute, with no means of supporting their families.

One such family is that of the hero of the play, the revenger, **Vindice**. We learn in his opening speech to the audience that **Vindice's** fiancée, **Gloriana**, was poisoned by the **Duke** for refusing to sleep with him and that **Vindice's** father, having lost his place at court due to the malice of the same **Duke**, died of 'discontent'.

The plot of the play revolves around **Vindice's** determination to be revenged upon the perpetrator of these two evil deeds. However, as the play progresses, he widens the scope of his revenge and determines to purge the entire court of its corrupt and loathsome inner circle.

Fig. 1.1 *Kris Marshall as* **Vindice**, *with Linda Marlowe as* **Gratiana** *and James Howard as* **Hippolito** *from a 2006 production of* **The Revenger's Tragedy** *by Meredith Oakes*

Genre

It is difficult to offer a single generic description of *The Revenger's Tragedy*. We have already used the following words to describe the play's action:

▨ grotesque

▨ comical

▨ satirical

and yet, the play's title points very clearly to its being a tragedy and a specific type of tragedy, a revenge tragedy.

The tragedy of the play is, as the title suggests, **Vindice's** tragedy. As his schemes become more elaborate and he moves from one successful strike to another, he begins to display hubris (excessive pride) in his own murderous ingenuity. In confessing his hand in the murder of the **Duke** and his vile son, **Lussorioso**, to the incoming, wholly good, new **Duke Antonio**, **Vindice** effectively writes his own death warrant.

In attempting to destroy the immorality of the court, **Vindice** himself has become amoral and, recognising this to be true, he goes willingly to his death. The fall of the good man, **Vindice**, into misery, because of his moral degeneration, is the stuff of tragedy.

What makes *The Revenger's Tragedy* so different from classical forms of the genre is the wit and ingenuity of **Vindice** as he adopts successive disguises to enable him to carry out his revenges.

The drama is constructed in a witty, comical fashion as a sequence of theatrical **set-pieces**. For example, at one point **Vindice** is contracted by the sinister **Lussurioso** to kill the character that he has been pretending to be!

In another scene **Vindice** acts as a pander (pimp) to the **Duke**, and he even dresses up the skull of his dead fiancée to resemble a young woman fit for the **Duke's** pleasure. It is by kissing the poisoned 'lips' of **Gloriana's** skull that the **Duke** meets his gruesome end.

While the **Duke** lies dying, **Vindice** forces him to watch his **Duchess** cavorting with his own bastard son.

Recent productions have tended to highlight these comically grotesque aspects of the play rather than the tragedy of **Vindice's** moral fall.

ⓘ *Tartuffe*, 1664

Jean-Baptiste Poquelin Molière (1622–1673) is generally considered to be one of France's greatest dramatists, responsible for producing some of the finest comedies in the history of European theatre. At the height of his career, Molière enjoyed the patronage of **Louis XIV** of France, who was one of the most powerful monarchs in Europe during the 17th century.

Period and production context

Molière's chief contribution to theatre lies in his comic invention. His early plays were farces based on the style of **commedia dell'arte** but he is most famous for a series of more mature comedies, which were written and performed before the king between 1658 and 1673.

Molière took the farcical situations and style of the broad comedy that he found in the work of classical and European predecessors and crafted

▨ Link

Look back at the material about the genre of tragedy in the AS coursebook, Chapter 12.

▨ Further reading

Keith Sturgess, *Jacobean Private Theatre*, Routledge, 1987

G Blakemore, ed, *Elizabethan-Jacobean Drama*, Black, 1989

Martin White, *Middleton & Tourneur*, Macmillan, 1992

Una Ellis-Fermor, *The Jacobean Drama*, Methuen, 1936

www.filmeducation.org. Go to 'Film Library A-Z', then select 'R' and find *The Revenger's Tragedy*. You will find a useful study guide.

www.izzardlounge.com. Click on 'Films', then *Revenger's Tragedy* (2001)

▨ Who's who

Louis XIV: the king of France from 1638–1715. He was known as the 'Sun King'. During his reign he replaced the old feudal system with a centralised form of government and attained military and political pre-eminence in Europe.

▨ Key term

Commedia dell'arte: a comic genre that originated in Italy in the 16th century and was popular across Europe until the end of the 18th century. Performances were improvised around a series of stock characters and skeletal scenarios. Characters such as Pantalone, the Capitano and the comic servants – the Zanni – crop up again and again and were immediately recognisable by their distinctive costumes and masks.

these into a form of social satire that had not been seen before. He has been credited with 'bringing comedy indoors' (traditionally comedies tended to have outdoor settings) and exposing the hypocrisy and folly underpinning bourgeois family life.

Tartuffe represents one of Molière's finest achievements. Molière first presented *Tartuffe* in 1664 as part of a lavish festival of entertainments, including drama, ballets and operas that he organised for the king and court at the Palace of Versailles.

The play, which, though immensely funny, also contains a scathing attack upon religious hypocrisy, caused great offence amongst a section of the audience, who saw the play as an attack upon religion itself. The performance provoked moral outrage and Louis XIV, despite being a devoted supporter of Molière, thought it prudent to ban any further performances of the play in order to appease the religious zealots (extremists) who opposed it.

However, the play was frequently performed in private houses and Molière finally gained the king's permission to give public performances of a re-worked version of his masterpiece in 1669.

Context to the play's action

While *The Revenger's Tragedy* is set within an ostentatious court setting, presided over by a corrupt **Duke** and his debauched family of sons, the action of Molière's *Tartuffe* is presented within a contemporary domestic setting in the mid 1660s.

Molière invites his audience into the Parisian family home of **Orgon** and his wife, **Elmire**. The cast is small, comprising the foolish **Orgon**, his pious mother, his wife, his brother, **Cléante**, and his two children, **Mariane** and **Damis**. **Mariane** is in love with a perfectly suitable young man, **Valère**, who has already gained **Orgon's** permission to marry his daughter. The family is served by the witty maid, **Dorine**, who, in the tradition of commedia dell'arte, has a good deal more sense than her employer.

Into this apparently normal household, the hypocritical and fraudulent character, **Tartuffe** has insinuated himself and persuaded both **Orgon** and **Orgon's** mother, **Madame Pernelle**, that he is sincerely religious and virtuous. **Orgon** decides to marry his daughter to **Tartuffe** and to disinherit his son in favour of the hypocrite. The rest of the family are not deceived by **Tartuffe's** odious nature but watch powerlessly as the head of the family, **Orgon**, is thoroughly tricked.

Orgon's family, though presented as loyal subjects of the king, are not in any way connected to life at court. It is only in the final moments of the play, when **Orgon** appears to be about to lose everything he possesses to the repulsive, **Tartuffe**, that catastrophe is averted by the arrival of an officer, bearing a warrant for **Tartuffe's** arrest signed by the king himself.

The speech of the officer at the end of the play commends the king as a monarch 'who can read men's hearts, whom no impostor's art deceives'. This speech was undoubtedly added to the play before its revival in 1669 and reveals how significant it was for Molière's survival as a playwright to pay homage to his king in the play.

Fig. 1.2 Paul Eddington as Orgon, hiding under the table while John Sessions, as Tartuffe, seduces Elmire, played by Jennifer Ehle in a 1991 production of Ranjit Bolt's translation of Tartuffe

Genre

Tartuffe is a comedy that draws upon both commedia dell'arte and satire, resulting in a drama that contains comedy of character as well as comedy of situation. In seeking to expose and ridicule vice, Molière, follows a long line of satirical writers. Many commentators describe the genre of the play as **comedy of manners.**

The play contains a serious message in its withering attack on religious hypocrites, but most audiences remember the play for the hilarious, farcical set-piece which sees Orgon's mounting frustration as he watches helplessly, from his hiding place under a table, while Tartuffe, thinking himself alone with Elmire, abandons his façade of piety and attempts to seduce her.

The Recruiting Officer, 1706

George Farquhar's play, *The Recruiting Officer* is generally considered to be one of the last examples of **restoration comedy,** containing many of the features that made the genre so popular.

It is a play that was first performed in 1706 and has rarely been absent from theatre repertoires ever since.

Period and production context

Farquhar wrote a series of successful comedies for the late Restoration stage, the most famous pair being *The Recruiting Officer* (1706) and *The Beaux Stratagem* (1707).

Audiences in the Restoration period were one of the most uniform in English theatre history and largely comprised the wealthiest and most apparently refined members of their society. Nevertheless their behaviour was decadent and J.L. Styan in his book on Restoration comedy suggests that the regular theatre audiences were the same folk that regularly attended the 'parks, brothels and gaming tables' of the time and that they classed a night at the theatre as pure entertainment.

Even in the early 18th century, when Farquhar was writing, the price of a theatre ticket was beyond the reach of most ordinary citizens. The audience continued to be made up of the wealthy classes who paid good money to see people like themselves portrayed on stage.

Farquhar's play was unusual in its time because it offered a different perspective on society. His cast list included a significant number of characters from the middle and working classes.

Context to the play's action

The Recruiting Officer deals with the twin themes of love and war. Farquhar based the play upon his own experiences of having been a Recruiting Officer in Shrewsbury. He therefore created a realistic setting of Shrewsbury, and presented the realistic action of officers recruiting men to fight for their country. He used this premise to explore two themes: the relationships between men and women and the methods used by unscrupulous officers to entice ignorant men to enlist into the army.

These are universal themes, but for the 18th century they had particular relevance. In the 1700s, women were not free to choose the men they wished to marry, since marriage amongst the gentry was linked directly to financial considerations. The 18th century was a time of international political instability and England's national security depended upon ordinary soldiers to support military action abroad.

The social context of the play's action is the provincial world of Shrewsbury, and Farquhar peopled the play with a variety of characters

▮ Theatre trivia

Molière died on stage in 1673. Ironically, he was playing the title role in his biting satire on hypochondriacs, entitled *The Imaginary Invalid.*

▮ Key term

Restoration comedy: comic drama written and performed in England after the restoration of the monarchy in 1660. Once Charles II was firmly established on the throne and the Puritan laws prohibiting theatre were lifted, a new form of comedy, full of vigour and risqué humour, was developed.

▮ Further reading

In *Letters to George*, Nick Hern Books, 1989, Max Stafford-Clark offers an insight into his production of the play, which he presented as a companion piece to the first production of *Our Country's Good*, at the Royal Court in the same year.

▮ Link

Refresh your memory about the Restoration Theatre by looking again at the section on *Playhouse Creatures* in the AS coursebook in Chapter 12.

▮ Further reading

J.L. Styan, *Restoration Comedy in Performance*, Cambridge University Press, 1986

Max Stafford-Clark, *Letters to George*, Nick Hern Books, 1989

from the middle and lower classes. In addition to the witty maid, **Lucy**, the cast includes potential recruits, a **Butcher**, a **Blacksmith** and a **Constable**, as well as the country wench, **Rose** and her stupid brother, **Bullock**. This was quite a departure from conventional characters found in Restoration comedy who usually represented the leisured classes.

Fig. 1.3 *Alex Jennings as* **Plume**, *with Sally Dexter as* **Sylvia** *and Desmond Barrit as* **Brazen** *in the 1992 production of* **The Recruiting Officer** *at the National Theatre*

Nevertheless, some of the standard Restoration features are easy to identify. They are:

- a heroic lead figure who is depicted as a rake (a man who lives an irresponsible, immoral life) – **Plume**
- a romantic second leading man – **Worthy**
- a witty girl – **Melinda**
- a serious but ingenious girl – **Silvia**
- a clever maid – **Lucy**
- implausible plot devices such as forged letters and improbable disguises. **Kite**, the astrologer, is one such invention; **Silvia**, disguised as a man in breeches, is the more common comic device of the Restoration genre.

Genre

The Recruiting Officer is recognised as one of the last examples of the Restoration comic style before it gave way to the more sentimental comedy of Sheridan and Goldsmith.

ⓘ *The Servant of Two Masters*, 1746

Although *The Servant of Two Masters* was written by **Carlo Goldoni** nearly eighty years later than Molière's play, *Tartuffe*, it also has its roots in the **commedia dell'arte** tradition. Goldoni was a prolific dramatist whose contribution to the theatre was to reform the improvisational nature of the commedia dell'arte form, harnessing its comic energy to a more realistic style of theatre.

▓ **Link**

The site indicated below allows you to explore the exterior and interior of several Restoration theatre buildings as well as providing further useful information about them. Once you get to the St Andrews University homepage, do a search for 'Theatres', then select the result entitled 'Theatres', which is a webpage designed by a member of staff.

www.st-andrews.ac.uk

▓ **Theatre trivia**

Farquhar began his career as an actor rather than a playwright. It was only after seriously wounding a fellow actor in an on-stage duel that he decided that writing was a less dangerous occupation!

▓ **Who's who**

Carlo Goldoni (1707–1793): born in Venice, he became a lawyer but his chief love was for theatre. He is credited with transforming the commedia dell'arte style from an improvisational jumble of styles and ideas to a scripted comic form capable of revealing character as well as delivering laughs.

Period and production context

When Goldoni began to write comedy, the commedia dell'arte form had been fully established for nearly 200 years. Commedia was a popular form of entertainment, often performed outdoors, by groups of travelling players. The fact that the acting troupes travelled all over Europe, as well as to England, meant that their influence was felt far and wide and different countries evolved different variants on the original form.

In Italy, each commedia company contained performers who would play only one role and they would play the same role again and again in different **scenarios** throughout their careers.

Stock characters included young lovers, greedy old men, boastful captains and cheeky, energetic servants. These characters even had the same names from scenario to scenario. For example, a young lover was commonly called Silvio, an old man, Pantalone, a doctor or lawyer would be Il Dottier and comic servants were often known as Brighella and Arlecchino – a 'stupid' fellow from Bergamo.

Although there were hundreds of commedia scenarios invented by different companies, many of the plot-lines were very similar. The stories often depicted young lovers prevented from marrying by parents, or some other obstacle to their affection, yet invariably, helped by their comic servants, their story ended happily. According to Lee Hall, in the introduction to his adaptation of *The Servant of Two Masters* (entitled *A Servant to Two Masters*), the recurrent themes of these scenarios were 'food, sex, love and money'.

Apart from the young lovers, the rest of the commedia characters wore masks that instantly signalled their stock characters to the audience.

Fig. 1.4 *Commedia dell'arte masks*

The scenarios were performed in the open air in town and village squares, on raised platforms, with a minimum of scenery consisting of a backdrop and wings. These scenes often depicted a town square like the one they were performing in.

The audiences paid for the privilege of watching skilled comedians performing familiar situations in an inventive way, improvising both verbal exchanges and physical knockabout comedy within scenarios that depicted everyday life in a highly exaggerated form.

Before Goldoni introduced the idea of a fully scripted play, the commedia actors used to memorise speeches, poems and essays from a range of contemporary and classical writers in order to be able to draw from them during their performances. The actors would also rehearse **lazzi**, which were set-pieces of comical business, often performed with acrobatic skill.

Many features of commedia dell'arte appear as ingredients of Goldoni's play:

- The characters, **Pantalone**, **Brighella**, **Dr Lombardi**, **Clarice** and **Silvio** have stepped directly out of a typical commedia scenario.
- **Truffaldino** and **Smeraldina** are the cheeky young servants.
- The obstacle to the marriage of **Silvio** and **Clarice** appears in the form of a suitor, presumed dead, who suddenly appears to claim 'his' bride.
- **Truffaldino's** scheme to serve two masters is born of hunger and greed – two motivating forces in commedia; his ingenuity combined with a form of stupidity that originates in Bergamo.
- A number of lazzi, including the business with the trunk and the old porter, **Truffaldino's** re-sealing of **Beatrice's** letter, the hectic serving of the meal to two hungry 'masters' at once.
- Both sets of lovers are united at the end of the play, either because of or in spite of **Truffaldino's** dishonesty; **Truffaldino** also 'gets the girl' in **Smeraldina**.

Context to the play's action

In common with all commedia scenarios, the play is set in the period in which it was written – in this case the middle of the 18th century – to reflect the experiences of its original audience. The location is Venice and the play opens in the home of Pantalone and his young daughter, **Clarice**. Much of the later action takes place outside **Brighella's** inn in a public square. The action concerns the proposed marriage between **Clarice** and **Silvio** both from respectable families. **Beatrice** and **Florindo** are also members of the Italian gentry; the servant figures complete the picture of provincial society that the play reflects.

Genre

Clearly, the play is a comedy. It is worth remembering that Goldoni, in adapting the traditional commedia dell'arte style, was breaking new ground. Although not a realistic play, *The Servant of Two Masters* presents a set of characters who express some genuine feelings of loss, jealousy and longing, in the course of the action, albeit within a fairly implausible scenario which is punctuated by a series of potentially hilarious lazzi.

i Lady Windermere's Fan, 1892

Oscar Wilde is known equally for his work as a playwright and for his sparkling wit and his decadent lifestyle which scandalised his contemporaries.

Oscar Wilde's off-the-cuff quips are famous. On being asked by Customs' Officers when he arrived in New York if he had 'Anything to declare?', he is reported to have replied 'I have nothing to declare except my genius'. When asked about the first night performance of *Lady Windermere's Fan*, he responded 'Oh, the play was a great success but the audience was a total failure'.

His plays are strewn with similar epigrams (short witty sayings).

Further reading

John Rudlin, *Commedia dell'arte: An Actor's Handbook*, Routledge, 1994

Mel Gordon, *Lazzi: Comic Routines of the Commedia dell'arte*, Johns Hopkins University Press, NY, 1983

Barry Grantham, *Playing Commedia: A Training Guide to Commedia Techniques*, Heinemann, 2000

www.commedia-del-arte.com

Who's who

Oscar Wilde (1854–1900): an Irish playwright and poet famed as a society wit and for his decadent lifestyle. His most famous play is *The Importance of Being Ernest*. He was imprisoned for homosexual offences when at the height of his career and endured two years' hard labour in Reading gaol.

Oscar Wilde's plays are difficult to categorise because Wilde himself appeared so completely unwilling to take life seriously that even the serious issues that he explores in some of his dramas are treated comically.

Period and production context

Wilde began writing for the theatre towards the end of the Victorian period. Theatre buildings and facilities had changed enormously over the preceding century and with the increased standard of living of all classes of society, theatre-going had become a truly popular form of entertainment.

Audiences grew to record numbers and included a greater diversity of people than ever before. London theatre attracted new audiences and melodrama became a staple of the London stage, catering for more popular tastes.

Towards the end of the century, however, a new type of drama emerged that was concerned with social issues and problems and which attracted a more refined audience. These plays were partly influenced by developments in modern European drama, and the plays of Ibsen in particular, and partly by the structure of **the well-made play** that English playwrights had been extensively copying since the middle of the century.

Ironically, it was this stale dramatic formula that Wilde completely revamped and used as a vehicle for his witty social dramas, *Lady Windermere's Fan*, *A Woman of No Importance* (1893) and *An Ideal Husband* (1895).

In Wilde's hands, however, the exploration of social injustice is both immensely entertaining and deeply cynical. *Lady Windermere's Fan*, while apparently exposing the hypocrisy of society and the inherent virtue of a 'fallen woman', actually celebrates the selfishness and cunning of the two 'sophisticates' Mrs Erlynne and the wicked Lord Darlington by giving them the majority of witty lines and rewarding them with a continuation of their lavish lifestyles.

Lady Windermere's Fan was first produced by actor-manager, George Alexander. It was staged at the St James Theatre, in a meticulously realistic box set, mirroring, in both furnishings and costume design, the world of the fashionable society who made up the audience for the play.

Context to the play's action

The context of the action of *Lady's Windermere's Fan* is Wilde's contemporary society, the English upper classes at leisure. The action takes place over a period of 24 hours, beginning with Lady Windermere preparing for a dance party in honour of her birthday and ending the following day after what could have been a disastrous decision to leave her husband. The events of the play are tied completely to a specific social class and to a specific period of time in London at the end of the 19th century.

In the course of the play the audience is invited to consider whether it is right or wrong to condemn adulterous women and to exclude them from society. They are also invited to consider whether Mrs Erlynne is a good woman or not. Wilde's sub-title to the play is 'A Play about a Good Woman'.

In this respect the play might be considered very dated, but Wilde's treatment of the situation is so completely 'tongue-in-cheek' that the issue retains its freshness despite the shift in the contemporary moral climate.

Link

See Chapter 2 in your AS coursebook for a summary of the changes to the fabric of the buildings.

Link

See Chapter 12 in your AS coursebook to refresh your memory about Ibsen's social drama.

Key term

The well-made play: this was a label given to plays with a formulaic structure which originated in France in the early 1800s. The chief exponent of the form was Eugene Scribe. The form was so mechanical and the dialogue so feeble that, eventually, no self-respecting actor wished to appear in his plays.

Fig. 1.5 *Vanessa Redgrave as* Mrs Erlynne *and her real-life daughter, Joely Richardson, as* Lady Windermere *in Peter Hall's 2002 production of Wilde's* Lady Windermere's Fan

■ **Further reading**

Richard Ellman, *Oscar Wilde*, Vintage, 1988

Oscar Wilde's Wit and Wisdom: a book of quotations, Dover Thrift, 1998

H. Montgomery Hyde, *Oscar Wilde: A Biography* Penguin Books, 2001

www.oscarwildesociety.co.uk. Click on 'Publications'.

Genre

The play is a witty social comedy and it has the structure of a well-made play. Despite the limited depth of characterisation (several characters are named after English place names) it takes a world view so completely at one with that of its playwright as to place it, almost, in a genre of its own. Wildean comedy is like no other.

■ **Activity**

Watch Mike Barker's 2005 film adaptation *A Good Woman*. It stars Helen Hunt as Mrs Erlynne and Scarlett Johansson as Lady Windermere. The play's action has been transposed from fashionable London to the Amalfi coast in Italy.

ⓘ *The Seagull*, 1896

Anton Chekhov (1860–1904) is Russia's most famous playwright. Although trained as a doctor, and famous for his short stories, Chekhov's reputation rests on four full-length major plays, *The Seagull* (1896), *Uncle Vanya* (1899), *Three Sisters* (1901) and *The Cherry Orchard* (1904). All of these plays have stood the test of time and continue to be produced and to fascinate audiences in theatres all over the world.

Period and production context

■ **Who's who**

Nikolai Vasilievich Gogol (1809–52): a Russian playwright and novelist, famed for his realistic style and his satirical insights into contemporary Russian society.

Ivan Sergeivich Turgenev (1818–83): a Russian playwright and novelist, famed for his realistic portrayal of everyday life and his sensitive revelation of the inner feelings of his characters.

The repertoire of Russian theatre at the end of the 19th century was not dissimilar to that of London. Audiences enjoyed melodrama, light comedy and musical pieces as they did all over Europe. Russian playwrights also 'borrowed' heavily from the French well-made plays.

In contrast to the English stage, however, Russia had seen the emergence of more serious drama in the course of the 19th century. Gogol's biting satire, *The Government Inspector* had caused such a stir that **Gogol** left the country in fear of reprisals. **Turgenev** wrote *A Month in the Country*, which was first performed in 1872, and anticipated Chekhov's style in its exploration of the theme of unrequited love, as well as in its focus on a group of characters rather than on one individual.

Chekhov himself was scathing about the state of Russian theatre which he described as both mediocre and outdated. His own early plays were one-act comedies but it is for his later plays – the plays that have been categorised by David Magarshack as the 'plays of indirect action' – that he is most famous.

The Seagull was first performed in 1896 in St Petersburg and it was a spectacular flop. The audience at the first night virtually hooted it off the stage, finding the characters and their situation utterly preposterous. Chekhov and his cast were devastated by the response.

Two years later, in a production for the Moscow Art Theatre, directed by Constantin Stanislavski, the play was a triumph. This says as much about the importance of a director's interpretation as it does about how different audiences react to the same play. However, *The Seagull* is a remarkably difficult play to categorise, and therefore to interpret, as it consists of a mixture of moods and tones that take the audience on a sometimes bewildering emotional journey. It is not always clear which characters they are meant to sympathise with at any one time.

Chekhov's characters are all drawn in great detail. In *The Seagull*, as in his other major plays, the seemingly inconsequential detail of everyday life is presented on stage with great realism. However, the **subtext** reveals the momentous emotions of the seemingly ordinary people of the play. You will remember from Chapter 16 in your AS coursebook (page 111), that the subtext of a play refers to the unspoken thoughts, feelings and motives of characters that actors are able to express through non-verbal means, through their use of body language, eye contact, pause and use of space.

The Seagull is therefore a play that is best brought to life by the kind of truthful performance style advocated by Stanislavski, where actors immerse themselves in the lives of their characters.

■ **Background information**

David Magarshack's influential book, *Chekhov the Dramatist*, Methuen, 1980, divides Chekhov's plays into two main categories: these are plays of 'direct action', where much of the 'action' of the play occurs on-stage; and plays of 'indirect action', where it occurs off-stage and is reported through the dialogue of the characters.

Fig. 1.6 *Johnathan Hyde as Dr Dorn, Romola Garai as Nina, Frances Barber as Arkadina with Ian McKellan as Sorin in Trevor Nunn's RSC production in 2007 of The Seagull by Chekhov*

■ Background information

The Russian Revolution occurred in 1917 when the autocratic ruler, Tsar Nicholas II, was overthrown. Soon after, the country was taken over by the Bolshevik (Communist) party led by Lenin. The Tsar and his family were murdered and the structure of Russian society was so altered by the changes imposed by the Bolsheviks that historians divide the history of the country into pre and post revolutionary eras.

■ Further reading

David Allen, *Performing Chekhov*, Routledge, 2000

David Magarshack, *Chekhov the Dramatist*, John Lehmann, 1952

Patrick Miles, *Chekhov on the British Stage 1909–1987*, Sam & Sam, 1987

Laurence Senelick, *The Chekhov Theatre: A Century of the Plays in Performance*, Cambridge University Press, 1997

Maurice Valency, *The Breaking String: The Plays of Anton Chekhov*, Oxford University Press, 1966

Context to the play's action

The play is set in pre-revolutionary Russia and explores the lives of a group of people who have gathered at the lakeside estate of Sorin, one summer at the turn of the century.

The first three Acts of the play cover a period of no more than a few weeks. They focus on the interaction between Sorin, and the characters who live on or round about his country estate, and his sister Arkadina, a famous actress, now approaching middle-age, who has come to visit Sorin, and her son, Konstantin, who lives with him. Arkadina is accompanied by her lover, Trigorin, who is a famous writer.

Two years elapse between the third and the fourth Act. Arkadina and Trigorin return to the estate again to visit Sorin, now close to death.

Landowning families in Russia at the time were relatively wealthy, although throughout the country appalling poverty often existed alongside wealth. The main characters in the play have neither immense wealth nor are they aristocrats but they are educated and financially comfortable, despite what they may say themselves. Amongst the cast there are writers, actresses, a retired law-court official, a doctor, a schoolmaster, and an estate manager. Chekhov is reflecting the life of a particular class of artists and professionals living at the time that he wrote the play.

Genre

As suggested above, *The Seagull* is a difficult play to categorise. Chekhov himself, in writing to a friend as he was completing the work, described it as follows: 'A comedy – three f, six m, four acts, rural scenery (a view over a lake); much talk of literature, little action, five bushels of love.'

Commentators agree that the play has elements of both comedy and tragedy; after all, the play deals with the frustrations of unrequited love as well as stifled ambitions and it ends with Konstantin's suicide. The ambiguity of tone that characterises the writing has led to widely differing stage interpretations of the play, even over the past thirty years.

Perhaps the best description of the play is **tragi-comedy,** while individual productions of the play may emphasise one or other element, depending upon the director's vision.

2   The creative overview

In this section you will learn about:

- how to formulate a creative overview of your set text

- how to use your overview to inform your staging decisions.

Key term

Motif: an idea or theme that appears repeatedly within a piece of literature or music, representing a dominant strand in the author's/composer's intentions for the audience.

AQA   Examiner's tip

A creative overview can only be achieved through gaining complete familiarity with a text, with the twists and turns of plot and with the subtleties of individual characters. Re-read your set play several times during your course, making notes on your developing ideas about it.

Think

Intentions for the audience

- How are you going to horrify, entertain and instruct your audience?

- How will you cast the most repulsive characters in the play?

- How will you ensure that your audience understand the justice of Vindice's death sentence? How might the performance suggest his descent into barbarism?

The main distinction between the exam question that you answered on your AS set text and the A2 questions is the need for you to demonstrate your 'whole play' knowledge. This knowledge is based on your 'creative overview' of the play.

To formulate your creative overview, you will need to take account of:

- the playwright's intentions for the audience – as far as you can determine them
- the over-arching message/meaning of the play
- the key perspective of the play – whose story is it?
- the significance of individual characters within the structure and pattern of the play
- the relationships between the characters
- the action of the play
- the language of the play and its subtext, if appropriate
- the themes and **motifs** of the play
- the shape of the play: its structure and development from scene to scene
- the performance style of the play
- the staging demands of the text
- the relevance of the play to a modern audience.

Through detailed consideration of these aspects of your chosen play, as well as through your research into the period setting of the play, you should arrive at a full understanding of its potential in performance. You may also find it useful to look at descriptions and photographs of previous productions of the play.

You will then be in a position to consider the most appropriate design(s) and the casting for the characters in your production. You will also be able to decide how *you* would approach the director's task of conveying its meaning for an audience.

How to formulate a creative overview

The principles for uncovering meaning and formulating an overview of a play apply to both the pre-20th century plays and the 20th-century plays studied for Section A and B of Unit 3.

Plays are open to all kinds of different, yet appropriate, treatments. The example below is just one possible interpretation of one of the set texts. If you haven't already done so, read the section on the context, style and **genre** of *The Revenger's Tragedy* in Chapter 1 before looking at this example.

🔍 *The Revenger's Tragedy*

The playwright's intentions for the audience

Tourneur/Middleton seemingly intended their audience to be alternately horrified, entertained, and instructed about the corruption at court and its inevitable consequences.

■ **Think**

The play's message

■ How will you convey this central message?

■ How can costume and lighting suggest the excesses of courtly life and the relative simplicity of rural life?

■ How might you use props such as jewels, coins, chests of gold?

■ How might you use prayer-books, crucifixes and other religious symbols?

■ **Think**

Perspective; whose story is it?

■ How will you create the relationship between Vindice and the audience? Think about his stage positioning, use of voice and accent, tone and demeanour during his asides.

■ How often will he engage in eye-contact with the audience?

■ Will this change as his actions become more bloodthirsty?

■ How might he be lit?

■ **Think**

Character groupings; court v country

■ How will you show the depravity of the court? Think about the costumes you might use to signal the difference between the women at court and the virtuous Castiza.

■ How might you emphasise the rapacious sexual appetites of the Duke, of Lussorioso, and of the Duchess? Think about suggestive movement and lewd gestures.

The audience is likely to support **Vindice** in his mission to take revenge on his fiancée's murderer and to applaud the inventiveness of the murders he commits.

However, when **Vindice** and his brother are finally sentenced to death by the noble **Antonio**, the audience are invited to question their earlier, morally dubious, reactions to a catalogue of grisly acts.

The over-arching message/meaning of the play

The play's message is that power and money corrupt, and that corruption can dissolve both family ties and public duties. The corruption in this play emanates from the court of the old **Duke**.

The play explores the contrast between the vices found amongst the rich and powerful characters at court and the virtues of those poorer characters, who live in the country.

There is also a clear message about the inevitability of death, irrespective of a person's rank, authority and wealth.

The key perspective of the play – whose story is it?

The story is predominantly **Vindice's**. We watch him develop from a moral avenger to what appears to be a deranged, cold-blooded murderer. His frequent **asides** to the audience engage their support.

Nevertheless there are several scenes, such as those involving the **Duchess's** sons, which do not include **Vindice**, so the story is not his alone.

If the play is about corruption, then the story belongs both to those who corrupt and those who become corrupted. Only **Castiza** remains pure.

The significance of individual characters within the structure and pattern of the play

Vindice is the most significant character in the play as he attempts to cleanse the court of corruption.

The court is dominated by the **Duke** and his family; each family member is utterly immoral. The **Duke** represents the source of corruption in the court, while the behaviour of his heir, the lascivious **Lussorioso**, suggests the perpetuation of corruption in the next generation.

The **Duke's** bastard son, **Spurio**, is so depraved that he sleeps with his step-mother, the **Duchess**. The **Duchess's** own sons are also morally repulsive, consisting of a rapist (**Junior**) and, in **Supervacuo** and **Ambitioso**, a pair of brothers so intent on gaining ultimate power for themselves that they destroy each other.

The country characters, **Gratiana** and **Castiza**, are significant in their relative abilities to resist the temptations of the court. **Vindice** and **Hippolito**, while representing the virtues of the country, are themselves corrupted by their bloodthirsty revenge actions.

The relationships between the characters

Most of the characters in the play are blood relatives. They belong either to **Vindice's** family or are part of the extended family of the old **Duke** and his second wife, the **Duchess**. **Antonio** is the exception, who becomes a duke in the closing moments of the play.

There is a contrast between the loving relationships of the siblings in **Vindice's** family, where the brothers attempt to preserve their sister from harm and assist one another, and the jockeying for favour, power and position that goes on between the two sets of brothers in the **Duke's** household.

There is no romantic love story in this play.

The action of the play

There are two strands to the action of the play. The first foregrounds the revenge action of **Vindice** against both the old **Duke**, who poisoned **Vindice's** fiancée ten years earlier, and **Lussorioso**, who has sinister designs on the virtue of **Vindice's** sister, **Castiza**.

The second concerns the **Duchess** and her sons. We see the **Duchess** conducting an illicit sexual relationship with her step-son, **Spurio**. We see her elder sons, **Ambitioso** and **Supervacuo**, first attempting to save their brother 'Junior' from being executed for the rape of **Antonio's** wife and, secondly, scheming to prevent one another from becoming the next **Duke**.

By the time the final curtain falls, **Vindice** has had his revenge, **Junior** has been executed and all the remaining sons of the **Duke** and **Duchess** have died in the bloodbath at the end of the play.

The language of the play and its subtext

The language of the play is unusual in its blend of **blank verse**, **rhyme** and **prose**, sometimes used all together in one speech! The use of blank verse for the speech of the courtiers is an Elizabethan/Jacobean convention, while the frequent use of rhyming couplets gives the play its distinctively witty flavour.

Prose is also used conventionally in the country, for example, in Act Two, Scene One, in the exchange between **Castiza** and her servant, **Dondolo**.

Because **Vindice** appears in three separate guises – as his true self, disguised as the villain, **Piato**, and disguised as his malcontent self – he has different styles of language to match his separate personas. When he is talking to his family, undisguised, he is at his most natural. He assumes a more cynical turn of phrase when he assumes the part of **Piato** with **Lussorioso**. When he returns to **Lussorioso** later in the play, as his malcontent self, his language is curt and he speaks in shorter phrases, saying little.

In this play, the **subtext** is mainly delivered through asides and **imagery** rather than through non-verbal means, as **Vindice** has no need to disguise his feelings from the audience.

There are numerous individual words that are repeated in the play. For example, 'sin', 'damnation', 'blood', 'lust', 'poison', and 'pleasure' appear in many different contexts and help to build up the impression of the concerns of the court. Words associated with time, the present minute, and the transitory moment are also frequent and suggest the speed with which the characters are hurtling towards *eternal* damnation.

The themes and motifs of the play

The themes of corruption, sensuality, lasciviousness, mortality and revenge that permeate the play have already been mentioned.

Transformation is another key concept in the play. Through the various disguises of **Vindice**, as well as through his ghoulish transformation of the skull of his fiancée into the means of poisoning the **Duke**, the audience sees the effects of transformation.

■ Think
Family relationships/resemblances

■ How will you identify the different groups of siblings for your audience? Think about casting ideas/wigs and/or make-up to reveal the family resemblances. Think about using costume to link **Ambitioso**, **Supervacuo** and **Junior** together and to the **Duchess**, their mother.

■ How might you contrast **Lussorioso** with **Spurio**?

■ Think
Presenting the two strands of action

■ How might you use lighting and sound to differentiate between the plot lines?

■ Would you create a distinctive setting for the scenes concerning the **Duchess** and her sons?

■ Are these scenes lighter or darker in tone than **Vindice's** revenge action?

■ How might you convey the shifting moods in staging terms?

■ Think
Speaking the verse

■ How would you direct your actors to deliver the rhyming couplets?

■ Think about the effects you want to create through the delivery of the verse.

■ How will you use elements, props, actions or gestures, to underline the significance of the frequently repeated words and images?

■ Background information

The Jacobean period was one of growing religious doubt. Nevertheless, the conventional teaching about the prospect of sin leading to an eternity of punishment acted as a deterrent for many people.

Think

Themes and motifs

- How will you use staging methods to convey these themes and motifs to the audience?
- How might you use masks?
- How will Vindice be disguised as Piato?
- How will you present the disguised skull on stage?
- How will you present Junior's head?

Background information

For the Elizabethans and Jacobeans, the skull, whether depicted in a picture or on the stage was a powerful reminder of their mortality. Another famous example of the skull used as a *memento mori* (a reminder of death) occurs in *Hamlet*, Shakespeare's 'revenge tragedy'.

Think

Style

- Will you emphasise the tragic or the grotesquely comic?
- Could Ambitioso and Supervacuo be presented as a comic double act?
- How will you portray the moral depravity of the court?
- How will the actors deliver the most outrageous lines?

Think

Staging issues

- How will you stage this play and accommodate the many different locations required for the action?
- How will you contrast the world of the court with life in the country? (for example, contrasting colours, lighting and sounds)
- How will you stage the two masques to add a spectacular finale?

Vindice's mother is transformed from virtuous to vicious (and back again). The old Duke's corpse is transformed, dressed up in 'Piato's' clothes to be 'murdered' in Vindice's place. The brothers, Ambitioso and Supervacuo have their triumph over the death of Lussorioso transformed to misery when they discover that it is Junior's head that has been delivered to them in the bloody bag, and not Lussorioso's.

As for motifs in the play, there are many skulls, brows, faces, masks and heads referred to in the language of the play. We actually see two decapitated heads in the action of the play: one a skull; and one fresh from the block!

Fig. 2.1 *Kris Marshall as* **Vindice** *with* **Gloriana's skull**, *in the 2006 production of* **The Revenger's Tragedy** *by Meredith Oakes*

The performance style of the play

The play ends with the death sentence pronounced on Vindice, the tragic hero of the play. He is the character who the audience have come to admire because of his ingenuity in destroying the thoroughly nasty Duke and his heirs. However, in spite of this, it is difficult to imagine a successful production taking an entirely serious approach to Vindice's 'tragedy'.

Modern productions tend to adopt a darkly comic approach to the catalogue of murders and sexual transgressions that the play depicts, while remaining faithful to the playwrights' bleak vision of moral bankruptcy.

The shape of the play: its structure and development from scene to scene

The play's conventional five-act structure is divided into many individual scenes that shift the action from the court to the country, and from indoor to outdoor settings. Scenes involving Vindice are interspersed with scenes that portray the various schemes of the Duchess and her sons, so that the main impression of the unfolding action is its rapidity.

Although there are two plots in the play, they come together in the final act when successive masquers perform their dance macabre to mask their intentions to murder their enemies.

The staging demands of the text

Although many productions of the play emphasise the lavish excesses of the court through the use of design elements, the actual staging demands of the text are very few. Some key items that would be useful are:

- a throne or chair of state for the Duke in Act One, Scene Two, and a chair for the Judge
- a bier (display platform) for Antonio's wife's corpse when she is revealed to Antonio's friends
- a bed for the Duke and Duchess when they are surprised by Lussorioso
- a furnished banquet table for the final scene
- various portable props, including swords, daggers, torches, gold coins, prayer books, a skull, a head, a signet ring, a censer (for dispensing incense).

The relevance of the play to a modern audience

Moral depravity and corruption in high places are themes that never go out of fashion. It is easy to see the relevance of the play to a modern audience at a time when interest in the lavish lifestyles enjoyed by royalty, celebrities and some politicians is keen.

The gulf between the rich and the poor and the virtuous and the vicious is always relevant to societies that are composed of both.

Conclusion

Once you have carried out a detailed exploration of your text – as shown in the example above – and given thought to the practical issues raised by it, you will be able to plan your 'production' with confidence. Create a detailed blueprint which will enable you to answer any question set on your chosen play.

Think

Settings

- You do not have to confine yourself to the settings suggested by the text.
- In an RSC production in the 1960s, Vindice's 'interviews' with Lussorioso were conducted in a fencing school, a massage parlour and finally a torture chamber. How might such settings help you to create meaning for your audience?

Think

Relevance

- How might you bring your production bang up to date?
- Think about design elements that you might use to depict the contrasting values of the court and the country and the excessively lavish lifestyle enjoyed by the Duke and his family.

Theatre trivia

William Archer (1856–1924), dramatist and critic, described Vindice as 'a sanguinary maniac with a gloating appetite for horrors'. He did not like the play.

3   The director's interpretation – comedy

In this chapter you will learn about:

- features of comedy
- how directors apply comic methods.

Key terms

Comedy: a form of drama which usually explores the absurdities of life and which ends happily – generally, with a reconciliation or marriage. The audience are expected to respond with laughter, recognising, in the exaggerated actions and troubles of the characters on stage, something familiar in their own lives.

Business (or 'biz'): a piece of action or interplay between characters that is not scripted but added for dramatic or comic effect. The term is a shortened form of stage business. Physical, comic biz is often termed knockabout business.

Link

Chapters 13 and 14 in the AS coursebook focus on the wider choices that face a director.

All the plays in Unit 3, Section A, contain **comedy** in varying measures.

Even *The Revenger's Tragedy,* although it cannot be classed as a comedy and ends badly for the protagonist **Vindice**, contains a very dark humorous strain.

Tartuffe, **The Servant of Two Masters**, *The Recruiting Officer* and *Lady Windermere's Fan*, though quite different in style from one another, are all what we might call 'laugh-out-loud' comedies, and conform to the comic convention of a happy ending.

These four plays are built around potentially difficult situations, threatening the happiness of the protagonists. However, the difficulties that beset these characters are resolved in the course of the action, either through their own ingenuity or through the intervention of others.

Like *The Revenger's Tragedy*, these four comedies also revolve around the theme of deception and mistaken identity. Each contains characters who have assumed a disguise of one kind or another, although none for the purpose of murder!

Both the odious **Tartuffe** and the sophisticate, Mrs Erlynne, in *Lady Windermere's Fan*, adopt false personas for personal gain. In *The Servant of Two Masters*, **Beatrice** disguises herself as her own brother in order to protect herself. **Silvia in *The Recruiting Officer*** disguises herself as a male recruit to be with her lover, **Captain Plume**. All the deceivers are eventually unmasked or choose to reveal themselves, except for Mrs Erlynne, who is destined to play a part for the rest of her fictional life.

Another hallmark of the comic genre that these four comic plays share is that each ends with the prospect of marriage, or the restoration of happiness to an existing marriage, for lovers who have somehow overcome the obstacles placed in their way during the unfolding of the plot.

The Seagull, although described as a comedy by the playwright, possesses few of the comic traits mentioned above. The audience is likely to laugh out loud only occasionally and, even then, it is likely to be triggered by a well-timed or wry delivery of a line or by some **business**, invented by the director, to satisfy the intentions of the playwright.

Far from ending with marriage and reconciliation, *The Seagull* ends with the suicide of one of the principal characters. Its 'comedy' lies in its portrayal of the absurdities of life and of the dreams and ambitions that people cherish. The characters might be described as 'disguisers' only in having to disguise their intense feelings of dissatisfaction from one another as they carry on with the business of everyday life.

The audience may find humour in the play if they recognise the impossibility of their own youthful aspirations. However, unlike conventional comedy, which builds to a happy resolution of the central difficulties of the characters, *The Seagull* ends in a mood of disappointment, resignation and loss.

A director of any of the plays mentioned above would have to give serious thought to the comic style required and to the degree of comic invention needed to convey both the playwright's intentions and his or her own interpretation of the play to the audience.

In the rest of the chapter, we are going to consider how a director might create comedy for the audience, using *The Servant of Two Masters* and *Tartuffe* as examples.

▓ Directing comedy

🔍 *The Servant of Two Masters*

Let us assume that you are about to direct *The Servant of Two Masters* and that, having carried out appropriate research into the original staging conventions of the play and Goldoni's debt to **commedia dell'arte** traditions, you have formulated your creative overview. You may have decided on the following key aspects:

▓ that Goldoni intended the audience to laugh – and this is *your* main aim

▓ that the key message of the play is that 'appearances can be deceptive'

▓ that **Truffaldino** has the key perspective in the play

▓ that the story hinges upon **Beatrice** and her search for **Florindo**

▓ that the action of the play must be fast-paced, physically energetic and comical

▓ that the language of the play is witty and comical and needs to be well-timed

▓ that the main theme of the play is that 'the course of true love never did run smooth'

▓ that the performance style of the play should be strongly influenced by commedia dell'arte, drawing both on its **slapstick** tradition and its use of individual **lazzi**

▓ that both the key message and theme are universally relevant.

These decisions will affect your whole approach to directing the play. Let us begin by thinking about casting ideas. If you are keeping strictly to commedia conventions you may choose to use masks for all the recognisable commedia stereotypes. However, for the modern stage, you may prefer not to use masks at all, but to reflect those stereotypes in the physical qualities of your actors.

The physical, knockabout nature of the style of commedia dell'arte means that you will want all your actors to be agile. There are special demands on **Truffaldino** and on the characters involved in the stage fight, (**Pantalone**, **Silvio** and **Beatrice**), who will need to be almost acrobatic in their physical skills.

These then are general casting requirements. What specific requirements might you have of individual characters?

The lovers, **Silvio** and **Clarice**, should both be young and conventionally good-looking. **Beatrice** and **Florindo** should also be attractive, although **Beatrice** has to look vaguely passable as a handsome youth! Appearances must be shown to be deceptive.

Both **Pantalone** and **Dr Lombardi** will need to look much older. In commedia plays, **Pantalone** was traditionally lean with a large nose while the Doctor was immediately identifiable from his long black gown and white ruff. His pedantry required a droning vocal tone.

Truffaldino and **Smeraldina** are the comic servant figures – the zanni – and would certainly not have refined features. They are not in the first flush of youth – many of **Smeraldina's** lines suggest that she feels she is 'on the shelf'. Nevertheless, they seem to find one another attractive and they are set to wed by the end of the play.

Truffaldino needs to have a mobile face to convey a range of expressions to the audience throughout the play. Since **Truffaldino** forges a bond with the audience, he should have an appealing, though not necessarily

▓ **Background information**

Beatrice disguises herself as her brother, **Federigo**, and travels to Venice to look for her lover **Florindo**, who has killed **Federigo** in a duel. She first visits **Pantalone** to claim her brother's bride and dowry. En route to Venice, **Beatrice** hires a rascally servant, **Truffaldino**, who acquires a second master – **Florindo**!

▓ **Think**

▓ What are the advantages of using traditional commedia masks?

▓ What are the disadvantages?

Think

Think about ways you could create more comedy from the appearance of the cast.

- Might **Beatrice** be exceptionally tall for a woman or very petite and feminine?
- Might **Truffaldino** and **Smeraldina** have similar exaggerated features?
- Might **Brighella**, be made up to look like a modern celebrity chef?

Link

Decide upon your performance space and how you are going to use it before you start planning comic action. Plays written in the 17th and 18th centuries contain few stage directions, so you need to establish your own settings. Refer back to Chapter 15 in your AS coursebook.

Think

- How might you stage this to extract maximum comedy? Where would you position **Smeraldina** and **Truffaldino** so that at each interruption **Truffaldino** has to turn, with increasing frustration, to face the equally frustrated **Pantalone**?
- Draw a sketch of your setting for this scene.

Think

How could you make this act of violence, and those that follow in the play, funny for your audience?

handsome, face. He is from Bergamo so should probably have a provincial accent, in contrast to the more formal pronunciation of the Venetian gentlefolk.

Although he is often quick witted and inventive, **Truffaldino** can't read and often gets into scrapes by speaking without thinking. His facial expressions need to register the rapid changes from despair to pride as he is alternately smug about his abilities and then suddenly desperate as the plot twists out of his control.

Activity

Whichever play you are studying, go through the casting process for each character. Note your ideas for each character and remember to justify your decisions from the text, as well as from your interpretation of the roles.

Fig. 3.1 *Clare Cox as* **Beatrice** *with Jason Watkins as* **Truffaldino** *in a 1999 production of* **A Servant of Two Masters** *by the RSC*

The plot of the play is slight, but it moves quickly and is punctuated by many opportunities for commedia-style lazzi as well as a comical sword fight. The scenes flow rapidly from one to another and much of the dialogue is comic banter. However, as a director, you will need to identify the sections where you could introduce comical routines, to provoke the audience's laughter. For example:

- When **Truffaldino** enters **Pantalone's** house, disturbing the betrothal scene between **Clarice** and **Silvio**, and catches sight of **Smeraldina**, he turns all his attention to her and begins to woo her. However, he is constantly interrupted, perfectly reasonably, by **Pantalone** firing questions at him about whom his master is.

- When the action moves from **Pantalone's** house to the street outside **Brighella's** Inn, **Truffaldino** addresses the audience directly. He explains how hungry he is – this is the basis of much of the comedy in the unfolding scenes – and needs to be developed into a **running gag.**

- **Truffaldino's** musings on his hunger are interrupted by the arrival of **Florindo** and a frail porter carrying **Florindo's** trunk that is clearly too heavy for him. **Truffaldino** takes the trunk on his own back and carries it into the inn. **Florindo** dismisses the original old porter with a kick up the backside.

Later in Act 1, **Truffaldino** is faced with the task of trying to re-seal the letter that **Florindo** has opened, before giving it to his first master, **Beatrice**. In the text of the play, the sequence involving **Truffaldino** sealing the letter with chewed bread takes up no more than half a page, however, on the stage this sequence should be a major lazzi and may take anything up to five minutes to perform, involving all kinds of physical comedy and even acrobatics before the letter is finally sealed.

In Lee Hall's version of the text, the scene (Act 1, Scene 8) goes like this:

> **Truffaldino** (very pleased with himself) I just can't help myself. Seeing how well I'm doing I may as well give this double service thing a proper run round the block. A man of my singular potential, it seems, is up to anything. But I can't get away with giving this thing (the letter) back in this state. Let's see if I can fold it so they won't notice.
>
> (*He makes a pig's ear of it.*)
>
> That's better but it needs sticking. How the hell do I wangle that? Maybe I could chew up a bit of bread as a sort of mortar, and then stick it like me granny used to do with her false teeth.
>
> (*He fishes in his pocket and pulls out a bit of bread.*)
>
> I'll give it a go. Well, there goes the emergency rations, but que sera sera as they say in England.
>
> (*He chews the bread but inadvertently swallows it.*)
>
> Oh bugger. There's hardly any left now.
>
> (*Chews it and swallows some more.*)
>
> It's just not natural to have to do this. One last go.
>
> (*He manages not to swallow it and unwillingly removes it from his mouth.*)
>
> Got you. Now to seal the bastard.
>
> (*He seals the flap with bread.*)
>
> Champion. Look at that. Top notch.

Jason Watkins, who played **Truffaldino** in the 1999 RSC production of this version of the play, executed the final sticking down of the letter with a run, a jump and a back flip, finally administering the 'seal' with an energetic bash!

In Act 2, **Pantalone** is insulted by **Silvio**, who is outraged that he has lost **Clarice** to 'Federigo' and the pair begin to fight. **Beatrice** arrives and joins in the fray. Once again, a page of text must be translated into a sequence of comical sword-play and violence lasting up to five minutes on stage. In the spirit of commedia, this should be a hilarious affair, with perfect comic timing, swords exchanged for umbrellas or sticks, feet landing in plant pots, characters fighting their own mirror images, and innocent bystanders grabbed to act as human shields. There might even be a chase sequence around the auditorium.

These are just a handful of moments from the play that require comic interpretation from an inventive director. The best way to plan your 'virtual' production is to try these out in practical sessions, taking great care!

Activity

Reread the scene in which **Truffaldino** simultaneously serves an elaborate meal to both of his masters, dining in separate (off-stage) rooms. Work out how you would direct this scene to achieve the funniest effects. Think about rapid entrances and exits, carrying tureens, plates and dishes, etc.

Key term

Running gag: a comic action, expression or routine that is repeated throughout a scene or throughout the whole play, to make the audience laugh.

Think

- How might you develop a running gag?
- Might you use a sound effect of a rumbling tummy that keeps embarrassing **Truffaldino**?
- Could **Truffaldino** salivate at every mention of food, or find a repeated gesture to show his hunger whenever food is mentioned?

Think

How would you direct your actor in this section to maximise the comedy of the situation?

Think

How would you bring this crazy fight to life? Work out a detailed sequence for your actors to perform.

Further reading

Barry Grantham, *Commedia Plays*, Nick Hern Books, 2006, contains a number of commedia-style scenarios and scripts and includes detailed descriptions of 67 different lazzi which should inspire directorial ideas for *The Servant of Two Masters*.

Background information

Tartuffe is a religious hypocrite who has conned his way into Orgon's house and has his complete trust. When Orgon decides to marry his daughter to Tartuffe and to disinherit his son in Tartuffe's favour, his wife, Elmire, takes drastic action and forces Orgon to witness Tartuffe's attempt to seduce her.

Key term

Exposition: usually the first scene of a play, which gives the audience much of the information they need to make sense of the unfolding plot.

Think

- How would you cast and direct Madame Pernelle in the opening act to ensure that the audience react negatively to her and empathise with the rest of the family?
- Consider her facial features, hairstyle, costume, accessories, vocal qualities and gestures.
- How might you create comedy here?

Tartuffe

As a director of *Tartuffe* your research and creative overview may have led you to the following main conclusions:

- that Moliere's intention for the audience is to make them laugh at the exposure of Tartuffe's villainy and Orgon's gullibility, but that the play is serious in its attack on hypocrisy
- that the over-arching message of the play is that 'appearances can be deceptive'
- that the action of the play is largely implausible and yet must be played with conviction in order to maximise the comic effects
- that the language of the play is both serious and comical and needs to be delivered accordingly
- that one of the themes of the play is the bringing together of the true lovers
- that the performance style of the play should reveal some of its commedia dell'arte origins
- that the play remains relevant today.

These conclusions will affect your casting ideas as well as your direction. There are some characters in *Tartuffe* who are indebted to commedia stock characters. It is possible, for example, to see Orgon as a **Pantalone** figure; Dorine, the cheeky maid, seems to belong to the tradition of the zanni servant figure, and, in Mariane and Valère, we find the stock pair of young lovers, whose love for one another is threatened by Orgon's decision to have Tartuffe as his son-in-law.

However, you may have decided that the exposure of Tartuffe's hypocrisy and Orgon's gullibility are important, so you might want to create these characters beyond the traditional stock characters of commedia. Elmire, Orgon's neglected wife, and her brother Cléante are also quite serious figures.

The opening Act is an example of dramatic **exposition**, where the departing Madame Pernelle gives an angry dissection of her visit to the house of her son, Orgon, criticising all members of the household (with the exception of Orgon and Tartuffe) in turn.

In the course of her tirade she identifies all the key characters in the play and, in the responses of the family members to her attacks, the audience are able to judge the accuracy of her opinions. She gives information about all the main players and their relationships both with her, with each other and with the absent Orgon and Tartuffe. This device enables the audience to adopt a sceptical attitude towards Orgon and Tartuffe, when they finally appear.

When Orgon arrives home from a short absence, in Act 1, we are able to see his foolishness for ourselves; he first appears as a loving family man as he insists on asking the maid, Dorine, about his family, before discussing anything else with Cléante, his brother-in-law, who is waiting to speak with him. However, as the dialogue progresses we begin to see his foolish obsession with his protégé, Tartuffe. The characters present are Cléante and Dorine.

[*Enter Orgon*]

Orgon: Ah, good morning brother.

Cléante: I was just going. I'm glad to see you back again. There isn't much life in the countryside now.

Orgon: Dorine – (*to Cléante*) a moment brother, please – excuse me if I ask the news of my family first and set my mind at rest. (*To Dorine*) Has everything gone well the few days I've been away? What have you been doing? How is everyone?

Dorine: The day before yesterday the mistress was feverish all day. She had a dreadful headache.

Orgon: And Tartuffe?

Dorine: Tartuffe? He's very well: hale and hearty; in the pink.

Orgon: Poor Fellow!

Dorine: In the evening she felt faint and couldn't touch anything, her headache was so bad.

Orgon: And Tartuffe?

Dorine: He supped with her. She ate nothing but he very devoutly devoured a couple of partridges and half a hashed leg of mutton.

Orgon: Poor Fellow!

Dorine: She never closed her eyes all through the night. She was too feverish to sleep and we had to sit up with her until morning.

Orgon: And Tartuffe?

Dorine: Feeling pleasantly drowsy, he went straight to his room, jumped into a nice warm bed, and slept like a top until morning.

Orgon: Poor Fellow!

Dorine: Eventually she yielded to our persuasions, allowed herself to be bled, and soon felt much relieved.

Orgon: And Tartuffe?

Dorine: He dutifully kept up his spirits, and took three or four good swigs of wine at breakfast to fortify himself against the worst that might happen and to make up for the blood the mistress had lost.

Orgon: Poor Fellow!

Dorine: They are both well again now so I'll go ahead and tell the mistress how glad you are to hear that she's better.

The climax of the comic action in *Tartuffe* occurs in Act 4. **Orgon** has already disregarded his wife's account of **Tartuffe's** attempt on her honour, as well as his son, **Damis'**, denouncement of **Tartuffe**, whom he overheard making indecent proposals to **Elmire**. **Orgon's** response was to disinherit **Damis**. In Act Four, **Elmire** persuades a reluctant and sceptical **Orgon** to hide under the table while she receives **Tartuffe** alone, knowing that **Tartuffe** will continue in his attempt to seduce her. The sequence that follows is a comic **set-piece**.

The director's job is to ensure that the audience see not only **Tartuffe's** mounting passion and increasingly physical assault upon **Elmire**, but her corresponding discomfort and fear that **Orgon** will not intervene early enough to prevent **Tartuffe** from achieving his desires. The audience must also be able to see **Orgon**, transfixed with horror in his hiding place, apparently unable to move as he watches his trusted **Tartuffe** fondling his wife. **Elmire** punctuates her dialogue with increasingly desperate coughs, to try to attract **Orgon's** attention and put a halt to her predicament.

Think

Think about the following points, then try directing this extract:

- **Orgon** is completely serious in his concern for **Tartuffe**.
- **Dorine** is laughing at **Orgon's** stupidity.
- **Cléante** is present throughout the exchange, dumbfounded by **Orgon's** responses to **Dorine's** account.
- Stage positioning; facial expressions; vocal delivery, gesture.

Key term

Set-piece: a carefully crafted piece of stage action that depicts a situation that is typical within the genre of the play. For example, in comedy, scenes of mistaken identity, concealment and chases and in tragedy gruesome murders, mad scenes or fights to the death might be set-pieces.

Fig. 3.2 *The seduction scene from the National Theatre's 2002 production of Tartuffe with Martin Clunes as Tartuffe and Claire Holman as Elmire*

Finally, just as **Tartuffe** is about to force **Elmire**, she asks him to check that they are entirely alone:

> *Elmire*: (*after coughing again*). Very well then, I see I must make up my mind to yield and consent to accord you everything you wish [...] The fault can surely not be accounted mine.
>
> *Tartuffe*: Yes, madam, upon me be it and ...
>
> *Elmire*: Just open the door a moment and make sure that my husband isn't in the gallery.
>
> *Tartuffe*: Why worry about him? Between ourselves – he's a fellow one can lead by the nose. He glories in our association. I've got him to the stage where though he saw everything with his own eyes he wouldn't believe it.
>
> *Elmire*: All the same, do go out a moment, please, and have a good look round.
>
> *Orgon*: (*coming out from under the table*). Yes! I must admit it! The man's an abominable scoundrel! I can't get over it! I'm in a daze.
>
> *Elmire*: But why come out so soon? You can't mean what you say! Get under the table again! It's not time yet. Wait till the very end and make quite sure. Don't trust to mere conjecture.
>
> *Orgon*: No! No! Hell itself never produced anything more wicked.
>
> *Elmire*: Good Heavens! You mustn't believe as easily as that. Wait until you are utterly convinced before you give in. Don't be too hasty! You might be mistaken! (*She puts her husband behind her as Tartuffe returns.*)
>
> (*Re-enter Tartuffe*)
>
> *Tartuffe*: Everything favours me, Madam. I've looked in all the rooms. There's no one there and now my rapture...
>
> *Orgon*: (*stopping him*) Steady! You are letting your amorous desires run away with you. You shouldn't get so excited! And ha, my godly friend, you would deceive me, would you? How you give way to temptation! You meant to marry my daughter and yet you coveted my wife! For a long time I couldn't believe that it was really true and thought to hear you change your tune: but the proof has gone far enough. I am convinced, and, for my part, I ask nothing further.

Think

Think about the following, then direct the extract:

- Tartuffe's frenzy of passion, believing in Elmire's consent
- Elmire's realisation that Orgon is not going to intervene
- Orgon's bewilderment at what he has witnessed
- Elmire's sarcasm towards Orgon
- Tartuffe's deflation when he realises he has been tricked.

Further reading

www.comedie-francaise.fr. On this website you can order video productions of *Tartuffe* (This site is in French so you may need some help to find your way around)

www.site-moliere.com. (This site is in both French and English)

www.theatrehistory.com. Select 'French Theatre'

www.louis-xiv.de. This site provides more details about Louis XIV

Activity

Improvise the earlier part of this scene, where **Tartuffe** attempts to persuade **Elmire** to give in to him, while she must appear encouraging although still resisting his physical advances. Remember to include an increasingly amazed **Orgon**, watching his wife struggling with **Tartuffe** at the height of his passion.

If you are studying *The Recruiting Officer*, *Lady Windermere's Fan* or *The Seagull*, try to identify the central comic situations or potentially comic moments within the piece. *Lady Windermere's Fan* depends more upon language for its comedy than the other plays. *The Seagull* does contain potentially comical moments, too, despite its more serious tone overall.

The director's interpretation – rehearsal methods

In this chapter you will learn about:

- directorial strategies in rehearsal

- bringing scenes to life on stage.

This chapter looks at some of the strategies that directors employ when they are working towards staging a play. It refers to specific productions of two of the set plays: **Katie Mitchell**'s production of an adaptation (by Martin Crimp) of *The Seagull*, produced in 2006 at the National Theatre; and Max Stafford-Clark's production of *The Recruiting Officer*, produced in 1988 at The Royal Court in tandem with the first ever production of *Our Country's Good*.

Whichever play you are studying, you will find the rehearsal methods referred to in this chapter relevant to your Unit 3 studies and also to your preparation for Unit 4.

The Seagull

Katie Mitchell is well known for the meticulous research that she undertakes into the plays that she directs. According to Helen Manfull, Katie Mitchell 'begins by reading the play probably twenty-five to thirty times'.

But this is only the starting point.

As part of her pre-rehearsal preparation, Mitchell explores the original context of the play in terms of the social, political and economic conditions that existed when it was set, and she steeps herself in the art and architecture of the period. Wherever possible she visits the location of the play, taking her designer and, where budget allows, the cast, too. On the research trip, the team take photographs and make audio recordings in order to build up a bank of authentic stimuli for when rehearsals begin.

The rehearsals themselves are exacting and involve a series of steps that are intended to enable the cast and production team to construct an entirely convincing 'imaginary world'. Katie Mitchell's research methods are based on a **Stanislavskian** approach to staging and are focused on the achievement of 'truth' on stage.

The rehearsals for Katie Mitchell's production of *The Seagull* lasted eight weeks, which is about twice as long as the average rehearsal time.

Rehearsal methods

Facts and questions

Katie Mitchell employs a rehearsal method entitled 'Facts and Questions'. This involves the cast sitting down together and combing the play to identify what Mitchell calls the 'non-negotiable' facts. These are then listed as Facts. This read-through will also throw up questions that the actors need the answers to, in order to develop their characters. These too are listed, under the heading Questions.

During a read through of the opening of Act 1, some facts emerge, for example:

- It is Russia.
- There is a house that belongs to Sorin set in an estate.

Who's who

Katie Mitchell: joined the RSC in 1988 as Assistant Director and worked with Adrian Noble on Ibsen's *The Master Builder*. Since the late 1990s she has worked predominantly for the National Theatre, where her productions have included Ted Hughes' version of Aeschylus's *The Oresteia*, Chekhov's *Three Sisters* and Martin Crimp's *Attempts on her Life*.

Link

Remind yourself of the staging decisions facing all directors by re-reading Chapter 14 in your AS coursebook.

Think

A 'non-negotiable' fact cannot be an opinion or an interpretation. For example 'Masha is in a bad mood' or 'the lake is beautiful' are not facts!

- The house is by a lake.
- Medvedenko has a mother, two sisters and a little brother.
- Medvedenko is a schoolteacher.

Some of the questions that need answers are:

- Whereabouts in Russia is the estate?
- How big is the estate? What does it comprise? What is Sorin's house like?
- Why does Masha always wear black?
- How long have Masha and Medvedenko known one another?
- Where did they meet?
- How long has Medvedenko been making daily visits to Sorin's estate to see Masha?

> ### Activity
>
> Try this method on the opening scene/act of your set play. Write down *all* the non-negotiable facts you can find.

Once the questions have been formulated, the director, cast and designers set out to find the answers to them. The questions can be divided into different types, each needing a different approach to find the answer.

Research questions

- Questions about the size of the estate, its extent and the number of buildings on it; what crops are farmed and when and how the estate is maintained.
- Questions about what a schoolteacher earned at the end of the 19th century, and how difficult it might be to survive on those earnings, the cost of living at the time; questions about the status of the teaching profession, the hours that Medvedenko had to work and the type of pupils he might have to teach.

These types of questions can be answered through historical research, using the internet or more specialised books about Russian history. The team then bring their findings to the rehearsal room.

Character questions

- Questions about the characters and their backgrounds: for example, how long Medvedenko and Masha have known one another, when and where they first met.
- Questions about the characters' feelings: for example, why Masha does not return Medvedenko's love; what each character is expecting to happen during this evening.

These types of questions can only be answered through the actors' imaginative exploration of their roles. Katie Mitchell first gets her actors to do some personal research about their characters: their social status; their family background; their profession, if they have one. Then they each create a time-line for their character, using any facts that Chekhov *does* supply about them, through what they say and what others say about them, and amplifying these through improvisations.

The characters playing Masha and Medvedenko might improvise a first meeting. The actors playing Masha and Konstantin might improvise a scene when they first met, perhaps as children, playing on the estate.

Other, simpler, improvisations create an imaginative life for the characters in the time leading up to when the action of the play begins. For example, Medvedenko might improvise part of his walk over to the estate – a three-mile walk – perhaps spent thinking of Masha and her indifference to him. While Masha might improvise getting ready for the evening ahead and Konstantin's play; although she always wears black, she may want to look attractive in Konstantin's eyes.

Activity

Choose a character who appears in the opening scene of your set play and try improvising a scene from your character's past with a partner. Then try an improvisation on your own, focused on something that you have done just before the 'play' begins.

Katie Mitchell's intention is that these improvisations give the actors a bank of 'shared memories' to draw on when they are acting, which makes their performances more believable to watch. Actors who have undertaken this factual and imaginative journey with their roles appear to be living in a 'real' world, because they are acutely aware of the context of their actions, on an estate in Russia at the turn of the century. They have constructed believable past experiences for themselves that have made each character who he or she is.

Fig. 4.1 *A scene from Katie Mitchell's 2006 production of* The Seagull *at the National Theatre, with Nina and Konstantin*

Titles for each act

Another of Katie Mitchell's methods is to give a title to each act of the play in order to concentrate everyone's attention upon the key event/ purpose of each one. In her production of *The Seagull* these were:

- Act 1 – The Performance of Konstantin's Play
- Act 2 – The Entertainment of the Celebrity Guests
- Act 3 – The Preparation for Arkadina and Trigorin's Departure for Moscow
- Act 4 – The Gathering to say Final Farewells to Sorin.

■ Activity

Give each act of your set plays in Sections A and B a title. It is a useful way of identifying significant chunks of action and of defining your emphasis. Compare the titles that you have created with those from others in your group.

The titles that Katie Mitchell used are interesting. For example, for Act 4, there is nothing in the title to suggest Nina's harrowing visit to Konstantin nor is there any reference to his suicide at the end of the play. The titles are intended to give the actors a realistic, solid situation to play and to help establish the mood of the act, rather than to highlight points of drama.

Time and season

Another of Katie Mitchell's methods is to establish the season and the time in which each act is set. Again, this helps the actors to create believable characters, as they can imagine and convey, for example, that they are warm or chilly; and this, in turn, might affect their moods.

In *The Seagull*:

■ Act 1 is set in a section of the park with the lake behind it, on a summer's evening after sunset, with the moon coming up. Masha finds it stifling and predicts a storm, while Polina remarks that 'it's getting damp', showing her concern for Dorn's health. There is a mood of anticipation.

■ Act 2 is set in the full heat of the midday sun; the characters sit in the shade of a lime tree, on the croquet lawn. There is a very lazy mood.

■ Act 3 is an indoor scene, but we know that it begins at lunchtime and there is a train to be caught at five-past two. There is an unsettled mood.

■ Act 4 is set two years later. Although the act takes place indoors, the bad weather is referred to throughout; the stage directions indicate howling wind in the chimneys and sighing trees; it is an autumn twilight when the act begins, but darkness soon falls. There is a sombre mood.

■ Activity

Improvise four different scenarios based on this information about the setting/season/time of the four acts in *The Seagull*. Use characters from your set play or invent your own. Note how these different external circumstances of time, season and place affect your characters in performance.

Place

Katie Mitchell's method extends the cast's understanding of 'place', beyond 'the park', 'the croquet lawn' or the 'dining room'. She encourages the cast to collaborate on constructing a complete physical context for the action.

In practice this means that the set is constructed with a shared knowledge of exactly where the other rooms or parts of the estate are located. The cast draw plans of the interior and exterior of the house and its exact position within the estate. So, for example, they will know exactly how far the croquet lawn is from the house and where it is in relation to the lake and to Konstantin's stage. They will know how far the house is from the railway station, from the next town and from Moscow. All this is a part of creating a believable world for the characters to exist in.

Theme

Katie Mitchell suggests that looking at the themes of a play with the cast provides the actors with 'additional creative fuel'. She explores the themes of the play with the actors in a practical way, and uses improvisations based on the play's themes and related to the actors' own lives to help add substance to their characterisation.

For example, in *The Seagull*, the symbol of the seagull appears to represent the theme of broken dreams. Although the notion of the seagull – as a symbol of wanton destruction – is associated most closely with Nina throughout the play, the presence of the stuffed bird in the final act appears to confirm that it is a symbol of the thwarted hopes and dreams of almost all the characters in the play, linking them together with this important theme.

The actors might be encouraged to improvise around the theme of their own unfulfilled dreams, before transferring the emotions stimulated by their improvisations to the portrayal of their characters within the play.

When you are formulating your creative overview of your set texts, consider how the themes that you have identified will modify the actors' performance of the play.

🔍 *The Recruiting Officer*

In 1988, Max Stafford-Clark embarked on an ambitious project at the Royal Court Theatre to create an acting ensemble that would take part in his production of *The Recruiting Officer*. The ensemble would also take part in his production of a new play, also set in the 18th century, to be developed collaboratively by the ensemble and Timberlake Wertenbaker, the playwright who was commissioned to write the new play's script. The play that emerged from this process was *Our Country's Good*. (See Chapter 15 for more detail about this play.)

Max Stafford-Clark's methods as a director include an emphasis on detailed research into the background to each play, combined with a very practical approach to staging, which he calls 'actions'.

Relevant research

In *Letters to George*, Max Stafford-Clark explains that any research undertaken must have a practical purpose and be utilised in the play. That means that the research has to feed into a practical exploration of part of the play and to influence the performance of one or more of the actors.

In his description of the rehearsal process for *The Recruiting Officer*, Max Stafford-Clark refers to a number of areas that had to be researched by the director and the cast, in order for the actors to understand their roles and be able to communicate some sense of period authenticity to the audience.

These included:

■ the conditions of war/battle – in particular the Battle of Blenheim in 1704
■ the process and legality of recruiting
■ the relative value of the money mentioned in the play to contemporary values
■ the relationship between money and marriage; money and sex
■ the significance of virginity in the 18th century

■ Link

See Chapters 3 and 21 in the AS coursebook for references to Max Stafford-Clark's work. His book, *Letters to George*, is a valuable companion to the study of *The Recruiting Officer*.

- the conventions of meeting and greeting between men and men, men and women, women and women, different classes/ranks in the 18th century
- the drinking habits of the gentry and the military at the time
- the conventions of duelling in the 18th century.

The purpose of specific areas of research

Let us look at the way that the research into money/marriage/virginity/sex actually affected the way specific scenes were directed and performed.

One of Max Stafford-Clark's early tasks was to discover the relative value of the sums of money that are crucial to the plot of the play, so that he could convert the precise figures quoted in the play into 1980s equivalents.

In the early stages of rehearsals, the cast were asked to read a chapter from a book of social history: Roy Porter's *English Society in the Eighteenth Century*. From this they learnt that multiplying the sums of money referred to in the play by sixty would result in equivalent sums in the 1980s.

Melinda's sudden and unexpected inheritance of £20,000 from her Aunt's will radically alters her relationship with Worthy. Before Melinda received her inheritance, Worthy thought her too poor to marry, but attractive enough to have as a mistress. He offered her an allowance of £500 per year to yield him her virginity and to become his mistress – a position which would have ruined her reputation and made her unwelcome in the best society. In 1980s terms, Worthy's offered 'settlement' was worth around £30,000 a year, but Melinda's inheritance was worth £1.2 million. Thus she suddenly becomes more desirable to Worthy as a wife than as a mistress.

Silvia, as Justice Balance's younger child, has a total fortune of £1,500 (£90,000 in 1980s terms), but once her brother's death is announced she becomes at once, the heir to her father's estate and receives an additional £1,200 a year (£72, 000 in 1980s terms).

These were huge sums of money which, given the social conventions of the time, placed both women beyond the reach of the men that they loved.

Justice Balance, while happy enough to have Plume as a son-in-law when Silvia had only a fortune of £1,500, ships her off to the country and out of Plume's reach as soon as she becomes heir to his entire fortune. While Melinda, although free from parental interference as she is an orphan, is not inclined to rush into a marriage with Worthy, a man who would have ruined her socially.

Stafford-Clark's research also highlighted the importance of a lady's chastity before marriage, as well as fidelity afterwards. This influenced how several scenes were played.

How the research is used in rehearsal and performance

Having undertaken specific research into the connection between money and sexual relationships in the period, Max Stafford-Clark had to find ways of allowing the cast to use the information in their performances.

He set up an improvisation that he called 'Moral Dilemma' in which the actress playing Melinda (Linda Bassett), was offered advice by the other members of the company over whether or not she should accept Worthy's offer of £500 and become his mistress or lose him completely.

The improvisation was set before the action of the play has started. After listening to a range of different views both for and against, the actress was given only a short time, alone, to make up her mind.

She decided Melinda had to agree to Worthy's terms, because this would have been her response to him had fate not intervened with her Aunt's death and legacy.

Fig. 4.2 *Jack McLaughlin-Gray as* **Mr Worthy** *and Rose Pickering as* **Melinda** *in the 1979 production of* **The Recruiting Officer** *at the Todd Wehr Theater*

This 'knowledge' of what Melinda's decision would have been, added new meaning to all the lines and exchanges that refer to her relationship with Worthy.

For example in Act 1, Scene 1, Worthy's explanation to Plume about Melinda's unexpected inheritance is tinged with frustration and, perhaps, regret that he had been so close to making her his mistress: he had given her a week to make up her mind about becoming his mistress, but the Aunt's death put paid to that necessity and turned Melinda into an attractive prospect as a wife, but also into a woman embittered about his treatment of her and unlikely to accept a marriage proposal.

In Act 1, Scene 2, Silvia responds to Melinda's insult of Plume by referring to Melinda's 'capitulating with Worthy for a settlement'. This hits a nerve because it reminds Melinda of the degrading position she might have found herself in, and the girls' quarrel degenerates into an argument and a suspension of their friendship, as a result.

Most significantly, the knowledge that the research supplied into both the value of money and of chastity in Farquhar's society adds real energy and emotion to Melinda's denouncement of Worthy in Act Five, Scene Three, before they become reconciled, as she exclaims:

> Oh Mr Worthy, what you owe to me is not to be paid under a seven year's servitude. How did you use me the year before, when taking the advantage of my innocence and necessity you would have made me your mistress, that is, your slave? Remember the wicked insinuations, artful baits, deceitful arguments, cunning pretences; then your impudent behaviour, loose expressions, familiar letters, rude visits; remember those, those, Mr Worthy.

Think

If you are studying *The Recruiting Officer*, think about the ways in which research into the other areas we have highlighted might affect the direction/staging of the play.

▧ Activity

List the areas of research that you think would help you to interpret your chosen play(s). For example:

▧ the historical background

▧ attitudes towards the role of women, marriage and fidelity

▧ class differences

▧ the importance of work and /or money

▧ dreams and ambitions.

▧ **Background information**

Max Stafford-Clark reveals that he has never studied Stanislavski; nevertheless he suggests in *Letters to George* that identifying a super-objective for the whole play, such as Silvia's objective to marry Plume, and using transitive verbs to express 'actions', are Stanislavski-based methods.

'Actions'

In *Letters to George*, Max Stafford-Clark outlines one of his directorial strategies, which he calls 'actions'.

He explains,

> 'An action has to be expressed by a **transitive verb** and gives the character's intentions or tactic for that particular thought'.

Let us focus on the exchange between **Worthy** and **Melinda** in Act 5, Scene 3, to see how this might work in practice. The objective of each character in this scene is to be reconciled to the other. The transitive verbs, that the cast might have used in rehearsal to help them in the delivery of their lines, appear underlined, in brackets, after each speaker's name.

> *Worthy* (<u>Entreats</u>)
> What pleasures I may receive abroad are indeed uncertain; but this I am sure of, I shall meet with less cruelty among the most barbarous nations than I have found at home.
>
> *Melinda* (<u>Disarms</u>)
> Come, Sir, you and I have been jangling a great while; I fancy if we made up our accounts, we should the sooner come to an agreement.
>
> *Worthy* (<u>Accuses</u>)
> Sure, madam, you won't dispute your being in my debt – my fears, sighs, vows, promises, assiduities, anxieties, jealousies, have run on for a whole year, without any payment.
>
> *Melinda* (<u>Attacks</u>)
> A year! Oh **Mr Worthy**, what you owe to me is not to be paid under a seven year's servitude. How did you use me the year before, when taking the advantage of my innocence and necessity you would have made me your mistress, that is, your slave? Remember the wicked insinuations, artful baits, deceitful arguments, cunning pretences; then your impudent behaviour, loose expressions, familiar letters, rude visits; remember those, those, **Mr Worthy**.
>
> *Worthy* (<u>Engages</u> – the audience, then <u>reminds</u> Melinda)
> (*Aside*) I do remember and am sorry I made no better use of 'em – But you may remember, madam, that–
>
> *Melinda* (<u>Reconciles</u>)
> Sir, I'll remember nothing – 'tis your interest that I should forget; you have been barbarous to me, I have been cruel to you; put that and that together, and let one balance the other. Now if you will begin upon a new score, lay aside your adventuring airs, and behave yourself handsomely till Lent be over, here's my hand, I'll use you as a gentlemen should be.

▧ **Think**

▧ How many words associated with money/commerce can you find in this exchange?

▧ Find similar exchanges in the play.

▧ Find another example in the play where similar use is made of references to military tactics.

▧ How will this affect your direction of the scenes concerned?

Stafford Clark stresses that the 'actions' suggested by the transitive verbs give the actors the direction as to how to deliver their lines in rehearsal. They may be altered as rehearsals progress, especially if the director feels that they are not serving the objective that has been identified, or that they are interfering with the clear expression of the subtleties of the lines and their meaning.

Activity

Apply the rehearsal strategy of 'actions' to your chosen play. Identify the objectives of the characters for a particular scene and see if giving each speech an 'actioning' verb helps you to interpret the characters' intentions.

Summary

Whichever play you are studying, you may find that some of the methods (listed below) for uncovering the meaning of a play, first to a cast and then, through the cast's understanding, to the audience, are useful techniques for you to apply as you explore your chosen text.

Exploration of text and characters

- Facts and questions: make lists of the non-negotiable facts and the important questions raised by each scene.
- Research questions: find out all you can about the context of your set play and the backgrounds of the characters.
- Character questions: use your imagination to discover more about the characters' feelings, intentions and motivations.
- Creating a character time-line/biography: comb the text for clues about each character's past from what they say about themselves and what others say about them.
- Improvisation of scenes from characters' lives:
  - in the immediate past
  - in the more distant past.
- Integrate what you discover through improvisations into your character biographies to create more rounded characters.
- Titles for acts or scenes: name each scene to help you find its central action and dominant mood.
- Time and Season: establish as precise a time of year and day as you can for the action of each scene, to help you understand the characters' situations more fully.

Practical application of your discoveries

- Go back through your research and select the findings that will have a real bearing on how characters interact. Apply your findings in practical rehearsal sessions.
- Break up individual scenes into small sections by identifying 'objectives' for each of the characters.
- Fit transitive verbs to each line in the section to map out a possible approach to the exchange; but be flexible and adapt the verbs where necessary.

The designer's interpretation

Link

Refer back to Chapter 15 in your AS coursebook before planning designs for your set plays for Unit 3. In particular, you may find it helpful to use the design checklists for your A2 plays.

Key term

Box set: a naturalistic set depicting a room created with three continuous walls with working doors and windows; the 'fourth wall' is the division between the stage and the audience.

Think

Lady Windermere's Fan requires at least three realistic settings, to indicate the luxurious family home of Lord and Lady Windermere, including their ballroom, as well as the more masculine apartments of the raffish Lord Darlington. How might you indicate the fashionable London society beyond the confines of these sets?

Link

Look back at the suggestions, in Chapter 15 of your AS coursebook, for creating an Italianate feel for the setting of *The Taming of the Shrew*. You could adapt some of these ideas for your virtual production of *The Servant of Two Masters*.

Your designs for the set plays for Unit 3 should reflect your interpretation of those plays: a strong design concept will help to clarify the meaning of the play for your audience. It is crucial then that when you are making design choices, you are aware of the potential of design to communicate your understanding and creative overview of the play.

The potential of stage space

Setting the scene

Before looking at some of the design demands of individual set plays, consider the potential of stage space to communicate with an audience. You are already familiar with the idea that a stage set can indicate *where* a play is set, *when* it is set and the *type of characters* that will people it.

In a conventional, **naturalistic** play, the director and designers can opt to replicate a realistic room or outside space on stage. For example, if a living room is the stipulated setting for the play, the set may contain carpets and fireplaces, sofas and occasional tables, lamps and pictures, etc. The director will decide whether to set the play in the period setting for which it was written or to transpose it to an alternative suitable setting.

However, even a realistic setting like this needs to suggest a world beyond the **box set.**

To be truly realistic it must have at least one door and at least one window (unless the designer is using an imaginary window in the **fourth wall** of the set). The designer needs to consider what lies beyond the room when the door opens, as well as what the characters see when they look out of the window. This may affect the way the characters behave within the confines of the 'room'.

The cast need to know where they are coming from as well as where they are going to, through the door or through French windows or in or out of any number of doors that the designer has incorporated into the set to fulfil the demands of the action.

Although *The Servant of Two Masters* is not a naturalistic play, contemporary designers often attempt to communicate the specifically Venetian setting of the play to the audience.

It is not unusual to see designs for the play that include detailed backdrops depicting the grand canal in Venice. Several recent productions have incorporated a moving gondola that appears to float by a landing stage at the back of the set, sometimes depositing various characters as passengers.

A bridge can also add to the illusion of Venice and may be used practically to emphasise the acrobatic skills of the actors, for example, in the sword-fighting scene.

In keeping with the comic style of the play, designers often incorporate shuttered widows that fly open or shut at strategic moments, preventing **Beatrice** and **Florindo** from meeting until the very end of the play. Hidden or swinging doorways can also be exploited for comic routines.

Meeting the functional demands of the play

Most settings are designed to be practical, in that they provide actors with places to stand, sit, lie, enter and exit as the text dictates. Plays written during and after the 19th century often have quite precise stage directions.

In *Lady Windermere's Fan*, for example, Wilde sets the opening act in the morning room of **Lord** and **Lady Windermere**, in 'Carlton House Terrace', and he offers the very specific direction for **Lady Windermere** to be at a table, stage right, and *'arranging roses in a blue bowl'*. Later directions include references to business with the bureau, to sitting on the sofa or to leaning on its back.

Act Two is set in the drawing room of the house. Wilde stipulates that, visible through a doorway, upstage right, is a *'ball-room, where band is playing'* while a doorway upstage left reveals *'an illuminated terrace'*. A further phrase in the directions states simply *'Palms, flowers and brilliant lights'*.

In addition to a playwright's design preferences (that a director or designer may wish to vary), some plays have specific functional demands that a designer *must* accommodate. For example:

- There must be hiding places for **Lady Windermere** and **Mrs Erlynne** in the apartments of **Lord Darlington**, to allow **Mrs Erlynne** to create a diversion when she steps out from her hiding place, and for **Lady Windermere** to effect an unnoticed escape from hers, as the diversion is in progress.
- In *Tartuffe* there must be a hiding place for **Damis** to overhear **Tartuffe's** first improper advances on **Elmire**, as well as a table, offering a hiding place for **Orgon** to witness the second attempt at seduction, without being seen.
- In *The Servant of Two Masters*, **Truffaldino** serves lunch to both of his masters at once, (in separate off-stage rooms). This scene might be staged with a set of swing doors, in the centre of the back 'wall', to indicate the kitchen beyond, and separate doors in the stage left and stage right 'walls' to allow **Truffaldino** maximum space to perform frenetic **lazzi** as he attempts to serve two demanding masters at the same time, as well as satisfying his own ravenous hunger.
- In *The Recruiting Officer*, **Plume** and **Worthy** need to be concealed during **Kite's** fortune-telling session, as they listen to proceedings and note down the particulars of what **Kite** predicts.

Accommodating the scenes

One of the most basic approaches to designing the production is to establish how many different locations are required by the action of the play.

Plays that are not confined to one location need a fluid use of space, as scenes may alternate between two locations or range across a number of different settings. A designer's task in these cases is to help the audience distinguish between locations by providing identifiable settings for the action in each place.

These settings don't have to be complete: different settings can be achieved very simply through the selection of appropriate hand-props for the actors, combined with a suitable lighting change. Alternatively, a full-scale scene change involving trucked or flown scenery, or even a revolve, might be a suitable design solution. Whatever method is selected the result should always help the audience to make sense of the play.

Think

- What do these directions suggest about the necessary size of the stage?
- Why do you think Oscar Wilde specifies that the house is on 'Carlton House Terrace'?
- What clues do these directions, taken together, give to a potential designer, about style, scale and suitable furnishings?

Fig. 5.1 *Darne N. Dhonnch (Lady Jedburgh), Katie Kirby (Lady Windermere) and Elizabeth Moynihan (Lady Plymdale) in* Lady Windermere's Fan *at the Gate Theatre in 2005*

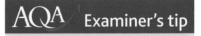

AQA Examiner's tip

You will need to make a note of all functional and scenic requirements of your set play before you begin to flesh out your designs.

Think

▪ How many different locations are there in your set plays? How will you create identifiable settings for each one?

▪ Does your set play require a change from an interior to an outdoor scene? How might you achieve this change without an elaborate set change?

The Recruiting Officer has numerous different settings, both indoors and out. The action moves from a market square to a series of indoor apartments belonging to various characters including **Melinda**, **Justice Balance** and 'Jack Wilful' (**Sylvia** in disguise).

The audience see the interior 'chamber' of **Kite**, disguised as a fortune teller and surrounded by books and globes. Later in the play there is a scene set in 'A Court of Justice' and there are others, set in fields and on a river walk beside the Severn.

In Max Stafford-Clark's production these separate locations were suggested quite simply. His designer, Peter Hartwell, used a slightly raked (sloping) stage and put a bench centre stage, with a working water pump behind it, to suggest the market square. Interior scenes were created by flying a Georgian-style window between the bench and the pump. Upstage there were two green Georgian doors with a straight-backed chair beside each of them.

To create the river walk, Hartwell placed a perspective painting of Shrewsbury against the length of the back wall, which was concealed by a gauze until needed in Act 3, Scene 2, when it was first revealed. These few furnishings were all that was used to create the various scenes.

Activity

For your set plays, try to create settings as economically as possible. Sketch and label your designs for each setting, using the minimum number of **flats** and furnishings, without compromising the demands of the play. In the exam, you can be as economical or as extravagant as you wish in your design ideas.

Fig. 5.2 *Nigel Cooke as* **Mr Worthy***, Julian Wadham as* **Captain Plume** *with Clive Russell as* **Kite** *in the 1989 production of Farquhar's* **The Recruiting Officer***. Design by Peter Hartwell*

Adding a time frame and meaning

A designer doesn't just have to think about place. He or she may also have to consider the passage of time during the course of the play.

In the previous chapter, we saw how a director, such as Katie Mitchell, considers how each act of a play may take place at different times and in different seasons, as well as in different settings. This affects the design choices as well as affecting the audience's experience of the play.

Katie Mitchell also works with her designer to find settings for individual acts that help to clarify meaning rather than just to indicate a place. She set Act 3 of *The Seagull*, which Chekhov sets in the dining room, in a corridor of **Sorin's** house. This meant that the emotionally charged

duologues, conducted between, for example, Arkadina and Konstantin, and between Arkadina and Trigorin, took place amid the hustle and bustle of servants and other characters preparing for the departure of 'the celebrity guests' to catch their train to Moscow.

The design team can add meaning to a play in a variety of ways.

In a recent production of *Tartuffe* the set consisted of four large pictures which had fallen out of their ornate frames. (The frames were over 5m high.) These pictures, which depicted the French court of Louis XIV provided raked acting levels for the show. Additional picture frames surrounded mirrors which also reflected the unfinished back of other frames. The designer seemed to be suggesting the artificiality of the times, and of course of Tartuffe. The empty frames and mirrors reminded the audience of the importance of projecting a fine image but suggested that there was no substance to them.

The National Theatre's 2002 production of *Tartuffe* also involved designs that extended the audience's understanding of the hypocrisy at the heart of the play. The set made a witty comment about the society it was satirising. At one point a character opens what looks to be a door into another room, to reveal floor to ceiling shelves of pretty satin shoes in a variety of pastel colours. The walls and ceiling of the set were decorated with elaborate murals depicting cherubs and surrounding a central picture of a **pietà**. The clash of interests between the fashionable material world and spiritual concerns was made obvious by juxtaposing these features.

Tartuffe's scandalous assault on Elmire took place beneath a dominating crucifix. The designer also introduced an **anachronistic** neon sign that flashed up some of the moralising **aphorisms** of the play, such as 'Hypocrisy is the homage which vice pays to virtue'.

As a finale, to the National Theatre production, the figure of the Sun King himself, Louis XIV, descended as a physical embodiment of the **deus ex machina** that Molière uses to ensure a happy ending to the play.

Think

- How would playing these emotional exchanges in a passageway, with the constant interruptions of other characters, affect the actors' performances and, consequently, the meaning of Act Three of *The Seagull*?
- What would be the specific effects of setting a section of your set play in a busy passageway?

Fig. 5.3 *Martin Clunes as* Tartuffe *(central) in the 2001 production of* Tartuffe *at the National Theatre*

Symbolic design

Both *The Revenger's Tragedy* and *The Seagull* invite a degree of symbolism in the design interpretation.

The Seagull

The Seagull, in spite of its naturalistic style, is dominated thematically by the symbol of the seagull that Konstantin shoots and then presents to a bewildered Nina in Act Two.

The dead bird gives Trigorin his idea for a short story about a girl, whose life is ruined by a man who casually comes by and idly destroys her – just as the seagull has been destroyed – for nothing. He then embarks on a course of action that leads Nina to the brink of despair.

In Act Four, just before Nina's dramatic reappearance, Shamrayev shows Trigorin the stuffed bird, but Trigorin has no recollection of it. Moments later, when Konstantin is alone, Nina returns. Her identification with the dead bird is both implicit and explicit. In her rambling speech she cannot disentangle herself from the bird in her own mind, *'I'm The Seagull … That's not right. I'm the actress. Yes!'*

As mentioned in the previous chapter, Katie Mitchell takes the seagull to represent the lost dreams of all the characters, but it seems clear that Nina, too, acquires a symbolic value of thwarted ambitions. Some designers have tried to capture something of the seagull in their costume designs for Nina, as well as ensuring that the stuffed bird itself is displayed prominently in Act Four.

The symbolism of the seagull drawn to the lake, as Nina says she is drawn, in Act One, has caused designers in recent times to make the lake a dominant aspect of the setting throughout the play. It has been suggested that it symbolises a 'lake of dreams'. The audience glimpse the lake through the curtains of Konstantin's stage in the opening Act. They also hear sound effects of water lapping the shore and see lighting effects to suggest the moonlight on the water.

Many of the characters have dreams that are largely unfulfilled by the end of the play.

In Act Two the lake can be evoked through Trigorin's fishing rods and waders, while in Act Three it can be seen through the dining room

Think

How far might this notion of the 'lake of dreams' apply to the various characters in *The Seagull*, as they journey through the play?

Fig. 5.4 *1994 version of Chekhov's* The Seagull *adapted by Pam Gems for the National Theatre. Set design by John Gunter, with lighting design by David Hersey*

window. In the final Act it might still be possible to see the lake in the twilight before darkness comes; we learn that there are waves on the lake, and when Nina arrives she is wet from the stormy weather.

The Revenger's Tragedy

The Revenger's Tragedy, because of its clearly defined intention to contrast extremes of goodness and evil, has frequently attracted a symbolic design interpretation.

In the 1969 production directed by Trevor Nunn, the court characters wore elaborate costumes in black and silver. The Duke was dressed almost entirely in silver, whilst lesser court members wore less silver and more black, according to their place in the hierarchy. The play was set on a large silver circle against a predominantly black background.

The opening scene was also designed to reveal the polar opposites of good and evil. It set Vindice above the court, in a gallery, while the court characters that he introduced entered into a pool of light and appeared to kneel and take communion at a communion rail. This symbolised their hypocrisy and Vindice's initial purity.

The skull was used as a repeated motif. Not only was the skull of Vindice's fiancée garishly disguised for her rendezvous with the Duke, but when Lussorioso invades the bedchamber of his stepmother, hoping to find her with Spurio, she was revealed in bed with the Duke, but without her usual finery, her wig or her make-up. She was horrified to be discovered, looking like death itself, with a bald head, whitened face and shrivelled body.

In Peter Lichtenfel's production in 1980, the stage was hung with purple and silver, but the scale of the setting was such that the actors were visually minimised. The Duke's throne was huge and carved in the shape of a skeleton wearing a bishop's mitre and carrying a sceptre – a grim reminder of the brevity of mortal life and the transitory nature of power. The Duke looked tiny sitting in the oversized 'lap' of the skeleton.

In this production, the closing masques also relied on distorting scale; the first was performed by four enormous puppets, each over twenty feet high – one of which was a skeleton. The revengers rushed out from under the skirts of the mannequins to murder Lussorioso and his fellow diners.

Lighting and sound

Remember to include your ideas for lighting and sound when you are considering design elements for your chosen play. These technical elements can make an enormous difference to the atmosphere of a production.

Changing lighting states and using different ambient sound can help to create a shift in location just as effectively as a change of scenery, if employed thoughtfully. Lighting and sound can also be used to accompany changes of scenery to further define a location.

In *The Revenger's Tragedy* lighting, and especially the use of shadows, dim lighting and silhouette, can be used to great effect to signify the treachery of the court. Blazing torches brought on to a dimly lit set can make the discovery of the dead body of the Duke especially effective. Vindice's 'bony lady' is generally presented in a shadowy meeting place for maximum impact.

The sound of music and revelling at court will contrast effectively with a brightly lit scene where we meet Castiza, perhaps with a sound effect of pure birdsong to suggest the countryside and its values.

> ### ▮ Think
> - What lighting states and/or effects would help you to create mood and atmosphere in your chosen play?
> - How might you use lighting and sound during transitions between locations?
> - Are there any lighting or sound demands that must be fulfilled to meet the requirements of the action?

■ Further reading

Websites for *The Servant of Two Masters*:

www.colby.edu/personal/j/jcthurst. Click 'Selected Resume', then '*A Servant of Two Masters*'. From here you should be able to view set design plans and production photos

www.paololandi.it/. Select '*Servant of Two Masters in Russian*' from the drop-down productions menu. Have a look at the set, costumes and plot using the links at the bottom of the page.

Websites for *Tartuffe* set and costume designs:

www.wfu.edu/theatre/archives/archivest.htm. Select 'Tartuffe' from the 1997-1998 productions.

www.greatlakestheater.org. Click on 'History and Production Archives', then select 2003-2004. Click on the reviews link for *Tartuffe*.

www.rfdesigns.org. Click on *Tartuffe*

www.du.edu/thea/designs/Design-Tartuffe.html

http://web.sau.edu/theatre/seasons/9899season/tartuffe/tartuffe.htm. Click on Theatre Department/St. Ambrose University, Davenport, Iowa. Then select title to see photos.

www.trinity.edu/sgilliam/TRINITY/TARTUFFE/homepage.html

www.courttheatre.org/home/plays/9697/tartuffe/PNtartuffe.shtml (information about the play and its background)

Websites for *Lady Windermere's Fan*

www.gate-theatre.ie/Lady_Windermere.html

A comedy such as ***The Servant of Two Masters*** will be enhanced by bright lighting and occasional sound effects to emphasise the comedy of the **pratfalls** and the lazzi. Music might be used to heighten the tension of the ludicrous swordfight.

Summary

To sum up, whichever play you are studying, consider how best you are going to use your stage space and which of the functions listed below your designs will fulfil.

- to signify period, place and time as well as the **social milieu** of the characters
- to create an authentic period setting or bring out meaning to a contemporary audience by using a specific transposed setting
- to allude to an off-stage world which could be immediate, for example, the next room; or more remote, for example, Moscow
- to accommodate the action, providing adequate space for the cast
- to fulfil any specific functional demands of the play
- to provide furnishings as indicated by the dialogue
- to facilitate comic action required by the play
- to symbolise the moral or spiritual qualities of the characters, or to suggest dominant thematic concerns
- to form an ironic comment on the action of the play
- to create an aesthetically pleasing (beautiful-looking) experience for the audience
- to create an appropriate mood and atmosphere for the action of the play.

6 The actor's interpretation of character

In this chapter you will learn about:

- building a character profile
- the contribution of individual characters to the creative overview.

Link

Refer back to Chapter 16 of the AS coursebook to revise the performer's checklist:

- Who am I? Where am I? Why am I here? How do I feel?
- What is my function?

Also revisit the sections on vocal qualities and physical expression.

This chapter builds on the skills acquired in your AS course and will extend your understanding of how to approach your set play from a performer's perspective.

Unlike at AS Level, however, exam questions about interpretation of individual characters from your set play will *not* refer you to specific sections of the text. You will have to select your *own* examples of the character in action, from different parts of the play, to support your ideas.

The selection of *appropriate* moments from the play will demonstrate your understanding of the character's role and purpose. How you approach a specific character will also reveal your understanding of the playwright's intentions for the role in relation to the meaning of the play as a whole.

The importance of research and character exploration

By now you should appreciate the importance of researching your set text, of understanding its period, context and genre. You should also realise the importance of finding out about previous productions of the play.

This wider knowledge will help you to build up a creative overview which will inform your interpretation of each aspect of the 'virtual' production that you are envisaging. The more you can discover about the role of an individual character, the better equipped you will be to find appropriate vocal and physical expression for it, and to bring that role to theatrical life in your answers.

Building a character profile for key characters

To prepare for the exam you will need to work through the major characters in the play in a methodical way, writing down information to help you construct a 'character profile' for all the major roles. You will need to consider:

- age and gender
- status and occupation
- self-perception
- position within (or outside) the social and/or economic framework presented in the play
- position within (or outside) the family network presented in the play
- initial relationships with other characters at the beginning of the play
- developments/changes in relationships with other characters during in the course of the play
- initial attitudes towards the main/other significant character(s) in the play
- developments/changes in attitude towards the main/other significant character(s) in the play
- initial attitudes/beliefs/ambitions/dreams/desires/aims/intentions
- developments/changes to attitudes/beliefs/ambitions/dreams/desires/aims/intentions in the course of the play

- ▓ reactions to events that occur in the course of the play
- ▓ relationship to the theme(s) of the play
- ▓ the character's 'past' (the 'before-time' to the play's action)
- ▓ the character's future (what the playwright indicates *will* happen to the character, after the play's action is concluded or what the audience is led to believe is *likely to happen* to the character).

▓ Activity

Experiment with improvisation to discover more about characters' attitudes. Remember to base your characterisation on how the playwright presents the character *within* the play.

Truffaldino from *The Servant of Two Masters*

If your chosen play is *The Servant of Two Masters*, you may feel that character analysis is not necessary because the characters are all 'stock' commedia figures. You might feel that Goldoni's intentions go no further than to make the audience laugh, so there is no scope for analysis and development.

However, although the primary intention of the play is to make the audience laugh, it also presents a microcosm of society, peopled by a wealthy middle-class and their servants. The portrayal of this society explores themes as serious as love and death, wealth and poverty, and loyalty and betrayal.

The play is comical in style, but the actors still need to present their characters as fully as is possible, to draw the audience into the world of the play and to convey Goldoni's central concerns.

If you were going to play the part of **Truffaldino**, for example, you would want to create a rounded character that your audience could identify with, rather than merely perform as a mouthpiece for a series of funny lines. The more the audience can empathise with **Truffaldino's** escalating trials and tribulations, gain pleasure from his successes, as he escapes detection, woos **Smeraldina** and, finally, eats a hearty meal, the more they will enjoy the play.

Follow the analysis below to see how a methodical approach to even the most comic of roles helps to define and flesh out the character.

Age and gender
- ▓ **Truffaldino** is a young man of marriageable age.

Status and occupation
- ▓ He is of lowly status, but as a servant to a wealthy gentleman he is admitted to the circle of his social superiors, to deliver and receive messages and to serve upon them.

Self-perception
- ▓ **Truffaldino** has a high regard for his own wit and ingenuity.
- ▓ He has confidence in his own abilities and in his interaction with others.

Position within (or outside) the social and/or economic framework presented in the play
- ▓ **Truffaldino** is an outsider in Venetian society.
- ▓ He is a servant from Bergamo (a region traditionally looked down upon by Venetians).

▓ **Think**

All the plays in this Section contain serious subject matter, however apparently frivolous the style or implausible the plots. Can you think of characters in your set play that need to be presented seriously in order to encourage an audience to engage with their situation?

▓ He is part of the economic framework however, employed by both **Beatrice** and **Florindo** and receiving wages in money and in kind.

▓ He is not poor in the conventional sense since his living expenses are met by his employer(s).

Position within (or outside) the family network presented in the play

▓ **Truffaldino** is excluded from the families of **Pantalone** and **Lombardi** and has to interact with them as a stranger and inferior (this does not appear to modify his cheekiness, however!).

Initial relationships with other characters, at the beginning of the play

▓ He is the servant of **Federico Rasponi** (**Beatrice**).

▓ He is immediately attracted to **Smeraldina**.

▓ He speaks directly to the audience and creates a confessional-style relationship with them.

Developments/changes in relationships with other characters during in the course of the play

▓ His interest in **Smeraldina** develops into courtship and, ultimately, a proposal of marriage.

▓ He insinuates himself into a further master/servant relationship with **Florindo**.

Initial attitudes towards the main/other significant character(s) in the play

▓ Respect for 'Federico'.

▓ Admiration of **Smeraldina**.

▓ Contempt for the **Porter**.

▓ Willingness to exploit **Florindo**.

Developments/changes in attitudes towards the main/other significant character(s) in the play

▓ Growing loyalty to each of his masters.

▓ Developing romantic interest in **Smeraldina**.

▓ Lack of respect for fellow servants and waiters at **Brighella's** Inn.

Initial attitudes/beliefs/ambitions/dreams/aims/intentions

▓ Self-interest.

▓ Intentions to earn more money.

▓ Dreams of satisfying his appetite for food.

Developments/changes to attitudes/beliefs/ambitions/dreams/desires/ aims/intentions in the course of the play

▓ Intention to avoid detection in his web of lies.

▓ Continued dream of financial security and the satisfaction of his appetite.

▓ Desire to marry **Smeraldina**.

Reactions towards the events that occur in the course of the play

▓ Horror when he is told by **Pantalone** that **Federico** is dead.

▓ Outrage at being misled about the death of his master.

▓ Romantic interest in **Smeraldina**.

▓ Frustration with **Federico** who has not fed him.

▓ Opportunistic attempt to get fed by becoming servant to a second master.

- Alternating complacency and fear of detection as he attempts to baffle each of his masters.
- Dismay over **Florindo's** opening of the letter intended for **Beatrice**.
- Opportunistic courtship of **Smeraldina** when she turns up unexpectedly at the Inn.
- Submissive reaction to two beatings.
- Increasing fear of being found out.
- Increasingly outlandish lying to escape detection.
- Optimistic reaction to all set-backs.
- Increasing good opinion of himself.
- Involvement of the audience at every turn.
- Final revelation of his deceit in order to secure **Smeraldina** as his bride.

Relationship to the theme(s) of the play

- The play explores the relationship between servants and their masters and their mutual obligations. **Truffaldino** is central within this theme. **Smeraldina** and the **Porters** also serve as examples of the situation of servants within society.
- Duty (both to masters and parents). **Truffaldino** is central in exploring this theme. **Clarice** is also important in relation to obedience to Pantaloon.
- The relationship between love and money (the arranged marriage and dowry; the dependence of servants on the good will of their masters). **Truffaldino** and **Smeraldina** cannot marry without the consent (and financial support) of their masters.
- Loyalty (in a range of guises). **Truffaldino's** loyalty is tested throughout. The theme is also communicated through the two pairs of lovers.

The character's 'past' (the 'before-time' to the play's action)

- **Truffaldino** seems to have worked for a number of different masters. **Beatrice** has hired him at some point on her journey from Turin to Venice. His past is vague but it appears that he has always been in service.

The character's 'future'

- Marriage to **Smeraldina**.
- Continued service to **Florindo** and **Beatrice** within their household, or to some other employer.

Fig. 6.1 *Jason Watkins as **Truffaldino** woos Michelle Butterley as **Smeraldina** in the 1999 RSC production of Goldoni's* **A Servant of Two Masters**

Using the character profile to create a performance of the role

Look carefully at the information about **Truffaldino** collected under the character profile headings. In each case consider how this information affects the way an actor would play the part.

Think about the actor's use of his body, his face and his voice and how these fundamental tools can communicate a rounded character within a believable, stage world.

You need to consider all the aspects of performance discussed in Chapter 16 of the AS coursebook. For example:

- **Truffaldino's** physical appearance and his demeanour which will alter during the course of the play
- his facial features and expressions, changing throughout the play as he responds to different events and interacts with different people: his superiors, his equals, his inferiors
- his use of voice, his distinctive Bergamo accent, delivery style and delivery of individual lines; the variety of his vocal expression as he converses with characters from different social backgrounds; his masters, **Smeraldina**, the waiters
- his movements, gestures, changing posture and eye-line, conveying different attitudes in the course of the play
- his energy levels, pace and tempo as he progresses through the single day of action: his exhaustion, hunger and contentment
- his use of space and the spatial relationships that he creates with the range of other characters
- his interaction with the audience: stage position, manner, eye-contact, response to banter
- his costume
- his handling of props, especially food and the various letters.
- You also need to consider the demands made by the style of the play, and address:
- comic timing
- comic invention
- **Truffaldino's** physical agility as he performs his **lazzi**.

In the exam

An example of the type of question that you might be asked in the exam about **Truffaldino** is:

> **1** How would you want your audience to respond to Truffaldino? Explain how you would perform the role, in at least **three** sections of the play, in order to achieve your aims.

In order to answer this question and to reveal your creative overview of **Truffaldino's** role in the play, you will need to refer to sections where he demonstrates different aspects of his character, where he is shown interacting with different characters and where he is showing a range of reactions to the unfolding events of the play. You *must* establish what response(s) you want to achieve from the audience in each instance or their response to **Truffaldino** overall.

Given the nature of the role, it would also be useful to include at least one section of interaction with the audience. A good answer will demonstrate your awareness of **Truffaldino's** place in the context of the microcosm of society that we have discussed as well as referring to some of the themes that he helps to highlight for the audience.

> ■ Activity
>
> Choose any character from your set play and find three sections where she or he appears in exchanges with different characters, or reveals different facets of the role to the audience.

Masha from *The Seagull*

As with the example on **Truffaldino**, your work on Masha should lead you to a fuller understanding of how you might play the role and equip you to answer any question set on Masha, in the exam.

Age and gender

- ■ A girl of twenty-two.

Status and occupation

- ■ Living as the daughter of the estate steward, Shamrayev, and his wife, Polina, she has no clear occupation although she helps her mother with household affairs.

Self-perception

- ■ Masha is full of self-pity which appears as self-knowledge/cynicism. She is in mourning for her life, and feels life is not worth living, because Konstantin does not return her love.

Position within (or outside) the social and/or economic framework presented in the play

- ■ Masha lives on the estate and is therefore entirely familiar with all but Trigorin and Nina.
- ■ She is dependent first on her family and then on Medvedenko.

Position within (or outside) the family network presented in the play

- ■ Masha acts almost like a servant to Sorin.
- ■ Once married to Medvedenko, she still appears to spend her time in Sorin's household.

Initial relationships with other characters, at the beginning of the play

- ■ It is hinted that Masha is actually the result of a long-standing affair between Polina and Doctor Dorn, who is her real father.
- ■ Masha is loved by Medvedenko whose love she does not return.
- ■ She is besotted with Konstantin.
- ■ She is loved by her mother, but she prefers Dr Dorn to her 'father'.

Developments/changes in relationships with other characters during in the course of the play

- ■ Masha marries Medvedenko, who she does not love, in an attempt to forget her love for Konstantin.
- ■ She continues to adore Konstantin.
- ■ She establishes a friendly, straightforward, relationship with Trigorin.

Initial attitudes towards the main/other significant character(s) in the play

- ■ She is mistrustful of Arkadina's treatment of Konstantin.
- ■ She adores Konstantin.
- ■ She is indifferent towards Medvedenko.
- ■ She dislikes Shamrayev and is fond of Dr Dorn.

Developments/changes in attitudes towards the main/other significant character(s) in the play

▧ No real change, despite having married Medvedenko and borne him a son.

Initial attitudes/beliefs/ambitions/dreams/aims/intentions

▧ She dreams of Konstantin returning her love.

Developments/changes to attitudes/beliefs/ambitions/dreams/desires/ aims/intentions in the course of the play

▧ She hopes that when Medvedenko moves away to take up a new job she will learn to forget about Konstantin.

Reactions towards the events that occur in the course of the play

▧ Indifference to Medvedenko's avowal of love.

▧ Stung by Konstantin's cruelty to her, she confesses her love for him to Dr Dorn.

▧ She responds passionately to Arkadina's musings about what might be wrong with her son.

▧ She drinks to forget her unhappiness.

▧ She is irritated by Medvedenko and wants him out of her sight. She reveals scant affection for her own child.

▧ She remains obsessed by Konstantin and is very protective of him.

Relationship to the theme(s) of the play

▧ The play explores the destruction of youthful dreams; Masha's dream of Konstantin's love is never fulfilled.

▧ Masha's unrequited (unreturned) love for Konstantin is part of a pattern of such relationships; Nina is destroyed by her unrequited love for Trigorin; Konstantin kills himself when he realises he has lost Nina for ever; Medvedenko wins Masha as his wife but does not gain her love; Masha's mother, Polina, lives an unfulfilled life, in an unhappy marriage despite her long-standing love for Dorn; Sorin who always wanted to marry, will die a bachelor.

▧ Another theme related to Masha is self-absorption.

The character's 'past' (the 'before-time' to the play's action)

▧ Masha has grown up in an unhappy family, loving Konstantin for many years.

Fig. 6.2 *Roger Allam as* Trigorin *with Katy Behean as* Masha *in Terry Hands' production of Chekhov's* The Seagull *for the RSC in 1991*

The character's 'future'

■ **Konstantin's** suicide may destroy her, or it may release her from years of unhappiness. She seems unlikely to find real contentment with **Medvedenko**.

In the exam

An example of the type of question that you might be asked in the exam about **Masha** is:

> **2** Explain how you would perform the role of **Masha**, in specific sections of the play, in order to achieve a sympathetic audience response.

Unlike the question on **Truffaldino**, which allows you to interpret the role in any way that you like, since you are invited to specify *your* preferred response to the character, this particular question on **Masha** *requires* you to present the role sympathetically.

To answer this question successfully you need to select sections from the play that enable you to build up a sympathetic character. This doesn't mean that you must ignore those moments in the play where **Masha** seems harsh to **Medvedenko**, or self-pitying about her love for **Konstantin**, but you will need to find ways of showing that harshness and self-pity in a way that does not alienate the audience but rather helps them to see **Masha's** inner torment.

Think carefully about how to use your body, facial expressions and line delivery to communicate **Masha's** unhappy inner life, even when she appears to be flippant with **Trigorin**, for example, or impatient with her unfortunate husband.

AQA Examiner's tip

You need to meet the precise demands of any question that you answer. Remember to be flexible in the exam and match your answer to the question rather than trying to twist the set question to suit your own pre-conceived ideas.

The Revenger's Tragedy, *Tartuffe*, *The Recruiting Officer*, *Lady Windermere's Fan*

Whichever play you are studying you will find it useful to create character profiles for all the key characters. You might begin with the character that appears in the exemplar question for your set play as given below. Look at all the questions here and note the variations between them. They each have slightly different requirements.

The Revenger's Tragedy

> **3** How would you want your audience to respond to the death of the Duke? Discuss how you would perform the role of the Duke, in **at least two** separate sections of the play, in order to achieve your aims.

Look carefully at this question, it is not simply asking you for a response to the **Duke** as a character; it is asking you to think about how you might play the part in sections *leading up to* his death in order to modify the audience's response to that death.

Your character profile for the **Duke** will have revealed his position within the court at the apex of the hierarchy and will have established his fragile relationships with his wife and extended family, as well as his thoroughly immoral attitudes to life and flagrant disregard for the feelings of others. The **Duke** is a character whom the audience are unlikely to sympathise with until his death, which is particularly unpleasant – and you may not want them to sympathise with him even at this point.

You will need to choose your sections with care, as each one must be 'played' to encourage a particular response to the *death* of the **Duke**.

Tartuffe

4   Discuss how you would perform the role of Dorine, in **two** or **three** sections of the play, in order to create comedy for your audience.

This question asks you to create comedy for your audience through your performance of the role of Dorine.

Within your overview of the character you may wish to mention the origins of Dorine's character as one of the cheeky servants or **zanni** from the commedia tradition. You will have no difficulty in finding sections of the play involving Dorine that have comic potential: her initial wrangle with Madame Pernelle in Act One reveals her determination to speak her mind; her robust intervention in Orgon's plan to marry Mariane to Tartuffe reveals both her concern for Mariane and her comic contempt for her master; her successful reconciliation of the young lovers in Act Two shows her comic ingenuity but also her real care for Mariane and Valère.

There are many opportunities for creating comedy through Dorine's facial expressions, her comic timing, the delivery of her jibes and ripostes to her master and her no-nonsense approach to the squabbling lovers as she physically drags them back together and forces them to make up.

Unlike the previous characters that we have looked at, Dorine has no romantic attachment, but her loyalty to the family she serves is evident throughout the play. The character profile that you draw up for Dorine may lack the complexity of those for other characters but will still provide you with clear ideas for performing the role within the social framework of the stage world that you create.

Fig. 6.3 *Felicity Kendal as Dorine attempts to reconcile Abigale Cruttenden as Mariane with Jamie Glover as Valère, in Peter Hall's production of Tartuffe*

The Recruiting Officer

5   Discuss how you would perform the role of Rose, in **two** or **three** sections of the play, in order to bring out your interpretation of the character.

This question asks you to state your interpretation of the character of Rose, so it's very important to draw upon your character profile here to reveal your understanding of the role.

Rose is young and innocent and socially inferior to Plume and Jack Wilful with whom she contracts a very unsatisfactory 'marriage'! Farquhar uses Rose as a plot device, but she is drawn in sufficient detail,

AQA Examiner's tip

Begin your answer to this question with a clear statement of your interpretation. For example, 'My interpretation of Rose is that she is inexperienced in the ways of the world, but, like most of the characters in the play, she is attracted by the prospect of wealth and position.'

with her notions and fantasies of becoming a lady, through marriage to a Captain, to make her an interesting character to play.

Apart from her relationships with **Plume** and **Jack Wilful**, **Rose** is important in relation to the play's concern with money and marriage. **Rose's** treatment by both men reveals a strain of misogyny which runs through the play and the way she is used as a tool to recruit soldiers suggests the cynicism of the military during war time.

Fig. 6.4 *John P. Connolly as* **Captain Plume** *and Dana Barton as* **Rose** *in the 1979 production of* **The Recruiting Officer** *at the Todd Wehr Theater*

Lady Windermere's Fan

> **6** How would you want your audience to respond to Lord Windermere? Discuss how you would perform the role, in **two** or **three** separate sections from the play, in order to achieve your aims.

Your character profile of Lord Windermere will help you to formulate your ideas about an appropriate audience response to his character.

Lord Windermere may not be a complicated role but Wilde puts him in a complicated position. He is presented as a good man, determined to protect his wife from disillusionment and humiliation at all costs. Out of these very best of motives, he becomes a victim of a subtle form of blackmail from Mrs Erlynne whom he alone knows to be his wife's real mother.

To create a rounded character in Lord Windermere you need to consider the central dilemma of the play as well as Lord Windermere's relationship with it.

Lady Windermere believes that her mother died when she was a baby and she idolises the memory of a mother she never knew. In fact, Lady Windermere's mother had abandoned her infant daughter to elope with a lover, and Lady Windermere's father tried to protect her from scandal by pretending that her mother was dead.

Lord and Lady Windermere have been married less than two years when Mrs Erlynne, hearing of her daughter's advantageous marriage to an extremely wealthy and titled man, returns to London after many years spent abroad avoiding the scandal that followed her elopement.

Her lover has long deserted her and she battens on to Lord Windermere, threatening to reveal her true identity if he does not provide her with an extravagant house and funds to maintain a lavish lifestyle.

Fig. 6.5 *Joely Richardson and Vanessa Redgrave as* Lady Windermere *and* Mrs Erlynne *in the final act of Peter Hall's production of* Lady Windermere's Fan *in 2002*

Wilde presents Lord Windermere's tricky dilemma. London society is shown to be a hotbed of gossip, and news soon reaches Lady Windermere that her husband is frequently seen in the company of the mysterious Mrs Erlynne and that he appears to be keeping her as his mistress.

When she confronts her husband about the rumour, Lord Windermere can do nothing but deny it. He continues to withhold from his wife the fact that her mother is very much alive, is what society considers to be a 'fallen woman', an adulteress, and someone who, simply by association, would contaminate her young daughter.

The events that unfold relieve Lord Windermere of the responsibility of solving the dilemma for himself, but in his character Wilde has created a good man as a counterpoint to the rest of the microcosm of London society which he depicts as, at best, superficial and, at worst, as morally bankrupt.

Activity

Whichever play you are studying, try improvising the following situations:

- Mrs Erlynne first reveals her true identity to Lord Windermere
- Lady Windermere accuses him of having an affair with Mrs Erlynne.
- Try playing Lord Windermere in different ways:
  - calm and collected
  - highly emotional.

Wilde's characters lack the emotional depth of, for example, Chekhov's, as he uses them to explore a moral issue. To a certain extent each character in the play represents a different attitude towards society and morality.

Lord Darlington, in particular, seems to be quite a shallow character, whose chief quality is his wit. However, you should approach your task of drawing up character profiles for all the key roles in *Lady Windermere's Fan* just as seriously as with any other play. Each one needs to be brought to life convincingly by an actor in order to engage the interest of the audience in the characters as well as in the social issue that the play debates.

7 Affecting the audience

In this chapter you will learn about:

- how decisions taken as director, performer or designer affect the audience's experience of the play

- what decisions you should make in preparation for your exam.

The audience's experience

You will know from your own theatre visits during this course that no two productions ever give you the same experience as a member of an audience. Your reaction to a comedy is very different from your reaction to a serious play. You may be absorbed by a realistic play or astounded and amazed by a piece of skilful physical theatre.

These different reactions are created by different types or genres of play. However, you will also find that no two productions of *the same play* affect the audience in the same way.

You might watch a production of *The Recruiting Officer*, for example, performed in an intimate studio space, with a basic set design that uses simple furnishings in a variety of configurations to create the transition from indoor to outdoor scenes. This would offer you a completely different experience from seeing the same play performed in a large auditorium with an elaborately designed open stage, perhaps with a revolve to shift the action from **Melinda's** apartments to the busy market square in Shrewsbury town.

You may see a production of *The Seagull* in a small studio space where you can see every facial expression and even the most subtle eye-contact between the characters. This will be an entirely different experience from watching the play in a large auditorium, where the actors have to make more emphatic gestures and moves to ensure that the audience can see and understand the **subtext** of the dialogue.

A production of *The Revenger's Tragedy* that depicts **Lussorioso** as a lecherous 'ladies' man' would affect the audience in a very different way from one in which his sexual preferences made **Vindice** as appealing a bed-fellow for him as the virtuous **Castiza**.

The potential audience's experience of any of the set plays will be influenced by the choices that you make in developing your creative overview of the play and the place within that overview of every character.

As director or performer you must make sense of the language of the play to ensure that the delivery of the text relays your interpretation of the play to your potential audience. As a designer you need to support your interpretation with concrete design ideas for all the visual aspects of the play as well as for any sound or other technical requirements of the text.

By the time you have completed the study of your text you should have made decisions, as director, performer and designer, about each of the following aspects that affect the audience's experience.

As director, designer or actor

- A creative overview of the play taking account of its style as well as its major themes and/or central issues

- Your intentions for the audience; your preferred audience response

Link

Look back at Chapter 2 to remind yourself how to formulate your overview.

As director/designer

- Choice of staging form, for example, proscenium arch, theatre in-the-round, traverse, thrust, promenade; the positioning of the audience
- Production style, for example, naturalistic, physical, stylised, symbolic
- Choice of period, authentic or transposed
- Setting ideas to create location/period
- Scenic devices to achieve transitions between separate settings or the use of a composite set
- Use of levels, ramps, balconies
- Choice and use of props
- Costume designs
- Technical design

As director

- Casting decisions for all characters in terms of their physical and vocal characteristics
- Directorial ideas for key scenes/sections/set-pieces in relation to intended effects
- The pace, mood and atmosphere of each scene
- Movement and vocal delivery of the actors; their interaction
- Groupings
- Ideas for creating comedy, if appropriate

As designer

- Design fundamentals: scale, shape, materials, texture, colour
- Setting design: backdrops, **cyclorama**, **flats**, levels, stairs, steps, entrances/exits, doorways, windows, traps
- Furnishings: period, style, scale, fabrics, condition
- Costume fundamentals: period, cut, line, fabric, fit, size, colour, condition
- Accessories: shoes, headgear, ornamentation, jewellery
- Props: authentic or multi-functional
- Masks, make-up, wigs
- Lighting: angle, intensity, speed of fade, use of shadow, colour, **gobos**, **specials**
- Sound: volume, direction, amplification, levels; music; effects

As actor

- The appearance of the character
- The physical appearance, height, build, facial features, colouring
- Performance style
- Gesture, movement, gait, posture, mannerisms
- Vocal qualities, volume, pace, pitch, pause, accent, dialect, emphasis
- Delivery of specific lines; delivery of verse, if appropriate
- Interaction with other characters and/or with the audience
- Eye-contact, physical contact, use of space, use of props
- Ideas for comedy, if appropriate
- Character development

How to be successful in the examination

▧ How to write a successful answer

In the examination, you must ensure that you select the question that appeals to your strengths. You must also ensure that you meet that question's demands precisely.

Your answer should show that you understand how your chosen play might work in performance and, through your treatment of the given task, that you understand the whole play. The questions in Section A will not refer *explicitly* to a creative overview, but it is a fundamental principle underlying Unit 3 that in *both* sections you do demonstrate this overview in your answers.

This requirement is stated in the specification as follows:

> In Section A of the examination, questions are focused on the interpretation of the plays from a performance perspective. In addition to their consideration of the performance and production elements that are stipulated for Section B of Unit 1 (see 3.1), candidates are required to demonstrate a creative overview of their chosen play in answer to questions which may require a director's, an actor's or a designer's perspective. Candidates are expected to select appropriate sections from their chosen play to illustrate their answers.

You will demonstrate that you have this creative overview by referring to the central concerns and themes of the wider play in the course of your answer, whatever its main focus.

Your answer should contain inventive ideas for a virtual production that will communicate meaning to a potential audience. Your understanding of the play's original period and genre must be evident in your answer through *explicit* reference to it as well as through the suitability of the staging decisions that you make.

You gain marks for:

▧ maintaining focus on the demands of the question

▧ appropriate selection and use of textual examples to support your answer and bring the play to life

▧ evidence of 'whole play' knowledge within your answer, whatever its focus

▧ relevant reference to period and genre

▧ creativity in your interpretation of character/action/design requirements

▧ precise detail in your staging or performance ideas

▧ clear practical suggestions

▧ consideration of how your ideas will affect the audience experience

▧ purposeful, labelled sketches to support design ideas, where appropriate

▧ reasonably equal treatment of each of the sections of the play that you have chosen to illustrate your answer

- accurate use of specialist theatre terminology
- fluency, good organization and development of your ideas.

You lose marks for:

- evident lack of planning
- poor selection of sections of text to support the answer, for example, if you choose all your illustrations from the same part of the play
- a narrative approach to the question, lacking precise practical detail
- generalised statements of intention, without specific examples
- inadequate use of quotations to support your ideas
- irrelevance; deviation from the focus of the question or answering only part of the set question
- inappropriate or unjustified suggestions that appear unsuitable to the period setting or style of the play
- absence of specialist terminology or inaccurate use of it
- colloquial expression
- under-developed suggestions
- ignoring the play's original period and genre
- absence of a sense of overview of the play.

Choosing the right question and focusing on its demands

Section A of Unit 3 offers you a choice of two questions on your set text. Choose the one that you feel most comfortable answering, or the one which asks for the perspective that you prefer writing about, whether that is a director's, a designer's or a performer's perspective.

Make sure that you understand the demands of your chosen question and that you continue to focus on these throughout your answer. Consider the questions below and make a note of the precise requirements of each one. It doesn't matter which play features in the question. Questions like this are routinely set on all the plays.

Director's questions

Director's questions might be phrased in various ways. Each of the questions below requires a response written in the first person and from a director's point of view. However, note that although they all require a brief outline of your casting decisions for two characters, the questions are not exactly the same.

The Recruiting Officer

7 Briefly outline and justify your casting decisions for Worthy and Brazen and then discuss how you would direct your actors, in **at least two** scenes where they appear together, in order to highlight their rivalry for the love of Melinda.

This question requires you to focus your directorial ideas upon highlighting the rivalry between Worthy and Brazen, so all your ideas should be linked to this purpose. Remember to refer to the wider implications of their rivalry, for example, by mentioning attitudes to marriage and money in the 18th century and Melinda's inheritance. This will demonstrate that you have an overview of the play.

AQA Examiner's tip

Devote one hour to planning and writing your response to your chosen question in Section A of Unit 3. Use your time wisely. Do not begin writing until you have decided which parts of the play will be most helpful to illustrate your answer.

The Servant of Two Masters

8   Analyse the effects you would want to create for your audience through your presentation of the relationship between **Silvio** and **Clarice**. Briefly outline and justify your casting decisions for the pair and then discuss how you would direct your actors, in **at least two** scenes where they appear together, in order to achieve your aims.

This question requires you to identify the effects that you want to create for your audience through your directorial ideas for **Silvio** and **Clarice** *before* discussing the directing strategies capable of achieving those effects. Demonstrate your overview of the play by briefly relating these young lovers to Goldoni's presentation of love in the wider play or by making suggestions that match the comic style of the play.

The Seagull

9   Briefly outline and justify your casting decisions for Madame Arkadina and her son, Treplev, and then discuss how you would direct your actors, in **at least two** scenes where they appear together, in order to reveal your interpretation of their relationship.

(Note that in some editions of the play, Treplev is called Konstantin.)

In this question you need to give your interpretation of the relationship between mother and son and then to explain how your direction will communicate that interpretation to the audience. Place your ideas in the context of the theme of disillusionment and thwarted ambitions to show your overview of their relationship in the play.

Designer's questions

Designer's questions might be phrased in some of the following ways:

The Revenger's Tragedy

10   As a designer, discuss how you would achieve an appropriate style and atmosphere for your audience through your designs for the play, using **at least two** of the following elements: setting, costume, lighting.

Tartuffe

11   What are the challenges that face a set designer of Tartuffe? Discuss how your set design ideas would satisfy the demands of the play with reference to specific moments of action.

Lady Windermere's Fan

12   Discuss how your design ideas for the costumes and accessories of Lady Windermere and Lord Darlington would help to convey their characters to an audience, and suggest an appropriate period and style for your production of Lady Windermere's Fan. You should relate your designs to the characters' appearances in **at least two** specific scenes.

All three questions require a response written in the first person and from a designer's point of view, but each has distinct requirements. The first question demands that you identify an appropriate style and atmosphere for **The Revenger's Tragedy** before you begin to offer design ideas for *two* elements. The second question requires that you consider the design challenges of *Tartuffe* and requires a *set* design. The third asks for *costume* designs that will convey the characters of Lady Windermere and Lord Darlington to an audience.

Take great care to address the precise demands of the question in each case and remember to place your designs within the context of your overview of the play.

Performer's questions

We have considered how you might approach performer's questions in Chapter 6, where there are examples of different types of question.

Performer's questions often ask about:

- your preferred audience response and performance ideas intended to achieve that response
- your interpretation of a character and performance ideas designed to convey that interpretation
- ideas for creating comedy through your performance of a specific character
- performance ideas to elicit a specified audience response to your character, for example, sympathy, dislike, horror
- performance ideas designed to highlight specific qualities of a character, for example, virtue, vice, sadness, hypocrisy.

In each case you must have a *purpose* in mind when deciding on how you will perform a role. You will need to choose your examples carefully so that you are able to fulfil that purpose. Try to choose sections from different parts of the play to show your character in different situations or with different characters, if appropriate. Don't forget to place them in the context of their 'journey' through the play and their significance within its main themes and concerns.

Look back over Chapter 6 which discusses how to approach performer's questions, in relation to each of the plays.

> ## AQA Examiner's tip
>
> Ensure that you use quotations from the text (*not* page numbers or line numbers) to support all your practical ideas. This should help to enliven your answer for the examiner. You should also identify the sections that you choose by referring to the relevant Act and/or Scene.

9   Summary of Section A

In these chapters you have learned about:

- the differences and similarities between the AS and A2 course content
- the context, period and genre of your set play
- how to formulate your creative overview of your set text
- how directors might approach the creation of comedy on stage
- how directors interpret plays to create meaning
- how some directors approach the rehearsal process
- the importance of research in the rehearsal process
- the director's creation of time and place
- how directors reach staging decisions
- how designers contribute to the interpretation of a play
- the potential of stage space
- how designers meet the functional demands of a play
- how performers interpret their roles
- how to prepare a character profile
- how the choices made by the production team affect the audience
- how to be successful in the examination
- where to find information about the set plays and how they have been interpreted in previous productions.

These chapters are intended to build upon the approaches to directing, designing and performing that are described in the AS coursebook. Look back at that book to refresh your memory about the different practical methods to help you to prepare for your examination at A2.

10   Introduction to the set texts in Section B

In this section you will learn about:

- the demands of the examination question for Section B

- the different theatrical styles of the six set texts.

The set texts in Section B of Unit 3 each represent a significant style of theatre. Five of them were written during the 20th century, while the sixth, *Coram Boy*, was written at the beginning of this century. All the plays are accessible and likely to remain in theatre repertoires for many years.

You only have to study *one* of these texts, but it would be worthwhile to read at least some of the others. This wider reading will introduce you to modern styles of theatre that you might choose to explore in your practical unit.

Do not be tempted to skip the sections below, or the chapters that deal with the plays you are not studying. Each section contains valuable information about interpretative strategies that will help you to understand the staging possibilities of your own set text.

This is the question that you will have to answer in Section B of Unit 3:

> As a director, discuss how you would stage the following extract in order to bring out your interpretation of it for an audience.
>
> Your answer should include suggestions for the direction of your cast and for the design of the piece. You will need to justify how your suggestions are appropriate to the style of the play and to your creative overview of it.
>
> You should also supply sketches and/or diagrams and refer to relevant research to support your ideas.

In order to answer this question you will be drawing on the knowledge you have acquired during your whole AS and A2 courses to interpret whichever short extract from your set play appears on the exam paper. You will need to have formulated your creative overview of the play and be sensitive to its theatrical style.

You will have undertaken some research into the play's background and staging history and will have equipped yourself, just as a professional theatre director must do, with enough knowledge and understanding of the play's meaning and dramatic requirements to be able to translate the play from page to stage. The following brief introduction to each play summarises its theatrical style, its concerns and dramatic methods.

Blood Wedding, by Federico Garcia Lorca

Blood Wedding represents the theatrical style of **poetic drama**. Written by Federico Garcia Lorca in Spain in 1933, the play presents a true story of illicit love, told though a mixture of poetry, song and lyrical prose. Lorca's dramatic style challenged the prevailing realism of the early 20th century, blending believable characters with symbolic figures and relying as much on visual elements, for its effects, as upon dialogue.

The play explores the conflict between passion and duty, and depicts a bride who runs away with her married lover on the day of her marriage, with tragic consequences. The wedding guests join with the bridegroom to

Key term

Poetic drama: plays written in verse or in a heightened, poetic form of prose. In the late 19th and early 20th centuries a number of English and European dramatists set out to restore poetry to the stage, which they saw as impoverished by the realistic and naturalistic styles that were then prevalent.

hunt down the lovers and are guided to their quarry by the deathly figure of an **Old Beggar Woman** and a symbolic **Moon**. Both the **Bridegroom** and **Leonardo**, the lover, are killed. In the closing scene of the play, the **Bride**, the **Bridegroom's Mother** and **Leonardo's** widow grieve together.

▓ *The Good Person of Szechwan* by Bertolt Brecht

Brecht wrote *The Good Person of Szechwan* between 1938 and 1940 when he was in exile from Germany.

The play represents the style of **epic theatre** for which Brecht is best known. It is a **parable play** that explores the difficulty of being good in a wicked world.

The 'Good Person' of the title, Shen Teh, is a soft-hearted, young woman, whose kindness is exploited. Her innate goodness is recognised by three wandering Gods and rewarded with a gift of enough silver dollars to enable her to give up prostitution and purchase a tobacco shop.

The shop attracts hoards of grasping, good-for-nothing neighbours, who impose themselves on Shen Teh's kindness and quickly drain her resources. In order to protect herself, she invents and adopts the physical disguise of a 'hard-hearted cousin', Shui Ta, whose hard-nosed business sense and ruthlessness with the hangers-on ensures that she keeps her business and is able to survive.

In typical Brechtian fashion, the play has a narrator who speaks directly to the audience; there are multiple settings, multi-role acting and a series of songs.

▓ *A View from the Bridge*, by Arthur Miller

A View from the Bridge represents the style of modern **tragedy**. Miller originally wrote the play as a one-act verse drama. However, the original 1955 production was not especially successful and Miller re-wrote it, in prose, as a more conventional two-act play.

Miller retained the fundamental shape of the tragedy, which is tightly crafted, and he included the figure of **Alfieri**, the lawyer, who speaks directly to the audience, commentating on the play's action, in the style of a classical Greek Chorus.

In **Eddie Carbone**, Miller creates a representative character – a decent, hard-working, family man. However, like the protagonist of Greek Tragedy he has a flaw or weakness. Although he does not acknowledge the fact, even to himself, **Eddie's** affection for his teenage niece is bordering on the incestuous. Her decision to marry one of her Sicilian cousins brings **Eddie's** simmering feelings to the boil and, in an act of treachery, he denounces the cousins, both illegal immigrants, to the Immigration authorities. The play ends with a violent quarrel in which **Eddie** is fatally stabbed.

▓ *The Trial*, by Steven Berkoff

It is notoriously difficult to categorise Berkoff's work. However, in *The Trial*, we can identify both an **ensemble** approach and elements of an expressionist style.

Although *The Trial* is an adaptation of a novel by Franz Kafka, Berkoff's treatment of it is highly original. While incorporating elements of a modern form of **expressionism** into his productions, Berkoff's techniques capture the nightmare quality of Kafka's original short story, through gesture, movement, mime and exaggerated acting.

▓ Key terms

Epic theatre: a form of political drama designed to appeal more to the intellect than the emotions. The style has an episodic structure, which eschews the logical development of realistic dramas, and invites spectators to *judge* the actions of the characters presented, rather than empathise with their problems.

Tragedy: the downfall of someone from security and happiness to abject misery and, usually, death. The fall is caused by fate combined with the protagonist's weakness or 'fatal flaw'. The audience should react with pity and fear as the tragic figure recognises responsibility for his or her undoing.

Ensemble theatre: drama that is performed by a group of actors, making roughly equal contributions even where some characters perform named parts and others take on multi-roles. It is a dramatic method rather than a style of theatre.

Expressionism: a theatrical style that emerged in Germany around 1910. Expressionist playwrights represented the external realities of life in a stylised and subjective way. In contemporary forms of the style, dialogue is often written in verse or heightened prose, characters are not realistically drawn and the events of the play appear to be random rather than logical.

Berkoff's *The Trial* follows the misfortunes of **Joseph K**, a naïve bank clerk who is arrested, for an un-named crime that he has no knowledge of, and subjected to a nightmarish ordeal, involving the courts and a mystifying justice system, as he attempts to defend his name. **K's** 'trial', which involves a visitation from his dead father, an escapade with his lawyer's mistress and a bizarre encounter with an apparently deranged artist, ends unhappily.

Our Country's Good, by Timberlake Wertenbaker

Our Country's Good is a play that defies simple categorisation in terms of its style. In its episodic form of twenty-two scenes, it must be called epic. However, the playwright invites the audience to empathise with some of the characters and, although it is a highly political play, it has elements of romance, as well as comedy.

The play was commissioned by Max Stafford Clark to be performed at the Royal Court as a companion piece to *The Recruiting Officer*, which we have discussed in earlier chapters. It might be safest to describe it as a hybrid: a **historical dramatisation** and, in its use of multi-role casting, an ensemble piece.

In common with most historical dramatisations, *Our Country's Good* does not simply tell a story about the past. Timberlake Wertenbaker crafts a powerful drama that tells a story about the past, in order to teach the audience something about the present – this is another feature of epic theatre.

Set first on a convict ship bound for Australia, and then in the convict colony itself, the play traces the transformation of a motley crew of semi-literate convicts into a unified theatre group, capable of putting on George Farquhar's elegant Restoration comedy, *The Recruiting Officer*. It explores different points of view about crime and punishment and delivers an optimistic message about the redemptive power of theatre.

Coram Boy, adapted by Helen Edmundson

Coram Boy is an adaptation of the novel written for young adults by Jamila Gavin. It won the Whitbread Children's Book of the Year award in 2000. Playscript rights were bought by the National Theatre, which then commissioned Helen Edmundson to adapt the novel into playscript form. Edmundson is an award-winning playwright whose work with Shared Experience included adaptations of *Anna Karenina* as well as *The Mill on the Floss*.

The broad style of theatre that *Coram Boy* falls into is a **dramatised novel**. However, this type of theatre can take many forms. The collaborative nature of the work that was undertaken in preparing this play for its production at the National Theatre meant that its dramatic style is eclectic. It is the result of a six-week period of workshops involving the actors, the director, the composer and the adaptor, as well as Jamila Gavin.

The play is set principally in London and Gloucester. It explores social issues of illegitimacy, prejudice and exploitation, adolescent love and the power of music. The play covers a time period of nine years and has the episodic structure of **epic theatre**. It includes a full choir, a string quartet and has a large ensemble cast who between them play adults, children and an angel, and who may also represent gargoyles and mules in the course of the busy action of some scenes.

Key terms

Historical dramatisation: a popular style since Shakespeare wrote his history plays in the 16th century. Modern history plays include Peter Shaffer's *The Royal Hunt of the Sun* (1964) which explores the Spanish conquistadors' expedition to Peru, and *Speaking Like Magpies* by Frank McGuinness, (2005) about the Gunpowder Plot.

Dramatised novel: a play adapted from a novel. The style of these adaptations varies; some use a narrator to help compress the narrative, while others employ traditional dramatic dialogue. Adaptations of fantasy stories such as Philip Pullman's *His Dark Materials* and Tolkien's *Lord of the Rings* use stunning special effects.

Link

Refer back to Chapter 5 of the AS coursebook for more information about Shared Experience theatre company.

11   *Blood Wedding*

AQA Examiner's tip

Do read the introduction, written by Gwynne Edwards, in your set text. However, remember that in the exam you will only be credited for including biographical detail if it is relevant to your interpretation of the play.

Background information

The Spanish Civil War was fought between the left-wing Republicans and the right-wing Nationalists. The uprising against the established Republican government started in July 1936, supported by the conservative landowners, the Church and industrialists. After three years of violence, the right-wing Fascist dictator General Franco proclaimed victory.

Key term

Cante jondo (deep song): said to deal with love, pain and death. It was the simplicity of the form and the strength of the emotions contained in these poems which appealed to Lorca.

Background and research

Lorca's background played a significant part in shaping his work; it inspired his choice of subject matter as well as influencing his developing dramatic form. Therefore, you need to know about Lorca's world to understand the origins of his rural tragedies as well as to appreciate his style of writing.

Biographical detail

Lorca's family lived in the isolated Andalucian village of Fuente Vaqueros, about twelve miles from Granada. Lorca spent his early life there and in the nearby village of Valderubbio. Both villages are part of the 'vega', a fertile plain surrounded by the mountains of the Sierra Nevada. Although his family moved to Granada when Lorca was 11, he never forgot his roots.

As a young man Lorca mixed with some of the most influential artistic figures of the early 20th century. He travelled widely and visited London, Oxford, Paris and New York, as well as spending time in South America. Lorca lived a bohemian lifestyle and he struggled to confront his emerging homosexuality.

The 1930s were turbulent times in Spain in the build-up to the Spanish Civil War, and Lorca's liberal lifestyle and left-wing sympathies were frowned upon by the emerging right-wing party. In the summer of 1936, once the Spanish Civil War had started, Lorca's life was cut short in a violent manner when he was arrested by right-wing partisans and executed by firing squad.

Artistic interests and influences

Lorca developed a deep and wide-ranging knowledge of different branches of the arts. As well as being an accomplished poet, he could draw and he also made puppets. Lorca was a talented musician and he played the guitar as well as the piano. He was fascinated by the flamenco dance as well as **cante jondo**, the songs and lullabies of his native area.

Lorca knew some of the most influential figures in the arts of the 20th century and shared many of their artistic aims. For example:

- Salvador Dali (1904–1989) the Spanish painter and sculptor, one of the leaders of the surrealist movement

- Luis Buñuel (1900–1983) the pioneering Spanish film-maker, best known for the surrealist classic *Un Chien Andalou*

- Manuel de Falla (1876–1946) the Spanish composer, influenced like Lorca, by the traditional music of the country and best known for the ballet, *The Three Cornered Hat.*

- Pablo Picasso (1881–1973) one of the most important artists of the 20th century, who was born in nearby Malaga.

Lorca's artistic and musical background and his association with and admiration for these avant-garde figures helps to explain the distinctively 'modern' style of his drama. Lorca wrote plays in a range of different styles including plays based on the puppet traditions. However, in *Blood Wedding*, it was the countryside of his homeland that most influenced his writing.

Theatrical experience

The 'Barraca'

Lorca's skills as a playwright were firmly rooted in his own practical experience. In 1931, at a time when theatre in Spain was largely attended by the middle classes, Lorca set up *La Barraca* (The Caravan). This was a touring theatre group designed specifically to bring performances to a wider audience in the more remote areas of the country. La Barraca was a company organised as an ensemble of players. They travelled from venue to venue in a lorry from which they unpacked their rostra-style stage.

The Barraca's repertoire included the classical plays of the 17th century, such as *Life is a Dream*, by **Pedro Calderon** and *Fuenteovejuna*, by | **Lope de Vega**, great plays from the Spanish Golden Age period which were also a source of inspiration to Lorca as he was developing his own dramatic style. With their preoccupation with the theme of the Spanish **code of honour**, as well as the musical content of their plays, both dramatists influenced Lorca's *Blood Wedding*.

Blood Wedding – a rural tragedy

Lorca's three most important plays, *Blood Wedding* (1933), *Yerma* (1934) and *The House of Bernarda Alba* (1936) are usually referred to as the 'rural tragedies' because they are set so specifically in the Andalucia that he knew.

Lorca's rural tragedies are principally concerned with the lives of women. Each present powerful characterisations of the female figures and dramatise the challenges, dilemmas and restrictions within their lives.

Lorca often chose subject matter that he drew from the real-life stories of his neighbours and contemporaries. His ability to recreate the speech patterns of the people he grew up with and to blend these effectively with a more heightened form of expression resulted in a style of theatre that was at once both 'realistic' and 'poetic'.

In *Blood Wedding*, Lorca maintains his focus on the rural society with which he was most familiar, but he took the basis of the plot from a true story that he had read in a newspaper. Lorca adapted this raw material to highlight two of his recurring themes: honour and betrayal.

It is interesting to compare the details of the newspaper story with Lorca's artistic choices.

Newspaper account	*Blood Wedding*
A girl elopes on the day *before* her wedding was due to take place.	A Bride elopes on the day of her wedding, *after* the ceremony. This allows Lorca to set the action against the background of wedding celebrations; song and dance.
The bridegroom's brother, travelling to the wedding on horseback, meets the bride and her lover as they are making their escape.	Leonardo and the **Bride** escape on horseback. The **Bridegroom**, accompanied by two other young men pursue the fugitives.
The bridegroom's brother shoots the other man dead.	The **Bridegroom** and **Leonardo** use knives to kill each other; their deaths are presided over by a mystical character of **Death**.

Who's who

Pedro Calderon (1600–1681): Calderon began writing plays at the age of 14 and completed nearly 200 in all. He had the patronage of Phillip IV of Spain. *Life is a Dream* is considered to be his finest play.

Lope de Vega (1562–1635): Spain's first great playwright and a prolific writer, it is thought that he wrote over 1,500 plays, of which about 470 have survived. Most of his plays were written in verse and deal with an idealised code of honour.

Key terms

Code of honour: in Spain the code of honour insisted upon honourable behaviour at all times and placed extreme importance on the idea of upholding and defending family honour – even to the death. This concept has obvious relevance to the whole plot of *Blood Wedding*.

Activity

Read one of the other rural tragedies to give you a more detailed picture of the background, style and interests of Lorca's work.

Link

Use your online resources for more information about *La Barraca*.

Theatre trivia

Lorca based the central character in his play *The House of Bernada Alba* upon a neighbour. Bernada Alba was a tyrannical mother whose control over her unmarried daughters made them appear to Lorca to be little more than 'shadows', an aspect that he explores in his drama.

■ Further reading

Ian Gibson, *Lorca's Granada, a Practical Guide*, Faber and Faber, 1992

Lorca's changes to the original story are dramatically important. The use of the knife rather than a gun and the double killing clearly intensify the drama; in the opening scene, the **Mother's** obsession with knives is made to appear prophetic. The fact that in *Blood Wedding* the elopement happens *after* the wedding ceremony also emphasises the violation of the code of honour by **Leonardo**. This alteration also allows Lorca to incorporate the colour and music of a wedding scene into the play.

ⓘ Stage history

The original production

The first production of *Blood Wedding* in 1933 was directed by Lorca himself. As the stage directions in the text suggest, Lorca knew what he wanted and was very precise as a director. For example, he specifies 'a long pause', 'a slow curtain' and 'a loud knocking'. Lorca's original cast were unused to the blend of prose and poetry that is a feature of the play, and initially rehearsals were difficult, but after much hard work the play's opening night was a resounding success.

Fig. 11.1 *Cyril Ikechukwe Nri (**Bridegroom**), Helen McCrory (**Bride**), Gary McDonald (**Leonardo**) in the Royal National Theatre's production of **Blood** Wedding by Frederico Garcia Lorca, adapted by Gwenda Pandolfi, directed by Yvonne Brewster in 1991*

Later productions

Later productions have emphasised the universality of the play's themes and concerns. Here are just some of the different ideas that have been used:

■ A 1935 production used geometric and abstract designs to heighten the **surrealism** of the language.

■ A production at the Edinburgh Festival in 1986 used a far more realistic design while using a very stylised acting technique.

■ In 1987 a group of Mexican actors went to Fuente Vaqueros, Lorca's birthplace, and performed *Blood Wedding* in the open air. The acting area was extensive, real horses were used, and as the wedding guests form a large but tight-knit group of dancers in the centre of this arena, the **Bride** and **Leonardo** galloped across the stage, between the dancers and the audience who thereby witness the elopement.

- The National Theatre in London in 1991, transposed the setting to Cuba, another Spanish-speaking rural community. The production used powerful, vibrant music and interpreted the flower imagery in concrete terms by setting lilies in oil drums on the set.
- There have also been productions which use flamenco dancers, versions in which the songs were sung in the original Spanish and sets which represented the arena for a bull-fight.

Most successful productions depend on the actors' ability to convey the truthfulness of the emotions within the play, coupled with a directorial intention to create Lorca's theatrical 'poetry' on stage.

Fig. 11.2 *Clara Onyemere (**Leonardo's Wife**) and Gary McDonald (**Leonardo**) in the Royal National Theatre's production of* **Blood Wedding** *by Frederico Garcia Lorca, adapted by Gwenda Pandolfi, directed by Yvonne Brewster in 1991*

> **Think**
>
> The text is open to many different interpretations; Yvonne Brewster who directed the 'Cuban' production says that Lorca is: *'open to interpretation; if you are honest with him he will never let you down.'*
>
> What do you think she meant by 'honest'?

Characterisation

The characters in *Blood Wedding* are strongly differentiated. The main plot is semi-realistic; its characters are named to reflect their domestic relationships.

The **Mother** has strong opinions and emotions and is presented from the very beginning of the play as deeply disturbed. Her obsession with knives, her constant grieving for the dead, her fear for her son and her deep-seated loathing of the Felix family define her as a character.

The **Bridegroom** shows great affection for his mother but he is also dominated by her. In Act 1 Scene 3, the **Mother** refuses the **Bride's Father's** offer of wine on her son's behalf, saying that 'he doesn't touch it'. His attitude towards the **Bride** is completely trusting. Once his honour is offended when he discovers the elopement of the **Bride** with **Leonardo**, however, the **Bridegroom** is compelled to act.

The **Bride** is not a delicate heroine. She lives in a barren landscape which produces strong women. Her emotions are passionate and dangerous. Her **Father** describes her as 'soft as wool', but his reference to the fact that 'she can cut a piece of string with her teeth' hints at a steelier personality.

Only **Leonardo** has a name in the play, rather than a description of his function, and it is a name that inspires strong feelings whenever it is uttered. **Leonardo** is usually portrayed as a physically attractive, virile-looking man. His name combines the Spanish words for both 'lion' and 'burning', and it is his passion and fiery energy that appeal to the **Bride**.

Leonardo's Wife is depicted as an unhappy woman, fulfilling her destiny as a wife and mother. She is the antithesis of the **Bride**, but is doomed, like her, to become a widow prematurely. She joins the **Mother** and the **Bride** in the final tableau of grieving women.

In Act 3, Scene 1, however, Lorca introduces five entirely symbolic characters.

There are three **Woodcutters** who take on the role of a tragic chorus, commenting on the action and anticipating the terrible outcome of the elopement. They carry axes and are accompanied by the sound of two violins.

The **Moon** appears, dressed as a young woodcutter, whose whitened face appears to illuminate the forest setting with an intense blue light. His speech is full of foreboding and he conspires with the **Beggar Woman** to ensure that the **Bride** and **Leonardo** do not escape their pursuers.

The **Beggar Woman** is a fantastical character who represents **Death**. She emerges from the forest, dressed in green cloth, her face, barely visible. She takes delight in guiding the **Bridegroom** to find the **Bride** and **Leonardo** and, when 'Death' comes, she symbolises her predatory nature by opening her cloak to suggest the wings of a large bird of prey.

💡 Staging the play

Style

Certainly *Blood Wedding* is an example of poetic drama. However, the style might better be described as a hybrid (mix), as it has elements of real life as well as surrealism. The basic story line is rooted in reality, although it is a reality as filtered through Lorca's poetic vision. This part of the play deals with the code of honour and incorporates the dance and song styles of the area of the *vega* to create a vivid picture of village life. However, there is also the surreal quality of Act 3, Scene 1, involving the **Moon**, **Death** and the three strange **Woodcutters**.

This symbolic element of the play is continued into Act 3, Scene 2, where the **Girls**, dressed in blue, are presented winding the skein of red wool. This is a further reference to the mythological idea of the **Fates** spinning and eventually cutting the thread of a person's life.

In addition to the **symbolism** contained in the language of the play and in the strange characters of the **Moon** and the **Old Woman**, Lorca uses concrete images and specific strong colours to help to communicate meaning to the audience.

> **Key term**
>
> **The Fates:** in Greek mythology there were three Fates, Clotho who spun the thread of a person's life, Lachesis who influenced the luck which that life received and Atropos who dictated the inescapable fate. When the thread was cut, this meant death.

> **Think**
>
> Ensure that all your directorial decisions are based on a thorough understanding of the play and its style. You must always justify your decisions in these terms.

> **Activity**
>
> Go through the text, noting each time a specific colour is mentioned, whether it describes the setting, props or costumes. What do you think Lorca was trying to achieve by his strong use of colour?

A director has many choices to make about how to present Lorca's distinctive style which offers considerable opportunities for invention.

Music

Throughout the play the use of music is crucial to reflect the style, atmosphere and setting of **Blood Wedding**.

Lorca uses song, music and sound throughout the play to contribute to the distinctive moods of each scene. For example:

- In Act 1, Scene 2, the **Wife** and **Mother-in-law** sing a dark lullaby to the baby.
- In Act 2, Scene 1, the wedding guests and girls sing 'Let the bride awaken'.
- In Act 2, Scene 2, the action is played out against a background of music, dancing and gaiety.
- In Act 3, Scene 1, the **Woodcutter's** appearance is accompanied by the unsettling sound of two violins which represent the forest.
- In Act 3, Scene 2, the **Girls** wind wool and sing before the arrival of **Leonardo's Wife** and **Mother-in-law**.

When you are making your staging choices you will have to decide what kind of music to use and whether to have the songs accompanied or simply chanted or sung without accompaniment. You will have to decide whether to incorporate flamenco into the wedding scene and whether you want musicians to be visible on stage.

What is most important about the music is that it is in keeping with Lorca's intentions and your own directorial approach.

Activity

Find out more about the singing, dancing and, above all, the rhythms of flamenco.

Imagery

In poetic drama, the playwright's use of **imagery** is fundamental to the meaning of the play; a director needs to understand it before he or she can translate the verbal imagery into a concrete theatrical idea.

With all the references to the heat and the importance of heat in the *vega* area, it is hardly surprising that water is a recurring image of fertility in Lorca's plays. The sound of water had a musical quality for Lorca, and an abundance of water was always presented as a positive sign.

The play has many references to water and the suggestion, in the lullaby, that **Leonardo's** black stallion will not drink, is presented as a sinister and unnatural idea. In the final scene, the **Bride** describes the **Bridegroom** as 'a tiny drop of water' while she thinks of **Leonardo** as 'a dark river'.

Activity

Go through each scene and note down how many references there are in each to:
- water
- knives
- flowers.

There are also repeated references to flowers and weeds in the play. The **Mother** describes her dead husband as a 'carnation' and a 'geranium'; the **Wife** calls her baby a 'carnation' and the singers repeat the idea that the bridegroom is a 'golden flower'. The **Bride**, on her wedding day, feels herself to drowning in a 'bedspread of roses', while the **Wife** describes the way **Leonardo** looks at her as 'a thorn in each eye'.

This last image is one of the many painful and violent images in the play. The recurring idea of the knife is established in the opening lines, but there are also references to a man losing both arms in an accident and the **Bride** feels 'splinters of glass are stuck in my tongue'. The **Woodcutter's** axes also represent the fatal blades that rob the women of their men.

Having identified the significant images within Lorca's poetic text, the task of the director is to help the audience to notice them.

In performance, an actor's awareness of the importance of individual images or image clusters within their lines helps them to accent them for an audience using a slight change of pace, a glance held longer than expected, or by giving a fractional pause before the image is spoken.

The designer might also be asked to realise the imagery within the design. A designer for *Blood Wedding* might want running water on stage. This is possible, although it does cause practical and safety problems which need to be recognised.

Flowers and knives are easier to accommodate within a design. Flowers could be introduced quite naturalistically, as with the **Bride's** orange blossom, or perhaps the other wedding guests could be wearing flowers. They could even be embroidered on the skirts or shawls of the women.

One designer chose to make an enormous abstract flower as the dominant feature of the set, and to blend the imagery of flowers and blades by having blood run from the centre of the flower at the moment when the two men stab each other.

Set design

There are many different venues demanded in *Blood Wedding* and Lorca makes some very specific demands:

- the Mother's house – a room painted yellow
- Leonardo's house – a room painted pink
- the Bride's cave – interior – a cross of big pink flowers
- the Bride's cave – exterior – a large door
- a forest at night – great moist tree trunks
- a white room with arches and thick walls.

Following the exact detail of Lorca's description would create the need to be able to change the settings for each location with speed and slickness. This is possible using a revolve, trucks or flown scenery, but the extent of modern lighting facilities would enable you to consider using a basic set, perhaps with white walls, which can be varied by the use of coloured **gels**, projected images, **gobos** and a well-rehearsed stage crew who can change items of furniture or the fixtures on the walls.

You might also consider the use of sound to evoke the appropriate venue. The forest can be given either a surreal quality or a realistic one, by use of light and/or sound. The heat of Spain, the approaching wedding guests, the tragedy of the final scene can all be enhanced by the stage effects as well as the acting skills of the cast.

▨ **Think**

Think about ways you might present the water imagery on stage.

▨ **Think**

Remember that costume designs need to work against the colour you choose for the set. For example, the **Mother** in black will show up well against the yellow walls which Lorca specifies. But, strong coloured gels can change the colours of the costumes if the light covers the whole stage.

▨ Further reading

Ian Gibson, *Federico Garcia Lorca*, Faber and Faber, 1989

Gwynne Edwards, *Lorca, Living in the Theatre*, Peter Owen, 2003

David Johnston, *Federico Garcia Lorca*, Outlines, Absolute Press, 1998

Leslie Stainton, *Lorca, a Dream of Life*, Bloomsbury, 1998

12   *The Good Person of Szechwan*

Background

You have already come across the name of Brecht in your AS studies. He is a towering figure in the history of modern drama.

Brecht was a prolific playwright/practitioner who challenged the theatre of his day which he disliked for its **bourgeois** setting and audience, as well as its tendency to reaffirm the values of the ruling classes and to ignore the plight of what he called 'the little people'. His own drama overturned the conventions of what Brecht called 'dramatic theatre', which depends for its effects upon audience empathy with the play's characters.

Instead, Brecht wanted his style of **political theatre** to have a more radical effect on his audiences. He wanted the spectators at his plays to see society in a new light, to recognise its flaws and to go out and change things!

Brecht's theory of **epic theatre** was constantly evolving and it has had a huge influence on modern theatre practice. The key features of his theory, outlined below, will help you to place *The Good Person of Szechwan* in context and to understand it better.

Brecht's rejection of dramatic theatre

■ Brecht's theatre is political in impulse; he regarded dramatic theatre as 'culinary theatre'– designed to be gobbled up and quickly forgotten. Brecht wanted his audiences to understand and *remember* the political message at the heart of his plays.

■ Brecht wanted to destroy any theatrical illusion and a sense of escapism. He wanted his audience to remain constantly aware that they were sitting in a theatre, learning lessons from the past.

■ His adoption of Marxism led to the creation of plays which reveal man within a social, economic and historical context.

■ Unlike the plays of 'dramatic theatre', Brecht's plays do not examine human psychology, but human behaviour.

■ The focus of Brechtian drama is always upon the poor, the socially disadvantaged and the powerless members of society.

■ Brecht developed the concept of *Verfremdung* (distancing) which was intended to create an objective distance between spectators and the action of the play through 'making familiar events appear strange'.

■ Many of Brecht's plays are set in the past and in foreign settings. Brecht believed that this contributed to estrangement effect.

Epic theatre – the theory

■ Brecht adopted the term 'epic theatre' to describe the style of his work, stressing the need for the epic dramatist to convey details of the sociological background to the story.

■ Through 'epic' means, Brecht believed that the dramatist should tell his audience 'what happens next' and even 'how the story ends'. He can also reveal the unspoken thoughts of his characters, as they articulate their inner thoughts directly to the audience.

> ### Key term
>
> **Verfremdungseffekte:** this is the German word that Brecht used to describe the distancing effects that he wanted to achieve through a combination of performance methods and production elements. The term has been translated as 'alienation effects', referring to devices that make the 'familiar' appear 'strange' to the audience.

Brecht saw the theatre of illusion as confirming fatalistic attitudes which epic theatre challenges.

Some of Brecht's early works, the *Lehrstucke* (teaching plays), were intended to be purely didactic (morally instructive).

Later, Brecht came to believe that the most effective way of achieving an audience capable of change was by presenting ideas in a **dialectical** format, combining instruction with entertainment.

Brecht believed in the power of fun (**Spass**) to criticise figures of authority or bad characters, and thereby help the audience to appreciate his political message.

In epic theatre there is no attempt to create fixed, highly individualised characters. Instead, characters are defined by their social function, and act differently in different situations.

Epic theatre – the practice

The construction of an epic drama is loose-knit and episodic.

The story is paramount, and sometimes Brecht uses a narrator figure and sometimes signs and/or projections, to guide the audience through the story.

Brecht uses gestic dramatic language, including verse, subtle rhythms, pauses and Biblical overtones.

The total effect of the drama is achieved through a **montage** of the separate elements of the theatre which juxtapose (put side-by-side) different episodes and different elements.

Brecht insisted that the workings of the theatre were all on view to dispel the 'magic' of theatre; he used bright white lights throughout the performance and actors often changed costume in full view of the audience.

Brecht uses songs as a means of communicating his political messages. These musical numbers are not integrated into the action of the play but are performed directly to the audience, helping to make the action appear strange.

The songs generally express basic social attitudes, such as resignation, despair, defiance or submission.

The songs are accompanied by musicians who are always visible on stage.

Brecht's stage designers were not required to create a realistic location, but to build a set that offered a suitable dramatic environment for the actors and the action.

Brecht demanded the selection and accurate use of historically authentic props that looked like well-used museum pieces.

An individual actor's body language and the physical groupings of actors on stage were used to highlight the social relationships in the play.

Brecht's theatre encouraged a detached, critical spirit in his audience, who were led to view familiar situations in a new way.

Epic theatre – the actor's role

Brecht's working methods were chiefly collaborative; his actors were always part of an ensemble ethic.

The basis of Brechtian acting is that the actor is not impersonating a character but narrating the actions of a certain person at a definite time in the past.

Key terms

Spass: this German word for 'fun' has a particular meaning for Brecht, who uses it to describe a method of social criticism achieved through the application of comic or satirical methods.

Montage: Brecht uses the term to describe his method of juxtaposing different images and/or theatre elements to achieve particular effects, for example, when a scene is played against a background of a slide or film projection, or when an actor steps out of the action to sing a song.

- The Brechtian actor acts 'in quotation marks' – demonstrating rather than embodying the role.
- The actor must show his evaluation of the character he is playing within his performance. For example, a villain should be portrayed with a spirit of criticism.
- The actor must externalise social attitudes through his adoption of **gestic acting**.
- The inner life of the character is irrelevant, except in so far as it expresses their outward attitudes. In some of Brecht's plays the bad characters wear masks.
- The Brechtian actor must show the alternative choices open to his character at every turn. Brecht called this 'fixing the not ... but'.
- Rehearsal techniques were designed to enable actors to see beyond individual character to their social function within a community, for example:
  - acting in the third person
  - speaking stage directions.
- The Brechtian actor steps in and out of role and/or swaps roles (**multi-roling**) in full view of the audience. The actors often address the audience directly.
- Each scene is played for its own sake and does not attempt to produce a consistent reading of a character since, for Brecht, all characters consist of contradiction.
- In some productions, when not acting, the actors sit on stage and watch the other performers, again, to emphasise the fact that they are actor-demonstrators and not *really* the characters that they portray.

Key terms

Gestic acting: the actor's communication of the social attitude of the role in performance. It describes a combination of gesture and attitude involving deportment, intonation, facial expression and handling of props.

Multi-roling: occurs frequently in Brechtian drama, where casts are large and peopled by many characters representing the society of the play. Although the main roles are always played by a single actor, a range of 'incidental' characters is played by members of the ensemble who often swap roles on stage.

The Good Person of Szechwan – an example of epic theatre

The Good Person of Szechwan is a good example of Brecht's epic style of theatre. Set in pre-war China in the capital of Szechwan Province, the play is episodic, consisting of a prologue, ten scenes, seven short 'interludes' and an epilogue written in verse. It is written mainly in prose but there are also sections of free verse as well as six songs. There are over twenty characters in the play, many of them unnamed inhabitants of Szechwan.

The play explores the impossibility of being good in a materialistic world (a world which values money and possessions above spiritual and ethical considerations). By introducing the fantastical characters of the three Gods into Szechwan, Brecht highlights the stark reality of poverty, hardship and selfishness among the city's working classes. Wang, the water-seller, is the main narrator in the play, who introduces himself directly to the audience and, in a series of interludes with the Gods, offers a progress report upon Shen Teh and on the 'ruthless cousin' that she has invented, and impersonates, in order to defend herself from exploitation.

Shen Teh also speaks directly to the audience and articulates her dilemma. Brecht's plays regularly feature characters who have contradictory natures, but in Shen Teh/Shui Ta he has created a truly split character. When Shen Teh appears as herself, she is a gentle but defenceless young woman, but when she adopts the persona of her male cousin, Shui Ta, she becomes hard-hearted, stern and resourceful. The actress playing Shen Teh usually wears a mask when she plays Shui Ta, as well as having a change of costume. In Brechtian style the gestus that she adopts when playing Shen Teh is completely different from the one she uses as Shui Ta.

Practise transforming yourself from a humble, kindly and charitable character to a confident, exploitative one, simply using your posture, facial expression, gesture and handling of props.

Figs. 12.1 *and* **12.2** *Jane Horrocks as (left)* Shen Teh *and (right) her alter ego* Shui Ta *in the 2008 Young Vic adaptation of Brecht's play with the changed title,* The Good Soul of Szechwan, *directed by Richard Jones*

■ Research

The Chinese setting

Brecht wrote the play when he was in exile from Germany during the Second World War, and its creation seems to have taken place over an extended period. As always, he collaborated with others during the writing period; notably with Ruth Berlau, Margerete Steffin and the composer, Paul Dessau, who wrote the music for the songs.

Brecht's choice of settings for his plays is never random and it is always worth researching the period setting and context of any play that you are studying.

Brecht wanted to avoid any sentimental 'chinoiserie' (stylised Chinese decorative arts) in the play. In fact, he stipulated that the setting should suggest a 'Chinese city's outskirts with cement works and so on' and he also wanted it to look 'semi-Europeanised'.

Remember that Brecht tended to place his stories in unfamiliar times and places in order to provide the audience with a critical distance from the events on stage. This is not to say that the Chinese setting is *irrelevant* to the story but that it is mainly *incidental*, since the events represented in the play are supposed to demonstrate the circumstances and consequences of a materialistic society anywhere in the world.

Marxism

Brecht's political motivation is undoubtedly a significant aspect of his plays. Try to acquire at least a basic understanding of Marxist theory as you explore this play. However, you should bear in mind that when Brecht was living in America in the 1940s and was summoned to appear before the un-American Activities Committee in Washington, he was categorical in denying his association with the Communist party.

In fact, Brecht stated that his reading of **Karl Marx** helped him to understand his own plays rather than having inspired them. Such a statement is typical of Brecht's brand of honesty!

Style of presentation

All of Brecht's later plays lend themselves to being performed in an epic style, although directors do not always follow all of Brecht's principles and theories. *The Good Person of Szechwan* is a 'textbook' example of Brecht's mature style, however, and it is difficult to envisage it being played in a *completely* different way.

The use of the narrator, the songs, the direct address and the insistent presentation of a community whose basis for existence is materialism, each add a persuasive voice to the idea that a *form* of Brechtian style is likely to be most successful.

Unlike Brecht's other great characters, Galileo and Mother Courage, whose contradictions are contained within their own behavioural patterns, **Shen Teh** is presented as literally split in two by necessity. The actress playing the role might be directed to play **Shen Teh** in a slightly more natural style than when she imitates **Shui Ta**, but her frequent addresses to the audience – as she weighs up her evolving situation – make any attempt at **naturalism** impossible.

On the other hand, a slavish copy of Brecht's own production of the play is likely to result in a lifeless imitation. Brecht used historical settings to allow a production to reflect upon contemporary life, not to inspire 'museum pieces' without relevance to modern audiences.

Characterisation

The characters in *The Good Person of Szechwan* are types rather than fully rounded personalities. Although it is possible to identify individual qualities in the specific roles, each offers a comment on the inequalities within capitalist society. There are no unequivocally good characters in the play, since this is the irony of the play's title. **Shen Teh** is basically good but necessity requires her, initially, to earn her keep through prostitution and, latterly, to alternate between her generous and truly charitable self and her exploitative and mercenary 'cousin'.

Wang's water cup has a false bottom and he, too, is forced by poverty to play the system. **Yang Sun** turns from a suicidal jobless pilot into a greedy and dishonest capitalist. The **Policeman** is affable enough to the rich – he takes bribes – but is really only the custodian of those with property. He has no sympathy for the homeless or starving members of Szechwan.

Further reading

Antonia Finnane, *Changing Clothes in China*, Columbia University Press, 2007

Who's who?

Karl Marx was the German philosopher credited with providing the Communist party with its core ideas. His most famous work, *Das Kapital*, outlined his belief that capitalism, in exploiting the working classes for the benefit of the establishment and the bourgeoisie, was the root of an evil that would lead to revolution.

Further reading

Peter Singer, *Marx: A Very Short Introduction*, (Very Short Introductions), Oxford University Press, 1980

Francis Wheen, *Karl Marx*, Fourth Estate, 1999

AQA Examiner's tip

A rigorous application of Brecht's epic style is NOT the only option open to you as you interpret the extract set in the exam. However, remember that the question demands that your ideas are appropriate both to the 'style of the play and to your creative overview of it'.

The homeless and hungry that batten onto Shen Teh when she first earns her reward from the Gods and buys a shop, are not seen as innately vicious but as conditioned, by a society that has let them down, to exploit others as they have been exploited.

The ensemble of actors is likely to take on and demonstrate a variety of characters and display varying degrees of financial misery and avariciousness. Successful presentation of these minor roles, as well as of the central roles of Shen Teh and Wang, depend upon the actors' abilities to perform in a spirit of criticism allowing the audience to see the reasons *behind* their behaviour and not merely their behaviour.

The Gods are turned into figures of fun in the play. Rather than appearing all-powerful, they demonstrate that their search for a good person is undertaken to validate their own existence. When the Gods finally ascend into the heavens in the closing moments of the play, far from having provided a **deus ex machina** they abandon Shen Teh to her own devices, leaving her more perplexed than when they first visited her. Brecht's mistrust of religion, which pervades all his work, is presented here most clearly as the Gods disappear upwards, waving and smiling, leaving Szechwan and Shen Teh to their own capitalist devices.

The Songs

The songs play an integral part in conveying Brecht's political message. They are traditionally performed directly to the audience. The voices of the singers are not intended to be trained, but should be rough and 'ragged'.

- Scene 1 – The Song of the Smoke. Three verses sung in turn by the Grandfather, the Man and the Niece. The subject of the song is the pointlessness of intelligence, crime and youth to counteract the lack of opportunity in life for the working classes. They join together for the poetic chorus lines:

  'Like smoke twisting grey

  Into ever colder coldness, you'll

  Blow away.'

- Scene 3 – The Water-Seller's Song in the Rain. Wang sings a lament about the precariousness of his job: when it rains nobody wants to buy his water and he cannot afford to eat.

- Scene 4 – Shen Teh sings the Song of the Defencelessness of the Good and the Gods. She complains about the impossibility of remaining good when one has empty cupboards and exhorts the Gods to send an army to defend good people and to distribute 'nature's bounty' fairly so that friendship and pleasure may exist.

- Scene 6 – The Song of Green Cheese, sung by Sun on the day he was to have married Shen Teh. The song is a satirical, optimistic vision of the future and of what will happen when "*The moon is green cheese*". It includes the chorus line:

  'When the moon is green cheese

  The poor shall inherit the earth.'

- Scene 8 – The Song of the Eighth Elephant, sung by a Chorus of exploited workers. The song exposes the practice of one worker acting as a spy upon his fellows, reporting to his employer and receiving benefits. The 'eighth elephant' is seen as a betrayer of his class – it is an allegorical reference to Sun's relationship with Shui Ta.

- Scene 10 – Trio of the Vanishing Gods on their Cloud. The Gods sing this brief farewell as they appear to ascend into nothingness.

▮ Staging the play – design issues

Brecht's ideas about design, referred to in the summary of the epic theatre style above, are a significant aspect of his theory. Try to find out more about the designers that he collaborated with, for example, Caspar Neher and Teo Otto (who designed the original production of *Good Person*). However, remember that you are not *required* to adopt Brecht's approach to design, provided you have a justified alternative.

As in many of Brecht's plays, *The Good Person of Szechwan*, is located in a variety of settings, for example:

▮ the street

▮ the small tobacconist's shop

▮ under a bridge/under a culvert where **Wang** sleeps

▮ the public park

▮ a private room in a cheap restaurant

▮ **Shui Ta's** tobacco factory

▮ the courtroom.

You might use a composite setting for the action of the play, using adaptable staging and/or props. Or you might choose to create different locations through technical elements, using lighting and sound. If you are going to create several separate settings, consider the use of devices such as trucks, revolves and flown scenery to effect transitions between scenes.

Brecht used a revolve stage to solve some of his staging problems in his production of *Mother Courage* and he was also famous for using a 'half-curtain' which covered the bottom half of the stage only, so that transitions performed behind it could still be seen by the audience. He wanted to show the audience that the actors were not magicians, but workers.

The atmosphere of the working district of Szechwan can easily be created through authentic-looking costumes and props, or you might use placards, slides or painted backdrops to indicate a change of scene.

▮ Further reading

John Willet, *Brecht on Theatre*, Methuen, 1964

John Fuegi, *Bertolt Brecht: Chaos, According to Plan*, Directors in Perspective, Cambridge, 1987

Margaret Eddershaw, *Performing Brecht*, Routledge, 1996

Martin Esslin, *Brecht, A Choice of Evils*, Heinemann, 1984

Jan Needle and Peter Thomson, *Brecht*, Blackwell, 1981

John Willet, *Caspar Neher, Brecht's Designer*, Methuen, 1986

Ronald Spiers, *Bertolt Brecht*, Macmillan, 1987

13 A View from the Bridge

Background information

In the early 1950s, Senator Joe McCarthy led a 'witch hunt' against people in public life who had been associated with the Communist Party. Suspected communists were regularly denounced and brought before the un-American Activities Committee to answer charges of undermining the country's security.

Key terms

Theatrical censorship: British theatre has periodically been subject to political, religious or moral censorship. Originally, The Master of the Revels, (first appointed in the Court of Henry VII in 1494) acted as official censor of potentially offensive material. This responsibility then passed, in 1737, to the Lord Chamberlain who retained the function of censor until 1968, when it was abolished by the Theatre Act.

Background

The genesis of the play

A View from the Bridge has its origins in a screenplay entitled 'The Hook' that Arthur Miller wrote in collaboration with Elia Kazan, who had previously directed the playwright's *All My Sons* and *Death of a Salesman*. The screenplay dealt with corruption and delinquency on the New York waterfront (docks). However the initial idea for the film was eventually dropped in the wake of concern at the Hollywood studio that the story might be seen as anti-American.

In 1955, Miller reworked some of the ideas for the screenplay into a one-act verse tragic drama. This version retained the setting of the original, which was located in a slum area known as 'Red Hook', facing the Brooklyn Bridge. Miller incorporated aspects of a true story that he had heard about a Brooklyn dockworker who had informed on two illegal immigrants.

The verse drama was coolly received and Miller re-worked it again into the form of a two-act drama. This time it was written in prose, but it used some of the dramatic methods of Greek **tragedy** to create a tense and compelling drama.

The play charts the downfall of an ordinary dockside worker, **Eddie Carbone**, who willingly harbours the illegal immigrant cousins of his wife until the younger one, **Rodolpho** begins to pay attention to **Eddie's** niece, **Catherine**. **Eddie** is fiercely jealous of **Rodolpho** and unwilling to allow **Catherine**, who he has raised as his own daughter, to be used by **Rodolpho** to gain a much coveted 'green card'. A green card would be issued on **Rodolpho's** marriage to **Catherine** (an American girl), allowing him to apply for American citizenship.

Eddie's protectiveness of **Catherine** is complicated by two further elements – his own inappropriately strong affection for her and his suspicion that **Rodolpho** is not only using her but that he is 'not right', meaning that he may be homosexual.

The suggestion of homosexuality was so risqué in the 1950s that when the play moved to London for its debut in 1956, it had to be performed privately at the Comedy Theatre to escape the **theatrical censorship** of the Lord Chamberlain.

When **Eddie**, slightly drunk, returns to his apartment to discover **Catherine** and **Rodolpho** alone together and in the bedroom, his jealousy erupts into a disturbing display of lust for **Catherine** and contempt for **Rodolpho** when he kisses first **Catherine** and then **Rodolpho**, who is trying to pull him away from her.

Catherine's decision to marry **Rodolpho** pushes **Eddie** to his limit and having tried, unsuccessfully, to find some legal way to prevent the match, he can think of no other solution to his torment than to denounce **Rodolpho** and **Marco**, his brother, to the Immigration Authority.

Research

Italian immigration

In 1955 Italy was a very poor country that had not recovered from the economic ravages of its part in the Second World War. Poverty was particularly severe in Sicily, which was less industrialised than the North. With no jobs and few prospects, many Italians flocked to America, to try to escape poverty.

There was a thriving trade in illegal immigration, encouraged by the dockyard owners who exploited the desperation of the immigrants, using them as cheap labour. When the immigrants first arrived in America, often finding homes with distant family members, who had themselves emigrated to America before the war, they were more or less guaranteed work until they had paid for their passage. Once they had paid their fare, and paid off the people instrumental in finding them work, they were left to make their own way.

Many immigrant men, like **Marco** in the play, left their families behind in Italy and sent money back to them while they saved enough to be able to return to Italy and prosper. Single men, like **Rodolpho**, came to America intending to stay and pursue the 'American Dream'. All illegal immigrants had to avoid drawing attention to themselves in case they were reported to the authorities and sent back to Italy.

The only way that illegal immigrants could gain citizenship and entitlement to stay in America was through marriage to an American citizen. The fear of being denounced to the authorities by suspicious neighbours or jealous co-workers resulted in many unscrupulous young men trying to marry quickly, to be integrated into society and to be free to live openly. Often, these hasty marriages did not survive.

The 'American dream'

America's view of itself has always been that prosperity depends not upon class or inherited wealth, which was often the case in European countries, but upon one's innate abilities, hard work and determination. For many people, coming to America represented the opportunity to achieve more prosperity than they could in their own countries. Others saw it as the opportunity for their children to grow up with an education and good career opportunities; to be accepted in society irrespective of class, caste, race, or ethnicity.

Style of presentation

The tragic form

In **A View from the Bridge** Miller has adapted the model of classical Greek tragedy and combined it with a semi-naturalistic domestic drama that is set in the slums of New York, not in the palace of a mighty ruler.

In place of the 'great man', who in Aristotle's definition must fall from happiness to misery due to a tragic flaw in his character, Miller presents **Eddie Carbone** as an ordinary longshoreman (dock-worker) who lives with his wife and niece in a modest apartment in one of the tenement buildings bordering the docks. **Eddie's** flaw is his excessive affection for his niece and his obsessive jealousy of **Rodolpho**.

Eddie's tragic fall is partly narrated by the lawyer, **Alfieri**, who acts as a Greek Chorus figure preparing the audience that they are about to witness a tragic story 'run its bloody course'.

Think

Think about the relevance of this form of 'people trafficking' to modern society. Illegal immigrants live in constant fear of being found out and deported back to where they have escaped from.

Further reading

Jim Cullen, *The American Dream: A Short History of an Idea that Shaped a Nation*, Oxford University Press, 2003

Link

Remind yourself of the features of classical Greek theatre by looking again at the section on *Antigone* in Chapter 12 in your AS coursebook. If your AS set text was *Antigone* you will notice the similarities between the two plays in terms of structure and dramatic method.

As in a traditional Greek tragedy, the form of the play is tightly constructed. Two short acts are punctuated with sections of direct address to the audience from Alfieri, as well as short exchanges between Alfieri and Eddie, which reveal Eddie's attempt to find a legal solution to his problem. The sections involving Alfieri are located in his 'office' area which is permanently visible, albeit set apart from the main acting area.

Like a Greek chorus, Alfieri both narrates the background to the action and interacts with the protagonists. It is Alfieri who recognises the truth about Eddie's over-protectiveness of his niece. In his statement in Act One that his alarm about the situation has led him to confide in 'a very wise old woman' in the neighbourhood, there is even an allusion to consulting an **oracle** figure.

Like many a Greek tragic hero, Eddie, a respected member of the local community, embarks upon a course of self-destruction by breaking social taboos (something not done or talked about) and the unwritten laws of family loyalty. In his incestuous desire for his niece and his betrayal of his wife's cousins, Eddie offends not the Gods, but the very social fabric of his neighbourhood.

In denouncing Rodolpho and Marco, Eddie unwittingly betrays relations of a near neighbour to the authorities, resulting in deportation. When Marco, in turn, accuses Eddie of betraying them all and publicly spits in his face, friends and neighbours reject him too.

In a bitter twist of fate, Rodolpho is allowed to stay in America by marrying Catherine. Marco is determined to have revenge on the man who has both insulted his brother and ended his hopes of saving his family from poverty. A violent argument between Marco and Eddie brings the latter a moment of tragic recognition. In a futile attempt to preserve his reputation, he draws a knife on Marco which is deflected into his own body. He dies in the arms of his wife.

The tragi-hero's journey to self destruction is complete and Alfieri, in choric style, is left to reflect on a man who 'allowed himself to be wholly known'. Alfieri's final comment that it is better to 'be civilised' and 'settle for half', suggests that this is the way to live within society's moral laws.

Fig. 13.1 *The final fight scene from a production of* **A View from a Bridge** *by the University of South Carolina – Department of Theatre and Dance*

Activity

Re-read the play noting elements of the tragic form. Consider:

- the role of the women in the tragedy
- the role of the neighbours and co-workers
- the single setting
- the structure of the two scenes
- the language
- moments of 'action' in the play.

Language

Despite the heightened emotions in the play, which are fitting with the play's tragic form, the playing style for the actors, apart from **Alfieri**, is largely naturalistic.

Miller has captured the colloquial speech patterns of the Brooklyn characters that the play focuses on, and he characterises individuals within the story through their language as well as through their actions. **Alfieri**, the lawyer, speaks standard American English, while the Sicilian brothers speak a more stilted form of English. They speak in short sentences to reflect their limited vocabulary and fluency in a foreign tongue.

Despite the educational limitations of the major characters, Miller gives them a language which helps them to express and, in **Eddie's** case, suppress, passionate emotions.

Activity

Look closely at the language that each character uses and see how Miller distinguishes between the different generations, between the women and the men and between the educated **Alfieri** and the uneducated longshoremen.

Try to find appropriate accents for all the characters.

Miller presents the familiar rhythms of domestic life in the first scene set in **Eddie Carbone's** apartment. It gives the impression of a realistic family situation involving well-established relationships, and exposing some of the tensions that lie under the surface of such relationships in a wholly realistically way.

Characterisation

Miller's characterisation depends upon both language and stage action. Given the domestic scope and semi-naturalistic style of the play, *A View from the Bridge* has a surprisingly large proportion of dramatic incidents that involve action as well as words.

There are the shocking moments of action such as the arrest of **Marco** and **Rodolpho** and the street fight that ends with **Eddie's** death. However, there are also the more subtle, but equally significant, moments of action that help to create the characterisations.

In Act One after **Alfieri's** Prologue, there is a series of episodes that move the action through time, beginning with Miller's presentation of the family dynamic in the Carbone family between **Eddie**, **Beatrice** and

Catherine. Miller uses both dialogue and detailed stage directions to chart the emotional temperature of the exchanges.

Early in the Act, Eddie has to wrestle with his opposition to Catherine getting a job. In addition to the words that he speaks, Miller gives the actor playing Eddie a great deal of guidance about how to play the part, facially and physically. Look at the following two directions for Eddie, the first is a *reaction* to Beatrice's words, the second explains how he should look *before* delivering his lines; in the first Beatrice is coaxing Eddie to let Catherine take the job:

> Beatrice: Think about it a little bit, Eddie. Please. She's crazy to start work. It's not a little shop, it's a big company. Some day she could be a secretary. They picked her out of the whole class. (*He is silent, staring down at the table cloth, fingering the pattern*) What are you worried about?

In the second example, Beatrice has just finished a further attempt to change Eddie's mind when Catherine comes back into the room.

> Beatrice: ...I mean it, Eddie, sometimes I don't understand you; they picked her out of the whole class, it's an honour for her.
>
> (*Catherine enters with food, which she silently sets on the table. After a moment of watching her face, Eddie breaks into a smile, but it almost seems that tears will form in his eyes.*)

Miller's directions are so specific for actions, movements, body language, facial expression and eye-contact that they create a kind of score for actors to play.

Activity

Notice how Miller develops his characterisation of Eddie and Marco in Act One, through his detailed directions:
- when Catherine plays 'Paper Doll' and dances with Rodolpho
- as Eddie rolls the newspaper
- during the 'boxing lesson'
- during the second dance
- while Marco demonstrates his strength.

These directions create a naturalistic style in the domestic scenes of the play. However, the punctuation of its structure with interludes involving Alfieri draws attention to the essentially non-naturalistic structure, as does the setting as Miller envisages it.

Staging the play – design issues

Setting

As soon as we read the stage directions for the play's setting we can see that Miller has contrived an essentially theatrical set:

> The street and house-front of a tenement building. The front is skeletal entirely. The main acting area is the living-room-dining-room of Eddie's apartment. It is a worker's flat, clean, sparse, homely. There is a rocker down front; a round dining-table at centre, with chairs; and a portable phonograph.

At back are a bedroom door and an opening to the kitchen; none of these interiors is seen.

At the right, forestage, a desk. This is Mr Alfieri's law office.

There is also a telephone booth. This is not used until the last scenes, so it may be covered or left in view.

A stairway leads up to the apartment, and then farther up to the next storey which is not seen.

Ramps, representing the street, run upstage and off to right and left.

The words that indicate that this is a **representational** set and not a realistic one are highlighted.

The directions look quite detailed until you try to sketch a stage design using nothing more than Miller's words. As a designer you will have to decide upon the following:

- Where exactly will you place the telephone booth in relation to the apartment? Will it be covered? If so, what with?
- What will the ramps that represent the street look like, exactly?
- How can you make an apartment look both 'sparse' and 'homely'?
- How can you suggest a further storey above the Carbone apartment when it 'is not seen'?

You really need to establish a strong **design concept** for the play in order to flesh out Miller's suggestions into a detailed setting design. Your design style should take account of the following basic facts about the play:

- the period setting – 1950s
- the geographical location – New York's Brooklyn Harbour area
- the social context of the Carbone family – a working-class family.

You might also consider the following themes from the play:

- the American Dream
- the bonds of blood
- honour
- betrayal
- social taboo
- justice.

If your approach is going to emphasise Miller's *naturalistic* presentation of character, you might decide to complement this by placing the action within the Carbone apartment in quite a realistic setting. This might lead you to choose period furnishings for the apartment, influencing your choice of authentically 1950s-style chairs/table and you might select typical colours from the period to use within the set. You may want the doors that are mentioned in the stage directions – and used in the play – to be properly hung, serviceable doors, even though Miller stipulates that 'none of these interiors is seen'.

Alternatively, you might choose to emphasise the tragic form and *non-naturalistic* aspects of the play. You might decide that all aspects of your set will have an 'entirely skeletal' appearance to them. The 'sparse' interior of the Carbone dwelling might comprise simple cubes to represent tables and chairs, and the doors might be represented by open frames that the characters simply walk through.

Activity

Try sketching this set exactly as Miller has described it.

▦ Think

Never underestimate the effectiveness of using lighting to establish discrete areas of action. This might be especially useful where the scenes switch from the apartment to the street, or to Alfieri's office. Remember, too, the light glowing in the telephone booth – 'a faint lonely blue'.

▦ Further reading

Susan C.W. Abbotson, *Student Companion to Arthur Miller*, Greenwood Press, 2000

C.W.E. Bigsby, *Arthur Miller: A Critical Study*, Cambridge, 2004

Neil Carson, *Arthur Miller*, Macmillan, 1982

Martin Gottfried, *Arthur Miller: His Life and Work*, DaCapo Press, 2003 (Fullest biography)

Alice Griffin, *Understanding Arthur Miller*, University of South Carolina Press, 1996

Ronald Hayman, *Arthur Miller*, Heinemann, 1970

You might choose an *expressionistic* style to suggest the Brooklyn Bridge in a huge backdrop or use projections upon a stark **cyclorama**. You might use a design palette of monochrome shades in black, white and grey and swathe the stage in a mist at the beginning of each Act to suggest the unfolding tragedy and the dankness of the waterfront environment.

In short, you might do anything that is appropriate to Miller's blend of naturalism with non-naturalistic form. As with any other play, you should meet its challenges, giving appropriate attention to the following:

▦ the style(s) of the play

▦ your interpretation of the play

▦ choice of staging form

▦ provision of space to accommodate the actors and the traffic of each scene

▦ use of space to facilitate the actor/audience relationship envisaged by the playwright

▦ the requirements for a series of different locations

▦ consideration of entrances and exits

▦ setting design

▦ costume design

▦ lighting/sound design

▦ design fundamentals; scale, shape, configuration of space, colour, texture

▦ cyclorama/backdrops; use of period furniture/props.

14   *The Trial*

In this chapter you will learn about:

- the origins of *The Trial*
- features of its dramatic style
- staging possibilities.

Link

Look back at the section on Berkoff in your AS coursebook (Chapter 23).

Who's who

Franz Kafka (1883–1924) trained as a lawyer in Prague, but devoted his life to writing. His insecurity about his literary work led him to instruct the executor of his will to burn everything he had written. However, his final wish was not obeyed, and, as a result, many previously unpublished works, including *The Trial* were published. His writings influenced many people, including Albert Camus, Samuel Beckett and Steven Berkoff.

Steven Berkoff's play *The Trial* is based on a novel of the same name by **Franz Kafka**, a Czech writer and novelist, whose work has exerted tremendous influence on Western literature. Kafka's novel presents a nightmare world in which the central character, **Joseph K**, is accused of an unnamed crime. After a series of ordeals, during which he attempts to prove his innocence, he is eventually condemned to death, still ignorant of the crime that he is accused of.

The novel has been interpreted as reflecting the anxieties of modern society, of depicting people's isolation and helplessness. It also explores people's inability to understand and to escape from their existence. The novel has strong autobiographical elements, reflecting Kafka's relationships with women, his domineering father, and his negative views of society.

The adaptation

Berkoff says Kafka's work has always fascinated him and that this particular novel 'obsessed' him for years. The final version of Berkoff's play was developed over a prolonged period. Early work on the text began in the late 1960s when Berkoff was teaching mime and movement at the Webber Douglas Academy of Dramatic Art. Working with a group of twenty students, Berkoff took a page of text from *The Trial* and the group adapted it for theatrical presentation. The **ensemble** quality of the piece was strongly influenced by this first exercise.

A version of the whole play was performed at the Oval House, in London in 1970, and in 1973 the first major production was put on at the Roundhouse in London. In 1991 it was performed at the National Theatre and that version, while on tour in Japan, was filmed and is available on DVD.

One of the most remarkable aspects of this play and its productions is that, not only did Berkoff write it, he also directed it and, in both of the productions mentioned above, he played the part of Titorelli, the painter.

Activity

Many plays are adaptations of novels, for example, *Nicholas Nickleby*, by Charles Dickens, *The Woman in Black*, by Susan Hill and *His Dark Materials*, by Philip Pullman. Explore some of the issues involved in adapting a novel to the stage by choosing a short section of a novel and turning it into playscript.

Research

When studying *The Trial* there is a wealth of material to use and research. As well as the printed playscript, consider:

- the original novel by Kafka
- pictures and accounts of the 1973 production
- the DVD of the 1991 version, including Berkoff's own comments on the production.

AQA **Examiner's tip**

Ensure that your main study is on the published edition of the text; everything you decide should be compatible with that version. Note that some scenes on the DVD are omitted and there is some rearrangement of speeches.

■ **Think**

What initial image do you want to create in your production?

■ **Background information**

Salvador Dali (1904–1989) was a surrealist painter, whose work is often described as beautiful, disturbing, amusing and sometimes violent. Famed for his flamboyant lifestyle as well as for his striking art, Dali was the basis for Berkoff's portrayal of **Titorelli** in *The Trial*.

■ **Key term**

Surrealism: an artistic movement which started in the 1920s and creates its effects by juxtaposing incongruous images.

■ **Link**

Refer to your online resources for further sources of information about Dali.

Finally, you will make your own decisions, interpretations and inventions, based on your 'creative overview' of the play.

💡 Style of presentation

Ensemble

As mentioned above, one of the outstanding features of Berkoff's *The Trial* is its ensemble quality. The group of actors provides the setting, the atmosphere, the reactions and shape of the entire performance, as well as playing individual characters. Although the play focuses upon the experience of **K**, that experience is made up of his encounters with a host of major and minor figures, all represented by the ensemble, stepping in and out of the **Chorus**.

The positioning of the group of actors defines and varies the acting area. The sense of **Joseph K's** predicament is given a concrete realisation when **K** is surrounded and enclosed by the rest of the ensemble. A claustrophobic atmosphere is created but, when the group withdraw, **K** is left lonely and isolated.

In the opening moments of the original version **K** was standing while the group were seated around him. In the second production, **K** lies on the floor with the group in their frames behind him.

Mime

Berkoff's training in mime has had a strong influence on the style and production of his plays. In the playscript of *The Trial* there are several mimed sequences:

■ the **Bailiff's** arrival is described as 'perpetual running'
■ he and **K** mime going up and down stairs
■ **Huld** 'shits' and the clients 'clear it up with a shovel'.

The use of mime in this play is far more than a convenient way of avoiding using real props; the mime allows for rapid transitions between scenes and also creates 'impossible' ideas and images, drawing on the mime skills of the performers and the imagination of the audience.

Images

In *The Trial*, mime creates extreme and **surreal** images. In the images, the ensemble create instantaneous, stage pictures using their bodies and faces, capturing the essence of a moment's experience on stage without the need for words. For example:

■ **Mrs Grubach** puts the breakfast tray down on **K's** back, as though he is a table
■ **Leni** 'opens the door, using her arm as the door'
■ **Titorelli** appears as a painting in a frame from which **K** has to pull him.

■ Characterisation

The central character of **Joseph K** needs to be the focus of most scenes. His sense of isolation, the pathos of his situation and the surreal nature of his experiences all need to be created with precision. The part was first played by the actor Bill Stewart, who played **K** as though he was 'guilty' for just existing. Berkoff admired this performance which he describes as being like a 'panicked weasel'.

Other characters such as **Huld** (the Lawyer), **Leni** (**Huld**'s mistress), **Mrs Grubach** (**K**'s landlady) and **Titorelli** need to be portrayed in vivid detail. One of the challenges for the actors and the director is that these larger-than-life characters have to emerge from the ensemble and be created instantaneously.

Consider what vocal and physical qualities you would be looking for when casting *The Trial* in order to ensure you have actors who can work well in the ensemble but can also emerge suddenly as one of the highly individualised characters. Such actors require both physical agility and mobile facial features that can be manipulated into a range of expressions from the most neutral to the most grotesque.

Staging the play – design elements

Settings

The frames

Most of the major images in Berkoff's play involve 10 large frames which are constantly moved around to create different venues, such as:

- **K**'s room
- the bank
- the street
- the offices of the court.

The frames define the acting area, and at times they literally frame the actors, but they also form doorways and mirrors, present obstacles, suggest corridors and frequently help to create the nightmare quality of **K**'s experience.

When the original company started to work on the piece they intended the frames to have canvas stretched across them, so they would become screens. However, as they rehearsed, they discovered that it was useful for the audience to see the actors and their reactions 'behind' the screens, so they left the canvas off, and just used the frames.

Fig. 14.1 *The 1973 production of* **The Trial***, showing* **Joseph K** *trying to find his way out of the courtroom, surrounded by 'frames'*

Think

The wooden frames in the 1973 version were replaced with metal ones in 1991. What are the advantages and disadvantages of this change? (Think about weight and lighting.)

The frames need careful practical consideration to ensure they are stable, safe and manoeuvrable.

■ Who's who

Alwin Nicolais (1910–1993) was a 20th-century pioneering choreographer. His dancers often performed within restricted spaces, with obstacles in their way to force them to investigate the physical properties of space.

The rope

Berkoff was influenced by the choreographer **Alwin Nicolais**, who has been described as the father of multimedia theatre. His work incorporating the use of sticks, balloons and rope gave Berkoff the idea for the use of the rope within *The Trial*.

In the original productions of the play, Berkoff used the rope in a series of inventive ways, to create walls, angles, the 'finishing line' for the race with the **Bailiff** and, most powerfully, as the suspended frame from which the priest addresses **K** in the final scene. The text describes the **Priest** as 'a figure of Leonardo', a reference to the famous Leonardo Da Vinci drawing, 'Vitruvian Man'.

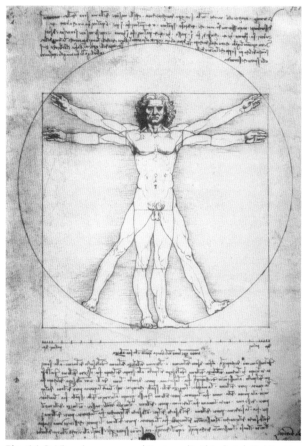

Fig. 14.2 *Vitruvius was an architect, and in this sketch Da Vinci is defining the architecture (the construction and the proportions) of the human body*

Fig. 14.3 *Alfredo Michelson as the Priest, in a frame, with some resemblance to Da Vinci's Vitruvian Man*

If you chose to use the same image in your production you need to decide what it is supposed to represent. For example:

■ Does the **Priest** represent mankind?

■ Does the shape suggest a crucifix and, if so, for what purpose?

■ Does the figure have to be suspended to be effective?

■ How else might this moment be realised?

Costume, make-up and masks

In Berkoff's own productions of the play, the costumes are designed in black and white, although those for the 1991 production are more individualised, varied and detailed. The costumes are basically simple and uniform, consisting of trousers or skirts worn with shirts and waistcoats, or with waistcoats worn like vests. They include different types of ties and collars, blouses, hats and shoes.

The limited amount of colour helps to create the ensemble effect.

Berkoff also used white face paint, typically a feature of mimes, to create a neutral mask-like appearance for the characters. In some sequences he used actual masks. Both of these design elements contribute to the nightmare feel of the play.

Fig. 14.4 *Masks being worn by characters, inside the Cathedral*

Sound

Throughout the text there are references to music, such as the 'Electronic Bach', the accompanying music for the Stripper and church music in the Cathedral scene. However, the play is also accompanied by a complex soundscape, some of it recorded and some of it created by the actors themselves. There are frequent sound effects, such as tapping, creaking and 'three enormous knocks', as well as vocal sounds to be made by the actors – such as 'the effect of a mad house'. Some sounds need particular care and research, for example, traffic, train and telephone effects need to evoke the appropriate period. Berkoff dictates precisely that the sound of the guards doing their officious search, opening and closing drawers, should be 'sharp'.

> **Activity**
>
> Create a soundscape for the play, using music, recorded sound effects, live effects and vocal sounds. Take care to plot the length of time the effect is used, its volume, and also note the reason for the choice and the desired impact on the audience.

■ Further reading

■ Steven Berkoff, *Metamorphosis*, Proscenium, 1981

■ Steven Berkoff, *In the Penal Colony*, Samuel French, 1999

(Both of the above plays are adaptations of Kafka novels)

■ Steven Berkoff, *Free Association: An Autobiography*, Faber and Faber, 1996 Steven Berkoff, *The Theatre of Steven Berkoff*, Methuen Drama, 1992

Lighting

Throughout *The Trial* lighting helps to define the acting area and to change the shape of it. Few lighting effects are suggested in the text, although a strobe effect is specified in the Offices of the Court scene to 'freeze' the action. In the final scene, there are several references by K to the darkness. As director, you may consider whether the audience are supposed to share K's sensations and perspective, whether the darkness is K's alone, or whether the references are more symbolic than literal. As with so much of this play, there are many options and opportunities for creativity.

Berkoff's definition of the play may give you inspiration when deciding on your directorial approach:

> 'K's guilt, for which he must die, is the guilt of betrayal: the guilt of betraying his inner spirit to the safety of mediocrity.'

> (From *The Theatre of Steven Berkoff* by Steven Berkoff)

The Trial itself is neither safe nor mediocre.

■ Activity

Watch these DVDs:

■ *The Trial*, directed and adapted by Steven Berkoff, produced 1991

■ *Salome*, written by Oscar Wilde, directed by Steven Berkoff, produced 1988

Our Country's Good

Who's who?

Max Stafford-Clark co-founded Joint Stock theatre group in 1974, having been Artistic Director of the Traverse Theatre in Edinburgh from 1966–1972. He became Artistic Director of The Royal Court Theatre in 1979, a post he left in 1993 to found the touring company Out of Joint.

Key term

Commissioning: employing a playwright to write a new script to a particular brief, usually for a specific group of actors.

Link

See references to the context of *The Recruiting Officer* in Chapter 1 and to Max Stafford-Clark's direction of it, alongside his production of *Our Country's Good* at the Royal Court in 1988, in Chapter 4.

Background information

The Recruiting Officer, written in 1706, became one of the most regularly performed plays on the English stage and was highly popular at the time when *Our Country's Good* is set.

Background

Our Country's Good is a play with a fascinating history. It came about as a result of a larger project initiated by the director, **Max Stafford-Clark**, while he was working as Artistic Director of the English Stage Company at the Royal Court Theatre in London in 1988.

Max Stafford-Clark assembled an ensemble of ten actors for a project which combined the production of Farquhar's 18th-century classic, *The Recruiting Officer* with the **commissioning** and directing of a brand new, but related, play, *Our Country's Good*, written by Timberlake Wertenbaker. The actors were to perform in both plays.

How are these two plays related?

Our Country's Good is based on real-life events described in the novel, *The Playmaker* by Thomas Keneally. Keneally's story is supported by the historical evidence in Robert Hughes' book, *The Fatal Shore: a history of the transportation of convicts to Australia 1787–1868.*

Both the novel and the history book describe the rehearsal and production of Farquhar's *The Recruiting Officer*, which was actually performed in Australia by a company of convicts under the direction of a Junior officer, Second Lieutenant Ralph Clark, who becomes the central figure in Wertenbaker's play.

It is the rehearsal of *The Recruiting Officer* and the subsequent personal development of both the convicts who took part in it, and the young officer who directed it, that form the basis of the play, *Our Country's Good*.

Timberlake Wertenbaker's script deals with a group of largely uneducated and uncouth convicts and a group of fairly disgruntled officers who arrive in Botany Bay (now Sydney) in 1788 to found a new colony, thousands of miles from their homes in England. They had endured a difficult eight-month sea voyage to reach their destination.

The play presents the development of that colony. It reveals the tensions that exist both within the officer community and the convict community, as well as in the relationship between the officers and the convicts, who have to find a way to live together despite the huge differences.

Presiding over the colony is Captain Arthur Phillip, whose liberal notions about the civilisation and rehabilitation of his convict charges set him apart from his fellow officers. His ideas for dealing humanely with the convicts are met with a mixture of misunderstanding and downright opposition from some of his officers.

However, with the co-operation of some of his more humane officers, and in spite of the fierce objections of one particularly unsavoury individual, Major Robbie Ross, Captain Phillip supports Ralph Clark's project to form a theatre company, using the convicts as his cast. Casting some of the most unpromising of actors to play the parts of Judges, Gentlemen and Ladies, as well as the parts of military officers, Ralph succeeds in turning an undisciplined rabble into a coherent and impressive theatre ensemble.

■ **Think**

Imagine having to leave your home and family for several years to live on the other side of the world with potentially dangerous criminals. The outward and return voyages alone would have taken nearly a year and a half! Little wonder that both the convicts *and* the officers are dissatisfied!

■ **Background information**

The concept of redemption is linked to the theological idea of 'saving souls'. Wertenbaker uses the term to suggest that, through participation in theatre, the convicts are in some way 'saved' and brought back into the community rather than remaining outsiders.

Like many plays, *Our Country's Good* deals with a range of issues and can be said to have many themes. The play deals with power relationships, both between the officers and the convict groups and within them. It explores the power within sexual relationships and the brutalisation that occurs when people are denied respect.

Another key theme of the play is the power of language. We hear a range of different voices and levels of articulation – from the vulgar convict cant of Liz Morden at one end of the spectrum, to the elegance of Farquhar's dialogue at the other. We are shown the effect of silence, both through Duckling's refusal to speak to Harry and in Liz's refusal to speak at her trial. We are shown how, empowered by language, some of the convict characters gain self-respect, and equally how characters such as Ross and Campbell are revealed in all their limitations by their inability to express themselves verbally, despite their more privileged backgrounds.

You will want to explore all these thematic areas in your study of the play. Wertenbaker herself has summed up the intention behind the play as being to 'explore the redemptive power of theatre'.

■ Research

You will need to undertake research before you draw together your ideas for staging *Our Country's Good*. This research should lead you to an understanding both of the historical context of the play's setting – a penal colony in 18th-century Australia – and of the genesis of the play itself.

You need to understand something of the British legal system in the 18th century that transported criminals, whose crimes were not considered to be punishable by hanging, to the other side of the world to serve their punishment.

With prisons overflowing with people whose crime might have been as petty as the theft of a tablecloth, the Authorities shipped over 150,000 convicts to Australia between 1788 and the mid-19th century.

Thomas Keneally has described the living conditions on the transport ships as 'atrocious'. Each of the convicts on the ships was given a space of less than half a meter wide, and was, effectively, lined up for travel, accompanied by provisions, including Bibles, kittens and dogs, pigs, geese and much more. The journey lasted for eight months, and 50 of the 800 or so convicts who set off in the first fleet died on the journey. This should give you some insight into the staging of the opening scene of *Our Country's Good*, 'The Voyage Out'.

Wertenbaker's play also focuses on the plight of the Aborigines whose lives were blighted for ever by the arrival of the British settlers. You will need to research their situation. The Aborigines had lived in Australia for at least 60,000 years before it became a dumping ground for Britain's criminal classes.

The first consequence of the arrival of the convicts and the establishment of their colony was the introduction, to the Aboriginal population, of European diseases such as chickenpox, smallpox, influenza and measles.

The settlers not only brought their diseases to the Aborigines. They also stole their land which took away their source of food and effectively turned them out of their own communities. This background should influence how you decide to present the Aborigine in the play.

The genesis of the play

Refer to the book *Taking Stock* (see the Further reading list), in which Max Stafford-Clark describes the process of the play's evolution through a series of **workshops** designed to stimulate the writer as well as to motivate and engage the actors in the creation of their own material.

Stafford-Clark charts the journey that the company embarked upon together which took them from his own original idea for the play to the full script; a journey accomplished through extensive reading, research, and improvisation before Timberlake Wertenbaker produced her first drafts that eventually became the published play.

Style of presentation

Ensemble playing

The play was originally written to be performed by a specific ensemble of actors. As these actors were also performing in *The Recruiting Officer* it is clearly intended for an ensemble that is comfortable in conveying a sense of period authenticity to the audience.

The episodic nature of the play and the suggested doubling-up of roles, including cross-gender playing, add up to a play that is non-naturalistic in style. However, the majority of characters, especially the convicts, are 'rounded' and most frequently played naturalistically – as far as the frequent changes between characters allow.

A production's success depends on its actors' ability to convey characters from the 18th century convincingly, both as officers/gentlemen of the period as well as convicts expelled from society. This is one of the many challenges of the play.

Wertenbaker originally wrote the roles for specific actors in the ensemble company and deliberately cast one actor, Ron Cook, to play both the characters of Captain Arthur Phillip, the humanitarian Governor-in-Chief of New South Wales and John Wisehammer, the Jewish convict who is persecuted by Robbie Ross. Mark Lambert played both the infamous Ross and Ketch Freeman, the colony's hapless and loathed hangman.

Activity

Go through the play's twenty-two scenes, referring to the original cast list. Note where each actor changes from one character to another. You will see how difficult it is to achieve a fluent style as actors take on their various different characters.

The sadistic Major Ross is something of a caricature and his sidekick, Campbell, is definitely a character that can be played in **cartoon style**. Wertenbaker has given them each a peculiarity of expression so that Ross invents numerous expletives when referring to the convicts while Campbell punctuates his speech with a series of splutters and meaningless phrases that render him incoherent.

Some of the scenes are undoubtedly comic, for example, the audition scene in Act 1, Scene 5 and the first rehearsal in Scene 11. Scenes involving violence and intimidation against the convicts are disturbing,

Key terms

Workshops: in relation to plays that are created collaboratively, these are rehearsals that explore the themes/issues/characters of the play in preparation. They can include improvisations based on research or on the actors' own experiences. The aim of the workshop is to supply the cast/writer with concrete ideas to develop/incorporate into the production.

Cartoon style: a highly exaggerated performance style, usually reserved for comic and villainous characters.

Further reading

Max Stafford Clark and Philip Roberts, *Taking Stock: The Theatre of Max Stafford-Clark*, Nick Hern Books, 2002

Alan Brooke and David Brandon, *Bound for Botany Bay*, National Archives, 2005

Max Stafford-Clark, *Letters to George*, Nick Hern Books, 1989

however, and require sensitive direction, as does the love scene between Ralph and Mary in Act 2 Scene 9, where the style is almost lyrical. There are frequent shifts in mood and atmosphere. The audience also sees intimate scenes played between two characters alternating with scenes involving almost all the cast. Some evoke laughter and others elicit tears.

When you are considering the style of the play, take note of Max Stafford-Clark's comment about the play in *Taking Stock*, where he recounts,

> 'My daughter, Kitty, is studying it at school now. She has to address all kinds of questions about whether it was influenced by Stanislavsky or by Brecht, which concerned us not one whit when we were working on the play'

This is an instructive insight into the play which appears to reject all stylistic labels other than 'thought-provoking historical drama'.

▓ Characterisation

The multi-roling of characters, especially when combined with an economical approach to costume, can create identification problems for an audience. However, in this play actors should use their vocal qualities to differentiate between roles.

Fig. 15.1 *Max Stafford-Clark's production of Timberlake Wertenbaker's* Our Country's Good *for Out of Joint Theatre in 1998*

Only one actor in the original cast played a single role, and that was the actor playing Ralph Clark. With the exception of Black Caesar and the Aborigine, all of the other characters are British, but they are distinguished by their regional accents. A variety of British dialects are indicated, including Received Pronunciation, Scottish, Irish, West Country, and Cockney.

Given that *Our Country's Good* explores the theme of language, these dialects, and their modifications as the convicts acquire more confidence, are crucial in establishing character within the multi-role play.

Activity

Make a chart of all the characters in the play, where they come from and their accent. Look at the cast list of the original production of the play and work out how many different 'voices' each requires. Do not overlook the civilising effect of the play and of the developing relationships within it.

Staging the play – design issues

What are the design challenges that face you as you prepare your ideas about staging *Our Country's Good*?

First, you need to think about how to accommodate your large cast and the play's 22 different scenes on your stage. You need to select an appropriate staging form for the play's scenic requirements.

The play features a variety of distinct locations which you might choose to represent by using adaptable staging and/or props. Or you might choose to create distinct locations through technical elements, using lighting and sound. If you want to create several separate settings, you might employ devices such a trucks, revolves and flown scenery to effect transitions between scenes.

The different locations within the play are as follows:

- the hold of the convict ship
- Sydney Cove
- Ralph Clark's tent
- an audition/rehearsal space – unspecified
- officers' quarters
- a rowing boat on the water
- a prison house
- a beach
- a court
- backstage area
- a separate area for the Aborigine.

Other important aspects to bear in mind are the frequent shifts from day to night that occur throughout the play and the movement of the action from outside to inside and back again.

The first scene is set in the cramped, dark and dank hold of the convict ship, but when the action moves to dry land the conditions are quite different. The Australian sun is hot, so, in addition to creating the effects of lamplight in the officers' quarters and in Ralph Clark's tent for the night-time scenes, you will also have to think about the immense glare of the daylight, for those scenes outside.

Remember the historical setting of the play; what did officers of the Royal Navy and the Royal Marines wear in 1789? You will need to do some research. Don't forget that, in addition to their convict costumes, the players in *The Recruiting Officer* will also require authentic looking costumes for their scene 'backstage' at the end of the play when they will be seen to transform from rags to finery for their first performance of Farquhar's play!

Activity

Think about how you might suggest these individual settings using key props rather than completely separate settings. Remember to take into account the historical setting of the play in choosing your props.

Think

How might you create these effects for the audience?

Activity

List the different sights and sounds that that might help you to create a sense of the Australian setting for your audience. Try matching these to possible lighting states and/or sound effects that you might use.

16 *Coram Boy*

Background information

In the 18th century, the word 'hospital' did not have the modern meaning related to medical services but referred to a charitable institution. The word relates to the concept of 'hospitality'.

Coram Boy, by Jamila Gavin, adapted by Helen Edmundson, is the result of a collaboration between the author, the adapter, a director and a group of actors from the National Theatre who created the play through six weeks spent in workshops on the project.

The resulting playscript offers directorial opportunities and challenges in equal measure.

The title of the play refers to a child, **Aaron**, who was brought up in the Coram Foundling Hospital, having narrowly escaped death at the hands of **Otis Gardiner**. In the play, this villainous character takes money from desperate young mothers in exchange for the assurance that their illegitimate babies will be accepted into the Coram Hospital. In fact, **Otis** murders the children, steals the money and the 'keepsakes' that the mothers entrust him with and amasses a fortune.

The action of the play takes place between 1742 and 1750.

Themes

The storyline of the play is fictional, but the background is historically accurate. Although some of the themes and issues which form the basis of the story appear to relate to conditions in the 18th century, such as the issue of slavery, there are others that invite modern audiences to reflect upon their relevance to contemporary society:

▨ illegitimacy and unwanted babies born to adolescent girls as a result of naïveté or exploitation

▨ the 'white slave trade' which sees orphans from the Coram Foundation sold into prostitution

▨ abuse of parental authority; cruelty to children

▨ the gulf that exists between the rich and the poor.

There are also many broader themes explored in the play, for example:

▨ friendship and loyalty

▨ the father/son relationship

▨ the fragility and vulnerability of children

▨ the power of music.

Who's who

Thomas Coram (1668–1751) was a prosperous ship builder and sea captain who settled in London, where he was appalled to see the corpses of little babies abandoned in the streets. He eventually succeeded in founding the Coram Hospital, to care for unwanted infants, supported by subscriptions from wealthy families as well as the approval of King George II.

Historical background

In the 18th century there was no reliable form of contraception, so the problem of unwanted babies was a significant one. There was no welfare state to support the poor or vulnerable, so an unmarried girl with a baby faced a bleak future. The social stigma attached to having an illegitimate child also spelt misery for girls from higher-class families who would be ostracised (cast out) from society if their 'mistake' came to light.

The play highlights the degradation associated with bearing an illegitimate child, showing how both **Miss Price** – abused and impregnated by her hideous guardian, **Mr Claymore** – and even **Melissa Milcote**, whose baby was fathered by **Alexander Ashbrook**, felt forced to rely upon the services of the unscrupulous **Otis Gardiner**.

All the mothers, rich and poor, who reluctantly handed over their babies to characters like **Otis**, believed that their children would be well looked after in the Coram Hospital.

Research opportunities

The Coram Foundation

The Coram Foundation, opened recently as a museum, offers opportunities to research the background of this play. It tells the history of the hospital, from its earliest days till the 20th century. For example, you can find out more about the use of coloured balls to decide which children would be taken in.

You can also view a cabinet which displays some of the items left with the babies by their distraught mothers, in the hope that one day they would be reunited. These include, as we might expect, lockets and brooches, indicating the wealth of some of the young mothers, while poorer girls left paltry items including buttons, a label from a beer bottle and a hazel-nut shell.

In the play, **Toby**, who is **Aaron**'s friend, is given the string of beads that his mother had left as a keepsake.

Fig. 16.1 *A portrait of Thomas Coram by William Hogarth (Foundling Museum)*

Activity

A visit to The Foundling Museum (40 Brunswick Square, London, WC1N 1AZ) is informative about the background to the play and is also a very moving experience.

For those who live too far away to visit the museum it has a helpful websites (www.foundlingmuseum.org.uk).

The museum also details the involvement of two famous men who contributed to the finances and upkeep of the Coram Hospital – William Hogarth, the painter, and **George Frideric Handel**, the musician and composer, who appears as a character in *Coram Boy*.

Historical/geographical settings

Many scenes in the play are set in specific locations that you may find useful to research when you are planning your design ideas. For example:

- Gloucester Cathedral
- the Ashbrook estate – an opulent Georgian country house set in its own extensive grounds (fictional, but typical of its time)
- the Coram Hospital building
- Mr Gaddarn's elegant London town house (fictional but typical of its time)
- docks on the Thames
- on board an 18th-century sailing ship.

Characterisation

There are over 20 named characters in *Coram Boy*, as well as others who are referred to simply as 'Boy' or 'Servant'. The ensemble also has to provide the background for particular scenes such as the guests and dancers in the ballroom in Act 1, Scene 20 and the mothers in Act 2, Scene 1.

Who's who

George Frideric Handel (1685–1759) was a German-born composer who spent much of his life in England. Handel produced an enormous body of work in various styles. He is best known for his composition, Messiah, an oratorio which was performed at the Coram Hospital in 1750 to raise money in support of the foundation.

Multi-role-playing is a key feature of this play. Both **Thomas** and **Alexander** appear as children and then as adults, played by different actors in the original production; while the actor who played the young **Alexander** also played his son, **Aaron**.

The play also requires strong **ensemble** work from the rest of the cast as they present characters from all levels of society, from aristocracy to servants; from 'desperate-looking mothers' to choirboys. Whenever the actors are playing characters (as opposed to representing gargoyles, mules or angels) they often have a relatively brief time to establish credible roles, for example, **Mrs Hendry** at the Coram Hospital or **Molly Jenkins**, one of the little Coram girls who is sold into prostitution.

Also, because the play is concerned essentially with the experiences of children and adolescents, a decision has to be made about whether or not to use child actors or to follow the original production and use women actors to play the parts of the young boys.

Whatever you decide upon you should consider the pace of the play, its many scene changes and the dizzying number of 'people' named and un-named that are needed for each scene. The play consists of some intimate scenes involving two or three characters only, but there are others when you will need every member of your company on stage, in some cases presenting a very different character from the one they presented in the scene before.

You will also need to consider the amount of music in the play. Some of your actors will have to be able to sing, not simple songs either, but Handel's famous music as well as specially written music for some of **Alexander's** songs and the **Coram boy choir's** performance.

The cast is also supplemented by the eerie presence of the puppet babies, who make a significant contribution to the atmosphere of the play.

Background to the first production

There is a wealth of material available related to the first production of *Coram Boy* in 2005, the revival in 2006 and its Broadway production, with an American cast, at the beginning of 2007. The reviews of both the English and the American productions are readily available and the photos illustrate many details of the staging and presentation.

Activity

The National Theatre has a DVD of the production in its archive, along with prompt/cueing copies and details of the designs. Although these cannot be bought or hired, it is possible to make arrangements to view them at the NT Archive, The Cut, London, SE1 8LL.

You can also access interviews with the director and adaptor and see extracts from the production on the National Theatre's Stagework website (www.stagework.org).

Staging the play

Style – epic theatre

The adaptation of the novel for the stage has resulted in a play which is epic in scale. The multi-role casting, the scope and episodic nature of the story-line, the shifting locations and the clear social message of the play also suggest that the term **epic theatre** is appropriate in describing *Coram Boy*.

Creating an overall style that is adaptable enough to accommodate both the scenes of intimate **duologue** and the scenes where the stage is filled with actors, musicians and scenery, is one of the main directorial challenges of a play. It has been described (by Adrian Sutton, the composer of additional music) as being 'only just this side of a musical or opera'.

In staging terms, it is simply not possible to create all the settings realistically, although there is a need to evoke an authentic flavour of 18th-century society through costume, furniture and props.

The play has 63 separate scenes and 30 different designated locations for the action of these scenes. These range from interior scenes set in Gloucester cathedral, in a dingy inn, in different rooms within **Sir William Ashbrook's** stately home, in various locations within the Coram Hospital and in **Mr Gaddarn's** townhouse to numerous exterior scenes set in Gloucestershire, in the grounds of the Ashbrook estate as well as in London, at the dockside, on a sailing ship and underwater.

A director may take inspiration from earlier epic theatre productions in merely suggesting the majority of these scenes.

Style – story-telling theatre

Because of the origins of the play in a story for young adults, the style of the play is also that of 'storytelling' theatre.

The plot is complex but can be seen as following two parallel stories, each of which concerns boys whose fathers dominate their lives. The two boys, **Alexander Ashbrook** and **Meshak Gardiner** could not be more different, however. **Alexander** is a gifted musician from an aristocratic background whose father disinherits him rather than let him follow his musical vocation. **Meshak Gardiner** is the simple son of the villainous **Otis**, the tinker and child murderer, who forces **Meshak** into the role of accomplice.

Alexander's obsession with music which leads him to experience music as colours and to live in an interior world is paralleled by **Meshak's** mental and physical affliction which manifests itself in his trances as he withdraws from the unpleasant realities of life. **Meshak** is also obsessed by the angel from a stained glass window in the cathedral that he comes to associate with **Melissa**, the young mother of **Alexander's** child.

The boys' fates entwine when **Meshak** saves the newly born son of **Alexander** from the murderous clutches of **Otis** and takes him to the Coram Hospital. His unlikely role as 'hero' of the play is confirmed when he saves the life of this child, **Aaron**, for a second time, and gives up his own life to prevent him from drowning.

Conveying all the intricacies of the plot, and the many relationships within it, is a director's first duty. You will need to think carefully about how you might deploy the design elements, technical elements and musical elements at your disposal to support your actors in the communication of this play's strong themes and story.

Stage design

Coram Boy must run smoothly through its 63 different scenes and the design requirements are as important as the demands on the actors.

There are many scenes which involve a large number of characters such as the ballroom scene in Act 1 scene 20 and the final scene, Act 2 scene 28 in the Coram Hospital chapel, and these need careful directorial planning to ensure the audience's focus is on the right area of the stage; some scenes even involve characters moving from one room to another.

Positioning of characters at crucial moments and appropriate levels of lighting are essential. In terms of planning your transitions between scenes you must appreciate that if each scene change took a minute, then more than an hour would be added to the running time of the performance. Rapid transitions, facilitated by minimal changes, are essential.

The intimate duologues must not be swamped by the complexity of the setting or the activity taking place elsewhere on stage. *Coram Boy* gains a great deal of its theatrical impact by the use of these two contrasting approaches; the opulence and scope of larger scenes versus the intimacy of the duologues.

The National employed exceptional facilities; a **revolve**, an **apron** stage, a gigantic acting area and the ability to fly both scenery and actors. The drowning of Meshak, for example, involved an enormous sheet of plastic, lit to represent water, with Toby, Aaron and Meshak flown behind it.

There are many alternatives to the facilities of the National, however. Projections, of both still images and moving ones, could be used to excellent effect. These can vary from a single photographic image on the back wall or **cyclorama** to a complex projection into which actors seem to step.

Other techniques to consider include:

■ physical theatre and/or mime
■ puppetry
■ lighting and special effects.

For example, Meshak's repeated vision of an angel can be enhanced by physical theatre; a puppet can be made to 'swim' or 'drown' (Act 2 scene 27); the hanging (Act 1 scene 35) can be suggested by the shadow of a man behind gauze.

In a production note to the script of the play, Helen Edmundson suggests that the apparent staging challenges in the text are in fact 'an invitation to invention'.

Fig. 16.2 *The puppet babies from the 2005 production of* **Coram Boy** *at the National Theatre, directed by Melly Still*

Activity

Re-read the final scene of the play, set in the Coram Hospital Chapel, noting its specific demands, such as Handel playing the organ, 'the packed and excited audience' and Alexander in a secluded corner.

Try three different approaches to setting this scene:

1. minimalist, bare stage
2. a composite set, with some appropriate detail
3. one which imagines all the facilities of a major theatre: revolves, flown scenery, trap doors, trucks, etc.

Assess the advantages and disadvantages of each approach.

Costume

It is hard to imagine that any production of *Coram Boy* could be successful without 18th century period costumes. The size of the cast and the need for historical accuracy, or at least a stylised representation of it, means that costuming this production is demanding and expensive.

Many outfits for both men and women are elaborate in design, using colourful, embroidered and rich materials, and the sheer number of costumes required is exceptional. Research into the period and style is essential. When you know what the real people of the day would have worn you can then decide whether you want to follow that style precisely or create your own interpretation.

You might also consider:

- the Coram children wore a very distinctive uniform
- the social status of individuals and groups can be clearly differentiated by dress
- the fashion for wearing wigs can help differentiate characters and in the case of Otis/Gaddarn, to effect a credible disguise.

Lighting

Apart from the obvious requirements of the lighting to illuminate the settings and suggest distinctive locations, there are specific requirements which make this text an exacting challenge for a lighting designer. The rapid changes from daylight to candlelight, from indoors to outdoors, and from enclosed to exposed spaces, demand imaginative lighting solutions. Changing lighting states will also facilitate the speed of transition between the scenes.

Specifically, consider the sun sinking in Act 1, Scene 3 and change 'from spring to autumn' in Act 1 Scene 26, and the need to create the illusion that the scene is lit by a moving candle in Act 1 Scene23.

The lighting plot for *Coram Boy* will make a significant contribution to any successful interpretation of the play.

Sound effects and music

Sound effects have their place to play both in creating individual locations and in effecting smooth transitions between scenes. Creaking doors, bells ringing and the sound of the bell that denotes the departure of the ferry all contribute to the rich texture of the play.

AQA Examiner's tip

As a director it is worth plotting a graph of the shifting moods and emotions expressed throughout the play.

■ Further reading

Jamila Gavin, *Coram Boy*, Egmont, 2000

The Foundling Museum Guide Book, 40 Brunswick Square, London WC1N 1AZ

War and Peace, adapted by Helen Edmundson, Nick Hern Books, 1996

The Mill on the Floss, adapted by Helen Edmundson, Nick Hern Books, 1994

Avril Hart and Susan North, *Historical Fashion in Detail: The 17th and 18th Century*, V&A Publications, 1998

Theatre Record, Volume XXV, Issue 23, see www.theatrerecord.org/

Since *Coram Boy* is a celebration of the power of music, however, no production would be complete without the careful integration of singers, orchestration, the playing of individual instruments and choral work.

We hear boys rehearsing, singing beautifully, going wrong, and even **Meshak** attempts to sing; **Thomas's** risqué songs add comedy to the play as well as signalling his lower-class origins.

Handel plays the organ: **Melissa** the virginal: **Thomas** the violin. In Act 1, Scene 20, **Alex's** beautiful singing for his mother changes the whole mood of the play as his voice breaks. The final confrontation between **Alex** and his **father** in Act 1 happens as **Alex** is playing the harpsichord.

Handel's music is pervasive in the play, culminating in a performance of *Messiah* conducted 'with great joy'. The additional music composed especially for the production by Adrian Sutton is also part and parcel of the creation of mood and period.

This is a play which makes quite extensive use of a variety of musical styles to support the textual demands, and the addition of the music to the adaptation of Jamila Gavin's original story was regarded by the director of the original production as vital to the emotional realisation of the piece. You will need to consider your use of music within your stage realisation of the play.

17   Preparing a blueprint for a production

In this chapter you will learn about:

■ how to prepare a blueprint for a theoretical production of your set text.

Link

When you are preparing your blueprint remember to look back over the chapters dealing with the director, the designer and the performer in your AS coursebook, as well as in this one. They contain checklists to help you to prepare thoroughly for the exam.

AQA Examiner's tip

Although you will have discussed and agreed suitable staging strategies with the rest of your group, as you studied the text, in the exam you are likely to gain more marks by offering your own individual response to the extract set.

The blueprint

As at AS Level, we suggest that you create a **blueprint** for a 'virtual' production of both the set plays that you are studying at A2 Level. However, because of the nature of the question that is set on your chosen play for Section B, it is important that you have given detailed consideration to every aspect of the Section B text's performance potential. You must make a scene-by-scene and section-by-section analysis of the play and be prepared to put forward your staging strategies for each one.

This blueprint should contain your personal ideas for interpreting the play as a whole and should give you a sense of having a complete understanding of how the play will look and sound on stage, from beginning to end. Remember that you need to have formed a 'creative overview' of your set play that will inform the staging strategies that you decide to employ, as a director of the play. Once you have a blueprint, you will be equipped to answer the exam question based on any section of the text.

Your blueprint should contain detailed sketches for the setting design(s) for the play. Make sure that you consider any scene changes that are demanded by the play and that you have taken into account the general **traffic** of each scene and made provision for entrances and exits. Note any furniture or major props that are indicated as necessary by the playwright either in stage directions or in the text itself.

In addition, you must also consider your creative overview. Your set design might be used to communicate the social position of the characters within it, or it might be used symbolically to draw the audience's attention to specific themes or issues within the play.

Your design decisions should take account of the period setting of the play (remember to justify any decision you have made to deviate from the play's actual period setting). Make sure that you do your research into period features that will help you establish authenticity – if that is your aim. You should also make sure that your design decisions are appropriate to your chosen style of presentation, your selected staging form and your intentions for the audience experience of the play.

Include sketches, or pictures, of your chosen costume designs for *all* the characters in the play and these, too, should reflect your chosen period and style. If you wish to achieve a realistic effect for your audience, you should undertake detailed research into the play's period when selecting authentic costume designs and consider suitable fabrics and accessories as well as appropriate individual garments for the characters to wear.

You will find it invaluable to supplement your own design sketches with pictures or diagrams of authentic or appropriate costumes and furnishings that you have found in the course of your research. These will support your understanding of the play and allow you to offer apt design ideas rooted in the play's original context. If you have transposed the setting of your production to a (justified), alternative period or location, you should undertake research into that alternative.

💡 Example of staging ideas for a section of text

The table below shows an example of how you might use a template grid to set out your blueprint. You will need a separate one for each scene of your chosen play or for each significant unit of action within a scene or act depending upon the way your set play is structured. Although time-consuming, it is a useful method for getting to know your set play in detail.

Staging decisions: *The Good Person of Szechwan* Opening Section of Scene 5	
Staging form	End-on, open stage.
Actor/audience relationship	Actors break the 'fourth wall' and engage directly with the audience when the text demands it.
Setting design	Brechtian influences approach – set looks 'temporary'. Oriental influence to indicate Chinese setting. Projections on cyclorama of busy contemporary 'Chinatown' shops and bars. Shen Teh's shop is trucked on – counter with tobacconist's 'goods'/stool for Shui Ta/shelves behind the counter. Shop sign written in Chinese characters is flown in above –also additional items: mirror, pipes, window flown in. Contrast between contemporary and traditional China intended to make a political point about the growth of China in 21st century.
Costume design	Oriental influence; all characters in Chinese padded jackets and wide trousers or long skirts. Shui Ta's black jacket is embroidered with a dragon. His trousers are black. He wears leather shoes. He wears a mask – plain white half-mask with frown. Mrs Shin wears a brown jacket without embroidery, a long brown skirt and brown fabric shoes. Yang Sun wears Chinese trousers but also a pilot's 'bomber jacket' (leather) and white scarf, helmet with goggles attached on his head. Purposeful use of anachronism.
Lighting	Plain white light.
Sound effects	Musicians on stage play Chinese instruments, for example, bamboo flutes, guan (clarinet style), and paiban (percussion) plus an electric guitar (modern allusion –twist on Brecht's historicisation) as Shui Ta saunters on and takes up his position in the shop.
Props	Goods on shelves and counter: boxes of cigarettes, cigars and tobacco; newspaper for Shui Ta; bucket and mop for Mrs Shin.
Mood and atmosphere/ pace/tempo	Fairly light and pacy.
Cast on stage – entrances and exits	Shui Ta strolls on and sits on his stool behind the counter.
Casting decisions/make-up	Shen Teh/Shui Ta: tall, average build, black hair. Shen Teh is pretty but wears a mask in this scene. Mrs Shin: tall, long nosed and thin/bony, hair in a bun. Sun Yang – handsome, slightly smaller than Shui Ta.
Direction – movement and delivery of lines	Shui Ta engrossed in reading the paper; Mrs Shin washing the counter, her bony bottom is towards the audience – some comedy as she cleans diligently all around Shui Ta – he ignores her and reads the paper as she talks and talks – sudden movement of paper when Mrs Shin mentions Shu Fu. Comic moments. Shui Ta jumps up to adjust appearance in the mirror when she hears Sun's voice; recovers, gruff cough. Comic moment. Yang Sun acts as if he already owns the place – constantly picking things up off the counter and examining them – puts cigarettes into inside pocket of his jacket. Jokey/matey attitude to Shui Ta – shows misogynistic attitude when talking disrespectfully about Shen Teh. Her stony response is quite amusing, also touching.
Interpretation/overview The significance of the scene to the play as a whole	Society is founded on materialism and should be changed. This is a key section in showing Shen Teh's split character. She can see that Sun is exploitative and grasping but her innate 'goodness' loves and forgives him. Sun's miserable existence has made him corrupt.
Research	Ideas are underpinned by research into Chinese culture (costume/musical instruments/setting) and Brechtian theory.
Intended effects	The audience will laugh at what is essentially a dreadful situation, then ask themselves questions about the materialism in 'Szechwan' – modern parallels should be perceived. Distance created through moments of humour.

18   How to be successful in the examination

In Section B of the examination, there is only *one* question on each of the plays and you are required to answer it from the perspective of a director working with designers and actors to communicate an interpretation of the section to an audience.

The question will relate to a short extract of about 70 lines of text (equivalent to two to three pages from your play). The extract will be printed on the examination paper and the question will always be as follows:

> As a director, discuss how you would stage the following extract in order to bring out your interpretation of it for an audience.
>
> Your answer should include suggestions for the direction of your cast and for the design of the piece. You will need to justify how your suggestions are appropriate to the style of the play and to your creative overview of it.
>
> You should also supply sketches and/or diagrams and refer to relevant research to support your ideas.

So, the demands of this question are:

- a director's perspective
- an interpretation of the extract – appropriate to the play's style and to your creative overview
- an explanation of the staging strategies required to convey that interpretation to the audience – including both direction of the cast and design ideas for the extract
- sketches or diagrams
- reference to relevant research

This is a lot to do in an hour, so thorough preparation is extremely important!

The director's perspective

You need to write your answers in the first person, from a director's perspective. This exercise demands that you write about your design requirements, as a director, too. Imagine that you and your designer have worked closely together and you are discussing the decisions that have been arrived at. You do *not* need to refer to the designer in your answer.

Look at the way the blueprint grid on page 102 is divided up. You should give attention to as many of the elements that appear in the first column as are relevant to your interpretation of the extract.

Interpretation

Your focus should be on interpreting the given extract within the context of your understanding/overview of the whole play. Don't be tempted to write too much about other scenes from the play but make sure that your interpretation is compatible with the play as a whole and that you indicate its significance within it. Your interpretation should give the examiner a sense of your knowledge and understanding of the performance potential of your chosen play and of its likely effect on an audience.

Staging strategies

By now you should be secure in knowing what staging strategies will serve your play. You should refer to:

- staging form
- set and costume design
- lighting and sound elements
- scenic devices for effecting transitions or changes of setting
- directorial ideas for your actors in terms of their appearance, their vocal, physical and facial expression; their interaction with each other and with the audience, if appropriate; their movement and use of space and of stage furniture and props.

Sketches or diagrams

You should support your ideas with relevant sketches and diagrams. For example, you will need to draw your set design; you may want to sketch an aspect of the set or costume that is difficult to describe. You don't have to be an artist, so don't worry if your design skills are a bit shaky, but you do have to provide *at least one* clear, labelled sketch, which can be of the set as seen from the audience perspective or a bird's eye view, in this part of the exam.

Allow about a third of a page of your answer book for each sketch that you draw.

Figs. 18.1 *and* **18.2** *Set design and a Chinese-inspired costume for* The Good Person of Szechwan

Research

While studying your set play you will have undertaken your own research, followed the online webquests (see p.iv) and acquired further knowledge about your play from your teacher. In the exam you should refer to aspects of this research that are relevant to the extract. For example, if you are studying *Our Country's Good*, your research into the transportation of convicts in the 18th century may well be relevant to almost every scene in the play. If you are studying *A View from the Bridge*, your knowledge about immigration policy in America in the fifties should inform your answer.

Look back at the chapter that deals with your set play to see various research suggestions.

Finally

Remember that this part of the exam is **synoptic** and that you are credited for evidence of your understanding of how plays work on stage. If you have prepared your play as thoroughly as we are suggesting, you will do well.

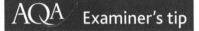

Examiner's tip

Avoid being too literary in your answer. Aim to bring the extract to theatrical life for the examiner.

19 Summary of Section B

In these chapters you have learned about:

- the background to your set play including its context, period and genre
- the style of your chosen play
- the design challenges/opportunities of your chosen play
- the special features of your set play
- the playwright's methods of characterisation
- the playwright's methods of communicating meaning
- the themes and issues of the plays
- research opportunities related to your play
- how to be successful in the examination
- where to find information about the set plays and how they have been interpreted in previous productions.

These chapters are intended to build upon the approaches to your text that are offered in the AS coursebook as well as in the chapters in Unit 3, Section A. You will find it useful to refresh your memory about how to interpret text by looking over selected chapters as you prepare for your extract-based question in Section B.

20   Introduction to devised drama

In this unit you will learn about:

- the importance of finding a suitable style in which to present your theatrical ideas.

Your choice

Devising drama is one of the most exciting and rewarding aspects of any drama course, because you will be working together to create a piece of original theatre.

As you begin work on your devised drama you face two important questions:

- What will it be about?
- What style will it be presented in?

You may decide on the content of your drama first, or you may decide on a style first, but the crucial issue is that the content and style work together. You must ensure that your chosen theatrical style:

- suits the chosen material
- suits the abilities of the group
- helps you to shape your ideas into a developed form
- adds clarity to the presentation
- is used to show your deeper understanding of a particular theatrical approach.

The options

The specification suggests a range of possible theatrical styles, although you are not obliged to choose any of them. The list includes broad categories, such as 'comedy', as well as more specific ones, such as 'verbatim theatre'. You need to consider very carefully which style is most appropriate for your group and your aims. The following styles are those listed in the specification:

- **comedy/tragedy/melodrama/farce**
- **commedia**
- **naturalism/realism/expressionism/symbolism**
- **epic theatre**
- **political theatre**/feminist theatre
- **Theatre of Cruelty**
- creative adaptation (of well-known stories or poems; not plays)
- **docu-theatre; verbatim theatre**
- **physical theatre**.

In the next chapter you will find material which will help you to make your decision about theatrical style. You will also find references to different styles throughout the AS and the A2 coursebooks, in chapters that explore live theatre as well as those relating to the set texts.

■ Think

Your devised drama is worth 40 per cent of your A2 marks, so think carefully about the choices you make. Some theatrical styles are more demanding of time and facilities than others, so be realistic about what you can achieve.

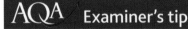

AQA Examiner's tip

Use of the theatrical style:

- know it
- show it.

21   Theatrical style

Link

Refer back to your AS coursebook (Chapter 6 Preparing for a theatre visit: style, and Chapter 12 Context, period and genre) as well as Chapter 1 in this book, to confirm your understanding of the terms 'genre' and 'style'.

Think

Most of the plays that we refer to here are full-length dramas lasting between two and four hours. Remember that, depending upon your group size, you have only between fifteen and forty minutes to present your devised piece. Choose wisely!

AQA Examiner's tip

Chapter 27 contains a case study tracing the development of the work of a group who have chosen physical theatre as their style. Use this study, or at least elements of it, as a model for your own group work.

This chapter will help you to choose an appropriate style in which to present your devised work for Unit 4.

Genre and style

We have used the term 'style' throughout the AS and A2 coursebooks to describe different types of theatrical production. We have also explained the context, period and genre of all the set plays at AS and A2, so you are familiar with classifying plays in this way.

The terms 'context', 'period' and 'genre' have separate meanings when related to plays. However, there is more overlap between the meanings of 'style' and 'genre'.

Most written drama belongs to a recognisable genre, and the genre of a play tends to be fixed. Comedy ends happily, tragedy unhappily; farce builds to a climax through a succession of ludicrous situations. The genre helps to define what a *reader* of the play is likely to discover, as well as to influence the audience's expectation of what they will experience in the theatre.

When we talk about theatrical style, however, we are thinking about text *in performance*. Theatrical style is created by the director, his designers and his cast, working together to present the text in a distinctive way and so shape the audience's experience accordingly.

In the AS coursebook we gave an example of different production styles of plays based on the Cinderella story. The style of these virtual productions (of essentially the same story) had the potential to affect the audience in very different ways.

So, when you decide upon your theatrical style, remember that you need to devise a piece that communicates your chosen meaning in a distinctive and recognisable *performance style*, whatever genre your devised script might fit in to.

Three examples of theatrical styles

This chapter focuses on three specific styles:

- **verbatim theatre**
- **'in-yer-face' theatre**
- **adaptation**.

However, the approach to working within a specific style, suggested here, will be applicable to whatever style you and your group choose to work in.

Research

To make an informed choice of theatrical style, you need to explore the style options in detail. Do some research using:

1 books, websites, articles
2 live productions of plays written and performed in your chosen style
3 published plays and DVDs of relevant performances.

Theatrical style can be identified through:

- the typical content, subject matter and themes
- the director's approach
- the acting style
- use of particular production elements.

Sources of information

With some styles, such as melodrama or revenge tragedy, there are good books devoted exclusively to that particular style, tracing its stage history, its development and possible variations within the style.

With other styles, the references may be in general books about theatrical presentation and stage history. Use the index and contents to find the information you need and refer to bibliographies which may suggest areas for further exploration.

The internet has a wealth of material, and, used with discretion, will provide both general definitions and up-to-date references. If you have chosen a style which is used habitually by particular theatre companies, their own websites will be a useful resource, especially those that include video clips.

Plays and performances

When you have identified the key features of the style of theatre you are considering, in a theoretical way, you will need to study relevant texts and watch relevant performances.

- Read one or more printed texts to increase your understanding of the potential of your chosen style.
- See a live production to help you understand exactly how the style, in performance, affects an audience.
- Watch a recording of a company that specialises in that style of presentation.

Only when you feel confident about the main elements of the style and how to achieve it, using the skills of your group, should you begin to devise your piece in earnest.

Verbatim theatre

Background

The theatre has always made extensive use of historical material. Sometimes, when an audience knows that the subject matter is based on reality, the immediacy of the drama is heightened. A contemporary version of 'historical theatre' has been named '**verbatim** theatre'. As the term suggests, the actual words of the play in this style of theatre are taken from the people who have witnessed or experienced the situation depicted on stage.

Research

A good place to begin your research into verbatim theatre would be Peter Weiss' play *The Investigation* (1964). This play is an early example of the genre and was based on the Frankfurt War Trials and the experiences of Auschwitz survivors. Weiss edited transcripts of the trial as he shaped his drama, but did not choose to stage the material as a realistic courtroom drama.

> **Further reading**
>
> These books offer a good starting point for your research:
>
> John Russell Brown, ed., *The Oxford Illustrated History of Theatre*, Oxford University Press, 1995
>
> Simon Trussler, ed., *Cambridge Illustrated Theatre: British Theatre*, Cambridge University Press, 1994.

> **Key term**
>
> **Verbatim**: word-for-word.

In contrast, *The Colour of Justice* (1999) by Richard Norton-Taylor for Tricycle Theatre, used details of the inquest into the notorious racist murder of Stephen Lawrence, in the nineties, to reconstruct the inquest for the audience in a completely realistic way. He used a realistic set and left the houselights up throughout the performance.

Other examples of verbatim theatre are included in the grid below.

Year	Play	Playwright	Topic/Event
2003	*The Permanent Way*	David Hare	A series of train crashes caused by negligence over safety after the privatisation of the railways.
2005	*My Name is Rachel Corrie*	Rachel Corrie, Alan Rickman and Kathryn Viner	The experiences of an American girl, who was killed in the fighting on the Gaza strip in Palestine, reconstructed from her letters and emails.
2005	*Talking to Terrorists*	Robin Soans	Interviews with people involved with terrorism.

Practitioners in this style

Verbatim theatre has become popular in recent years and productions in the style have been mounted by a variety of theatre companies and directors, including Max Stafford Clark, who premiered *The Permanent Way* and *Talking to Terrorists*, and the company, Tricycle Theatre.

One of the groups that specialise in verbatim theatre is Recorded Delivery. The playwright, Alecky Blythe has created several plays for this group, based on the transcripts of recorded interviews. The topics presented in the 'verbatim' style by the group illustrate how varied this medium can be:

- *Come Out Eli* (2003) is about a house siege in a notorious part of Hackney.
- *All the Right People Come Here* (2005) is about the Wimbledon tennis championships.
- *The Girlfriend Experience* (2007) presents the lives of a group of prostitutes working in a seaside town.

Fig. 21.1 *A scene from* **All the Right People Come Here**, *Recorded Delivery, 2005*

The distinctive feature of Recorded Delivery's verbatim work is that they adhere more closely than other practitioners to the actual words spoken in interview, all of which have been recorded.

Definitions: content and approaches

Verbatim theatre topics are broad and becoming broader. Based on interviews, diaries, court reports, parliamentary speeches, personal interviews, letters and emails, verbatim theatre starts from the actual words spoken or written. The degree of editing, shaping and selection varies from practitioner to practitioner, but in this type of work the intention is to represent the facts faithfully. The playwright or editor may wish to highlight a political or social message, but this is achieved by quoting the words of individuals describing their first hand experiences, it is not achieved by literary crafting, still less by distortion.

Acting style

The overall style in verbatim theatre varies although most will require a realistic delivery, at least at times.

In *The Permanent Way*, there are moments of **physical theatre** as the characters travel on a train. There is **impersonation** of the politician, John Prescott, but there are also very sensitive and moving speeches from the passengers who were injured in the crashes and from their relatives; these are delivered realistically.

My Name is Rachel Corrie, based largely on diary entries, is presented as a one-woman show. By contrast, in *Come Out, Eli*, five actors represent a total of 41 characters. This clearly cannot be achieved in a realistic style.

Production style

As with the acting style, production styles vary. The realism of the content may demand a degree of realism in the presentation. Costume design is usually in keeping with the occupations and positions of the characters being presented and is frequently completely naturalistic. Some plays are staged in a minimalist or representational way, others involve meticulous recreation of a court house or a prison cell, for example.

▨ 'In-yer-face' theatre

Background

'In-yer-face' theatre is a relatively modern term, first used by Aleks Sierz, to define a shocking and violent approach to the theatrical presentation of disturbing and challenging subject matter.

However, shock tactics in the theatre are nothing new. You will remember encountering reference to the writings of **Antonin Artaud**, in the AS course book. Artaud outlined his vision of 'The Theatre of Cruelty' as a form designed to assault the audience's emotions and to confront them with the darkest side of human existence. Writing in the 1930s, Artaud stated, 'The Theatre of Cruelty will choose themes and subjects corresponding to the agitation and unrest of our times.'

In the 1960s, **Peter Brook** adopted the term 'Theatre of Cruelty' to describe two of his productions, *Marat/Sade* by Peter Weiss (1964) and *US* (1966) a devised anti-Vietnam war play. *Marat/Sade* is based on the assassination of Jean-Paul Marat during the French Revolution and is

▨ Further reading

Rachel Corrie, Alan Rickman and Katherine Viner, *My Name is Rachel Corrie*, Nick Hern Books, 1995

Richard Norton Taylor, *The Colour of Justice*, Oberon Books, 1999

David Hare, *The Permanent Way*, Faber, 2003

Robin Sloan, *Talking to Terrorists*, Oberon Books, 2005

Richard Norton Taylor, *Bloody Sunday*, Oberon Books, 2005

Richard Norton Taylor, Will Hammond and Dan Steward, *Verbatim Theatre*, Oberon Books, 2008

Peter Weiss, *The Investigation*, Marion Boyars, 2005

Website of Recorded Delivery: www.recordeddelivery.net

Website of Tricycle Theatre: www.tricycle.co.uk

AQA Examiner's tip

Verbatim theatre is usually created by people who feel strongly about the chosen topic, and their passion is what infuses the play with its power. So do not choose this style unless you have a real interest in your chosen topic.

▨ Who's who

Antonin Artaud (1895–1948): a revolutionary theatrical theorist, author of *The Theatre of Cruelty and The Theatre and Its Double*.

Peter Brook (1925–): theatre director, innovator, author of *The Empty Space*.

AQA Examiner's tip

Some websites list playwrights who have been associated with the 'in-yer-face' theatrical style, but note that many writers, such as Alex Jones, may not use this style for all their work.

Further reading

Graham Saunders, 'Love Me or Kill Me': Sarah Kane and the Theatre of Extremes, Manchester University Press, 2002

David Tushingham, ed, Live 3: Critical Mass, Methuen, 1996 (a collection of excerpts of plays by Harwant Bains, Kate Dean, Sarah Kane, Phyllis Nagy, Joe Penhall, Philip Ridley and others)

Aleks Sierz has a website devoted to 'in-yer-face' theatre: www.inyerface-theatre.com.

performed as a shocking play within a play by the troubled inmates of a lunatic asylum.

US, a savage attack on America's involvement in the Vietnam war, is famous for the final moment in which a butterfly is set alight on stage – mirroring the desperate acts of self-immolation (burning sacrifice) performed by Buddhist monks in protest against the war.

In 1968, the abolition of censorship in the theatre meant that there were no longer any restraints on the style, content or language of plays that could be performed. However, it was not until the 1990s that a group of playwrights, who now best represent the 'in-yer-face' movement, came to prominence.

Research

Because 'in-yer-face' is such a relatively recent development in the theatre, its representation on the internet is particularly good. There are also references to this theatrical style in many books but the definitive one is Aleks Sierz, *In-yer-face Theatre: British Drama Today*, Faber and Faber, 2001.

Some major examples of works in this theatrical style are:

Year	Play	Playwright
1995	Blasted	Sarah Kane
1996	The Beauty Queen of Leenane	Martin McDonagh
1996	Shopping and F***ing	Mark Ravenhill
1997	Closer	Patrick Marber

Remember that these playwrights had opportunities which are not available to you. For example, these are all full-length plays, and so the subject matter can be developed slowly and subtly, whereas you have a relatively brief time in which to present your ideas.

Definitions: content and approaches

The picture of society presented by this style of theatre is profoundly disturbing. The audience is forced to face up to the depravity of which humans are capable. Violence, both verbal and physical, is a key characteristic of 'in-yer-face' theatre.

The language of this style of theatre is often heightened and even poetic, but it is equally obscene. The physical and sexual violence is also extreme and pervasive. For example, *Noise* by Alex Jones (1997) contains an attack with a Stanley knife on a pregnant girl; in *The Lieutenant of Inishmore* by Martin McDonagh (2001) there is a torture scene during which a man has his nails pulled out; in *Blasted*, by Sarah Kane (1995), a man is raped by a soldier who then sucks out his eyes and eats them. There is no taboo subject matter in 'in-yer-face' theatre.

If you are thinking of devising in this style of theatre you need to choose a topic that matters to you, as a group. The point of 'in-yer-face' theatre is not simply to shock the audience but to use shock as a method of raising audience awareness about a social or political issue that you care deeply about.

Fig. 21.2 *The torture scene from Martin McDonagh's play,* **The Lieutenant of Inishmore***; RSC production, 2001*

Acting style

Although 'in-yer-face' plays often contain the blackest of black humour, these horrific scenes are played with serious intentions and must be acted with complete conviction by the performers. Any hint of embarrassment will destroy the impact and sense of reality. Any group that sets out to shock for the sake of it will not be representing the style appropriately.

Style of presentation

However extreme the circumstances that are represented in these plays, the style required in the presentation, as with the acting, is realism. The settings may be urban or rural but they are frequently domestic. Because the content goes beyond the normal experience of the audience, the style of presentation needs to convince them of its reality.

■ Creative adaptation

Poems, films and novels

The two theatrical styles discussed so far in this chapter have distinctive characteristics and are relatively easy to categorise. The theatrical demands of creative adaptation are different. Devisers working in this style take an existing work in another medium – a poem, a film, a novel – and explore its dramatic potential, shaping it and adapting it to the demands of the stage so as to engage a theatre audience. Poems, such as Coleridge's *The Ancient Mariner*, have been successfully adapted into pieces of theatre, and several films, such as *The Theatre of Blood* (National Theatre, 2005) and *Brief Encounter* (Kneehigh, 2007) have become effective stage plays, finding their own style and identity, not merely being an imitation of the original.

The theatre company Shared Experience have adapted novels as diverse as Brontë's *Jane Eyre*, George Eliot's *The Mill on the Floss*, E.M. Forster's *A Passage to India* and Tolstoy's *War and Peace*. Such novels are used creatively; they are not simply presented as a drastically edited version of the original story.

In Shared Experience's production of Charlotte Brontë's classic novel, *Jane Eyre*, for example, Mrs Rochester (who in the novel is the mad wife of hero, Mr Rochester) was portrayed as Jane Eyre's alter ego (alternative personality) and was visible on stage for much of the performance. The central character in George Eliot's novel, *The Mill on the Floss*, Maggie Tulliver, was performed by three very different actresses, all of whom were on stage simultaneously at times.

These are good examples of how adaptation can be seen as a creative process. Devisers explore their chosen texts/poems or films in order to create something new; something which has its own artistic validity.

Research

Numerous novels have been adapted for the stage. Just a few examples are listed in the grid on page 114.

AQA Examiner's tip

'In-yer-face' theatrical style is not to be undertaken lightly or without the complete commitment of all members of the group.

Novel	Author	Detail
Nicholas Nickleby	Charles Dickens	Adapted by David Edgar into a stage version that lasted over eight hours. Available on DVD.
His Dark Materials	Philip Pullman	Adapted for the National Theatre stage by Nicholas Wright. The story has also been made into a film.
Lark Rise to Candleford	Flora Thompson	Adapted for a promenade production by Keith Dewhurst. The TV version is different again.
Noughts and Crosses	Malorie Blackman	Adapted for a studio theatre production by Dominic Cooke. Both novel and script available.

Other media are also adapted for the stage. Some examples are below.

Medium	Title	Playwright or company
Poem	*Hiawatha*	Michael Bogdanov, National Theatre
Painting	*Sunday in the Park with George*	Stephen Sondheim
Film	*A Matter of Life and Death*	Kneehigh

As with all styles you might choose for your A2 devised drama, remember that you are restricted in length and facilities. However much you and the group enjoy *Bleak House* or *The Lord of the Rings*, a 20–40 minute version of the whole story would have to be very superficial. However, a section from such books might give you inspiration and suggest *theatrical* opportunities.

Typical content, subject matter, themes and approaches

As the lists above show, every aspect of style will vary according to the nature of the piece chosen. The unifying element is the desire to create something which has its own individual worth.

The acting style

The acting style will vary according to the work you have chosen to adapt, but the challenge is to find a style that enables you to do justice to the characters and the situation in the original. If you are adapting a novel, then the number of characters may be greater than the number in your group. Pruning characters, focusing on just one, and multi-roling are methods for dealing with this. However, such methods should be part of your adaptation from the beginning. Discovering well into rehearsals that one particular character is outside the acting range of anyone in the group is disastrous.

The style of presentation

Remember that if you have chosen to do an *adaptation*, that is the challenge you have set yourself. Give plenty of thought to your choice of text before embarking on this time-consuming but rewarding devising project. If the original text presents problems, you have a clear choice: either choose another text or find a theatrical solution to the problem.

When the National Theatre announced they were preparing an adaptation of the children's book *War Horse*, by Michael Morpurgo, there was concern that a book which is written in the first person and from the

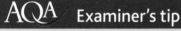

AQA Examiner's tip

In your devised drama, using a narrator who recites large sections of the unadapted text is not original. Your approach must be a creative one.

perspective of a horse might prove too difficult to achieve on the stage. However, the performance used exceptionally effective life-sized puppets, to play the horses – amongst other characters – and made no attempt to use the first person narrative. The end result was very different from the original story, but it proved to be a powerful, effective production in its own right.

There are numerous techniques that your group can use to adapt your chosen work into a theatrical medium, for example, you might use mime, projection, multimedia, puppets or masks, multi-roling, lighting and sound. You might use physical theatre techniques to allow you to compress aspects of the narrative. There are all kinds of ways of presenting the 'inner truth' of a text on stage and communicating with your audience in a way that does no disservice to the original but rather extends its meaning by using the medium of theatre.

Your key aim is to give your work power, clarity and, above all, theatrical effectiveness.

Further reading

Mervyn Millar, *The Horse's Mouth*, Oberon Books, 2007 (an account of the adaptation of *War Horse* for the stage).

22   Devising strategies

Who's who

Forced Entertainment: an experimental theatre company based in Sheffield, founded in 1984. Their work is diverse and uses live art, video and digital media, as well as movement, soundtrack and dialogue, to create a form of theatre that relates to contemporary living.

The art of devising

Although many contemporary theatre companies create their own new work, the idea of devised drama is far from new. As you have discovered, both in your AS coursebook and in this book, drama has to be devised by someone. Sometimes it is an individual playwright working alone, such as Chekhov; sometimes it is an **ensemble** working in collaboration with a writer, such as Joint Stock working with Timberlake Wertenbaker to produce *Our Country's Good*; and sometimes it is a group of individuals working in a company, such as Kneehigh or **Forced Entertainment**, who begin with a blank sheet of paper – or empty space – and end up with a complete theatrical show.

In the AS coursebook we considered the early origins of drama and traced its development from pre-historic man's early re-enactments of the hunt, through the religious drama of the Greeks, the re-telling of biblical stories in the middle ages, to the huge stylistic diversity of modern drama. In earlier chapters of this book we discussed the origins of **commedia dell'arte** – one of the most influential styles of 'devising' that Europe has ever produced. So, by now, you should be familiar with the concept of drama created by a group of collaborators.

The notion of 'newly devised' drama is, however, a little misleading. Just as commedia players drew on a bank of stock characters, stock **lazzi** and stock situations, to create their performances, so contemporary devisers draw upon a range of historical and contemporary cultural resources in order to create theatre.

Modern practitioners who specialise in devising often gain their inspiration or their subject matter from classical literature, children's fairy stories, folktales, major paintings or musical compositions, from important news stories, or from their own life experiences. Their task is

Fig. 22.1 *The World in Pictures, a production by Forced Entertainment in 2006*

to transform their various sources of inspiration into a coherent piece of theatre that communicates meaning to the audience.

Commentators on the art of devising often describe it as a process of creative collaboration, depending upon intuition, spontaneity and an accumulation of ideas.

Finding a style

Intentions for the audience

The specification requirement to choose a particular style of theatre in which to present your devised work will help you, in the early stages of devising, to make the transition from blank page to a complete piece of theatre. Your choice of style will partly be determined by your intentions for the audience and partly by the subject matter that you want to present to them.

Start by considering what effects you want to create for your audience.

- Do you want to make them laugh?
- Do you want to make them cry?
- Do you want to make them think?
- Do you want to make them uncomfortable?
- Do you want to keep them in suspense?
- Do you want to delight them?
- Do you want to horrify them?
- Do you want to educate them?
- Do you want to achieve a combination of two or more of these effects?

Most of these responses cannot be achieved through the *content* of your piece on its own. They are dependent upon the *style* that you adopt. Think about the effects that you have experienced when going to the theatre and try to analyse how the style of theatre helped the production team to create that experience for you.

Think

Think carefully about how much time you have to achieve these effects for your audience. If you are in a group of four performers, you have only 20 minutes to educate, delight, horrify or amuse your audience! Be realistic about what you can achieve in the time.

Matching the style to your intentions

Intentions for the audience	Choose from
Do you want to make your audience laugh?	comedy/farce/commedia/comedy of manners/physical theatre
Do you want to make them cry?	tragedy/verbatim theatre/realism/naturalism
Do you want to make them think?	political theatre/docu-theatre/epic theatre/feminist theatre/historicised theatre/symbolist theatre/realism/naturalism
Do you want to make them uncomfortable?	Theatre of Cruelty/realism/'in-yer-face' theatre
Do you want to keep them in suspense?	melodrama/story-telling theatre/physical theatre
Do you want to delight them?	comedy/musical theatre/story-telling theatre/physical theatre/puppet theatre/mask theatre
Do you want to horrify them?	puppet theatre/mask theatre/'in-yer-face' theatre/tragedy
Do you want to educate them?	political theatre/theatre in education/epic theatre
Do you want to achieve a combination of two or more of these effects?	tragi-comedy/black comedy/satirical comedy/physical theatre/story-telling theatre/total theatre

Some theatrical styles appear in more than one place in the table above because they are capable of producing more than one reaction from an audience. For example, you can achieve a variety of different effects in physical theatre and mask or puppet theatre because of the freedom within these styles to adopt a range of production tones, from utterly light-hearted to darkly macabre.

Before committing yourself to any particular style, think carefully about the individual strengths of your group. Do you have one or more natural comedians in the group? Are any of your group members skilled in dance and movement? When you are devising your own piece, you can play to the strengths of the group when you choose your style of theatre. Similarly you can avoid exposing any weaknesses by not choosing a style beyond the reach of some of your group members.

Finding subject material

Whether or not you have chosen your style first, selecting an appropriate topic area for your presentation is important. The possibilities are endless. Try to avoid staring at a blank piece of paper for too long!

Adopt a positive, democratic approach to choosing your subject matter. Remember that your intentions for your audience are as significant here as they are when you are choosing your style.

During the decision process:

- review all your shared experiences of watching live theatre and identify the main subject area that each production dealt with
- identify ways in which the style of each production helped to communicate the subject area
- consider the success of what you have seen
- decide whether you want your piece to be character-driven or action-driven
- decide whether you want the scope of your piece to be domestic (mainly about relationships) or public (relating to individuals' clashes with institutions, governments, laws)
- decide whether you want your piece to ask questions and provoke thought and challenge, or to provide answers and resolve issues
- use photographs or paintings to stimulate your ideas – the internet has thousands of images that you could access to help you here
- use historical incidents or news stories to stimulate discussion among yourselves
- use pieces of music to help you identify an appropriate mood or atmosphere or give you an idea for a story
- look at folktales from other cultures as stimuli for a story-telling piece
- come up with as many ideas as you can, no matter how bizarre, and record them
- assess each of your ideas in a positive way trying to think of the practical strategies you might use to bring the idea to life on stage
- make sure everyone has their say but also make sure that you listen and contribute in equal measure
- draw up a shortlist of ideas that lend themselves to being performed in a particular style and explore them in practical improvisations
- consider the design implications of each idea and match them to the skills of your group, your practical resources and the style you are likely to adopt
- make an informed choice about your short-listed ideas by undertaking sensible preliminary research *before* committing to the subject area.

Activity

Use the website Artchive (www.artchive.com) for access to thousands of art images from the Great Masters to modern poster art.

Try to avoid:

■ spending too long sitting around drawing up lists of what you might do
■ rejecting ideas out of hand without considering their theatrical potential
■ choosing a topic that is too complex to deal with in 15–40 minutes
■ choosing a topic that does not really interest you
■ trying to emulate something seen in a film or on television.

■ Devising strategies

Most contemporary devising groups divide the devising process into three main phases:

■ gathering and generating material
■ structuring and rehearsal
■ assessing, discarding, polishing material.

AQA Examiner's tip

Ensure that you allow sufficient and equal time for each of these important phases.

Gathering and generating material

Whatever your chosen style of theatre, in the early stages of your devising process you will need to accumulate ideas and use those ideas to fuel improvisations, to drive research projects and to provide you with the springboard for creating usable sequences of meaningful theatre.

Depending upon your chosen topic area you will have different sources for the 'gathering' phase. However, you will all have a common resource for *generating* material – your own imaginations and experiences. Applying your own ideas to your stimulus material, whether that takes the form of stories, art, music, history or newspaper articles, will transform it into something original and unique to your group.

Initially, you may have an idea for a plot, for a series of characters or simply an idea for a setting for your piece.

Plot

What is going to happen? You will need to create a sequence of potential events. Try to avoid cliché.

Characters

Who is involved in the plot? You will need to consider and invent the types of characters involved. Try to create individual, multi-faceted characters rather than stereotypes (unless you are devising in commedia style or using stock characters intentionally).

Setting

Where is the action set in terms of both period and location? You might make your work more original by setting your piece in a distant location and/or time period.

Experiment and improvisation

In the gathering and generating stage of devising, you need to experiment and improvise to help you to:

- build and develop characters
- create scenarios and situations
- establish apt settings – both geographical and in terms of period.

You will also find it useful as you accumulate and sift your material to consider:

- the creation of tension
- variety of pace
- sequencing
- climax
- the actor/audience relationship
- the combination of dialogue/monologue/duologue/narrative/silence
- the integration of physical action
- the timescale of the piece.

Research

Your research is a crucial part of the gathering of ideas. You can work individually on some aspects and together on others to ensure that *all* of your group have a shared understanding of your chosen subject and its context.

You should never embark on a piece that involves events or a setting that you have no personal experience of without undertaking research. This could apply to settings such as in a women's prison, in the law courts, in a hospital, on a cruise-ship or in an office.

Your research should enable you to integrate authentic situations into your piece as well as to craft appropriate dialogue. Remember that doctors and lawyers, for example, use specialised terminology in their work, many professions have their own **jargon** (specialist words) and groups such as soldiers or prisoners often share a distinctive vocabulary of their own. If you want to create a convincing piece of drama you need to ensure that the dialogue you write will be plausible for the context that you have selected.

If your piece is to be set in a hospital, for example, arrange to visit one, to soak up the atmosphere. If it is set in the First World War, go to a library or use the internet to research the period. If it involves a love story between a First World War soldier and his girlfriend, find access to collections of authentic letters between lovers in the period to help you with your dialogue and achieve the correct vocabulary for the era..

All pieces of drama benefit from research. The more meticulous the research, the more likely you are to achieve a convincing piece of theatre.

Development

As your ideas develop, or if you begin to feel stuck, bring in different stimulus materials. These can be abstract things like poems or songs, or concrete objects, like a watering can, a fan or a locked trunk. Almost anything can be used for an improvisation that might inject new life into your work and move it forward.

Improvisation is one of the most productive ways of transforming your stimulus material into living drama. Do not be discouraged if some of your improvisations lead to a dead end. Sometimes an improvisation lasting five minutes might throw up thirty seconds of really useful material that can then be developed into a significant portion of action and dialogue.

Many contemporary devising companies video all their rehearsals and explorations during the gathering and generating period, as this records all their best ideas. A video recording can remind you about how you developed certain improvisations and might reveal some viable moments that you have forgotten about.

If you do not have access to recording equipment, at least make detailed notes of everything you have done during the devising process.

Structuring and rehearsal

When you feel that you have accumulated all the material that you need and you have improvised and scripted a substantial amount of viable material, you need to put your piece together in a satisfying structure.

Experiment with the **transitions** between your scenes or sections of action or dialogue. Do not just think of these as pauses, punctuating your piece. If your transitions are handled smoothly they can enhance the effect of your work. If handled badly, they can destroy the effects you have created, breaking the tension and shattering carefully constructed illusions.

In this phase of the devising process you should also be finalising your selection of costume and setting ideas and sorting out technical support if you are working in a group without a technical designer. Whatever the skills of your group, you should never underestimate the potential value of well-chosen lighting and sound states to enhance the effectiveness of your work.

At the end of this period you will often find that you have more material than you need to meet your timing requirements. You can trim back in the final phase of your work, but at this stage all your material should be learned, lines known and moves plotted.

In terms of the rehearsal process, you should give your devised piece the same degree of respect and attention as you did when rehearsing a published script at AS. Just because the words and/or movements have been invented by yourselves, do not think it is acceptable to ride roughshod over your script once it has been finalised.

You will find it useful to break your piece down into individual scenes or units of action and ensure that each one is rehearsed carefully. This means thinking about the delivery of each line, the stage positioning and movement of each performer and the potential effectiveness of each moment within every scene or unit in your piece.

You also need to set yourself a realistic target for having all lines learnt so that the real work of breathing life into your piece can begin.

Assessing, discarding and polishing

The final stage of your devising process is very important as you need to evaluate the material that you have accumulated and shaped and to assess the success of your style of presentation.

Break down your work into individual units of action, dialogue or movement and subject each one to honest critical scrutiny.

Assess how completely you have achieved the following (as appropriate to your chosen style):

- an interesting plot-line
- believable characters or recognisable stereotypes

- an authentic setting/a suitable representational setting
- a suitable dramatic environment
- dramatic tension
- variety of pace
- believable/authentic dialogue/language
- focused and polished physical work
- fluent transitions
- a well-shaped, coherent structure with an appropriate ending
- a complete theatrical experience for your audience through a range of production elements
- a clearly defined style of theatre
- the potential to communicate meaning as appropriate to your style of theatre.

In the final stages of rehearsal do not be afraid to discard work that does not satisfy you, nor to re-work sections that you thought you had perfected weeks before. Remember that changes made to one scene may make lines elsewhere inexplicable or redundant.

Review your records or recordings of your rehearsals to see if there is anything you did better originally. Ask yourself if any of your material has become redundant. If so, cut it! Consider whether any aspect of your work is under-rehearsed. If so, polish it!

Show your piece to a critical audience and act upon any constructive criticism. You should be confident that your theatrical style is secure and that it supports your presentation.

AQA Examiner's tip

When planning your devising and rehearsal period, work backwards from the date of your exam. Allow time to present your piece to a critical audience, in advance of the exam.

23   The skills of the group

▧ Available skills and make-up of the group

This chapter looks at the skills available for you to choose to be assessed in for your A2 practical exam, and also outlines some of the guidelines that appear in the Specification booklet.

The skills available at A2 are the same as those at AS. You may choose to stay with the same skill, developing and improving your work, or you may wish to try a different skill and widen your theatrical experience.

As in your AS year, you will be working in groups and each member of the group needs to contribute to the devising process.

Here is a reminder of the skills that you may choose from:

▧ Directing (one candidate per group)

▧ Acting (at least two candidates per group)

▧ Costume design (one candidate per group)

▧ Mask design (one candidate per group)

▧ Design of stage setting(s) (one candidate per group)

▧ Technical elements: lighting and/or sound (one candidate per element or one candidate assuming responsibility for both elements)

The Specification offers guidance about how each exam group must be structured, stating:

> Candidates are required to work in groups to present for an audience a devised drama, performed in a theatrical style of their choice.
>
> The group size is to be between two and eight Acting candidates, plus, optionally, up to five candidates offering a design skill (costume design, mask design, set design or technical design (lighting and/or sound)), and/or one Directing candidate.
>
> Each group is to be self-contained and totally responsible for all aspects of the devised work which should realise clear dramatic intentions for an audience.

Although in theory you may choose any of the seven skills, in practice as a group, you need to follow the guidelines to make sure your group is the correct size and has the correct combination of skills.

This means that each examination group *must* contain a minimum of *two* and a maximum of *eight* acting candidates; *may* choose to work collaboratively as actors and *does not* have to include a directing candidate or any design candidates; *may* choose to add to their group any or all of the following:

▧ one director

▧ one set designer

▧ one costume designer

▧ one mask designer

▧ one lighting designer*

▧ one sound designer*.

* or one technical designer responsible for both lighting and sound.

So, to re-cap on the information given in your AS coursebook:

- ■ If your group contains the *minimum* number of actors, and *no* additional non-acting candidates, then the group, as a whole, will contain *two* of you.
- ■ If your group contains the *minimum* number of actors, but the *maximum* number of candidates offering directing or design skills, the group, as a whole, will contain *eight* of you.
- ■ If your group contains the *maximum* number of actors and the *maximum* number of candidates offering the other skills, the group, as a whole, will contain *14* of you.

There are many different permutations possible, but whatever the make-up of the group, the Specification stresses that:

> Whatever skills are chosen for assessment, it is assumed that all candidates in the group take an equal and active role in the devising and creative process and, accordingly, share responsibility for the effectiveness of the finished piece in performance.

■ Link

Refer to your AS coursebook to remind yourself about the demands of each skill as well as about the exam requirements. The demands are the same at each level.

■ Preparation time: the devising/rehearsal balance

In Chapter 22 we looked at the three main phases of the devising process:

- ■ Gathering and generating material
- ■ Structuring and rehearsal
- ■ Assessing, discarding and polishing

You need to create a realistic timetable to accommodate these three stages in your own work. The specification suggests that you spend ten weeks or 50 hours working together on your devised drama. This does not include time spent researching your subject matter or researching your chosen style.

Depending upon how many hours of Drama and Theatre Studies you have in your timetable per week, this represents about two and a half months of timetabled lessons. Most students also work outside lesson times, especially in the final run-up to the examination.

Beware of how time can slip away in the early stages of the devising process as you discuss and decide upon fundamental aspects of your piece. You need to be disciplined with the organisation of your time.

You should spend approximately half of your time gathering, creating and structuring your work and half rehearsing, assessing and polishing it. This does not mean that you cannot devise anything new after the half-way mark but it does mean that you should give as much attention to rehearsing and perfecting your work as you would if you were working on a published play. Once you move into the final weeks of your allotted time you should be working to a script or **performance score**. This may be a work in progress but, at least a week or so before your exam, the piece should be more or less fixed.

How long should the devised drama last?

The Specification offers the following guidelines about the running time of your extract:

> Playing time for the presentation of the piece should be approximately 15–40 minutes, according to the number of Acting candidates in the group; i.e., a group with only two Acting candidates should work to the lower limit, and a group with eight Acting candidates should work to the upper limit.

You may find it difficult to judge how long your devised piece is going to be when you first start work on it. Unlike working on a scripted play, where you might time a read-through of the extract/text to gain a rough idea of its playing time, when you are devising your own material, you may not be certain how long each section of your piece will last in its finished form. You may not even be sure which parts are going to be retained and refined and which cut out or re-shaped.

Make sure that you devise enough material for you to present developed ideas, to display your chosen style and to provide a meaningful experience for the audience. You also need to keep to the recommended timings and be prepared to prune your work to avoid repetition of ideas or devices which would diminish the effectiveness of your piece.

Your teacher and the visiting moderator will expect to see carefully rehearsed, detailed and engaging work which fulfils the timings suggested by the Specification.

Number of acting candidates	Recommended timings for the devised drama
2 or 3	15 minutes
4	20 minutes
5	25 minutes
6	30 minutes
7 or 8	35–40 minutes

Although the recommended timings are related to the number of actors in each exam group, remember that not all actors have to be on stage for the duration of the piece. Do not think in terms of each actor having a specific number of minutes to perform in.

Your chosen style will determine whether or not your group appears as an ensemble throughout or whether individual characters come and go at different points in the piece.

Now you are devising, rather than interpreting a play written by someone else, you should ensure that you create plenty of opportunities for demonstrating your chosen skill. If you are an actor, do not devise a role beyond your abilities or one with few opportunities for revealing your talents. If you are a designer, do not allow the rest of the group to devise a piece that requires little design input!

Building an ensemble of devisers

You will have experienced the importance of team work in preparing practical work for an audience and for an exam during your AS course. When you are devising, the need for creative co-operation and mutual support is even greater. You will begin your work with nothing but your own imaginations and experiences to build upon and it is vital that you create an atmosphere of mutual respect from the start.

However many candidates you have in your group, it is important that from the beginning you think of yourselves as a team of equals, each with a great deal to offer by way of creative suggestions, objectivity and constructive critical skills.

It is important when you choose your group that you feel able to work constructively with each other. However, that is not always possible.

You may find that some members tend not to contribute much or tend to be dismissive of all ideas except their own. You may find that some members attend rehearsals erratically and nothing is more frustrating, when you are trying to make progress with your piece, than having absentee co-performers.

You can avoid some of these problems by drawing up a devisers' contract that sets out the minimum requirements of each group member. If you do this as the outset and agree on the terms of the contract together you will find it beneficial to *all* group members. Even the most harmonious group should sign up to an agreed contract. Remember to involve your teacher in helping the group to monitor how well the terms of the contract are fulfilled.

The contract should include agreement to:

■ a devising/rehearsal schedule (working backwards from the date of the preview performance – *before* the examination date)

■ sign an attendance register for each rehearsal, unless prevented by illness or other unforeseeable circumstances

■ conduct rehearsals in an atmosphere of mutual respect

■ turn up for each session with at least *one* new idea per member in the early stages or later with a solution to one of the blocks that the group have encountered with the material (including design members)

■ give constructive consideration to all group members' ideas

■ undertake necessary research as required by the group

■ take it in turns to chair the rehearsal if there is no directing candidate or to nominate a chairperson each session or each week of the process

■ leave all personal problems/private differences behind you for the duration of each devising/rehearsal session

■ end each session or completion of a section of the piece with an *objective* appraisal of what has been achieved and of what needs to be done to improve upon what has been achieved.

Each student must be totally committed to the dramatic intentions of the group as a whole and to the style that you have chosen to work in.

Devising can be the most rewarding aspect of the whole Drama and Theatre Studies course. It can be challenging but it is also an immensely exciting opportunity for your group to make meaning and to impress an audience with your skills and invention.

The devised drama is your original work and you should take ownership of it, enjoy the process of making drama and be proud of what you create. Enjoy it!

■ Choosing skills: considering abilities and style

When you are devising your own work you no longer have to match your skill to the demands of a text but you still have to consider the demands of the chosen style and whether or not you have the necessary skills to meet those demands.

Whatever theatrical style you have chosen, be it **commedia, verbatim theatre** or **absurdist theatre** for example, you will need to ask yourselves the following questions:

What are the performance demands of the chosen style? Consider whether you need:

AQA Examiner's tip

For all skills, you need to think about the demands of your chosen theatrical style as well as of the demands of devising.

- naturalistic acting skills
- caricatured acting skills
- physical movement-based performance skills
- specialist theatre skills, for example, singing, dancing, mask work.

What are the design demands of the chosen style? Consider:

- **naturalism**
- **selective realism**
- **representation**
- **symbolism**
- **expressionism**
- **minimalism.**

If you are a group made up entirely of actors, make sure that you have the necessary skills and resources between you to create or acquire a setting and/or costumes in keeping with your chosen style.

24

The designers in the devising process

Initial ideas: gathering and creating

In this chapter we are going to look at the role of designers within the devising process. If you are one of the designers in question, or if you have one or more designers in your group, you need to ensure that throughout the devising process *all* members of your group are fully involved in the artistic decision-making that underpins your developing piece.

Unit 4 involves devising drama in a particular style, rather than interpreting someone else's script, so designers have greater freedom at A2 than at AS to shape the direction of the practical work. The designer has to work in a way that complements the evolving work of the director and performers but this does not mean that the designer(s) take a subordinate role to others in the team. Designers are crucial in helping the group achieve their chosen style and should take as much initiative in driving the piece forward as any other member of the group.

In the gathering and creating stages of the devised work, designers should contribute equally to the research and information gathering processes. In addition to thinking about design fundamentals, such as space and staging considerations, fabrics, colours, masks, costumes or technical elements, depending upon their chosen skill, designers should involve themselves in the search for a subject area and even participate in the early improvisations that start to shape the work.

However, designers should also start to affect the piece through design ideas so that the work of the performers and designers mesh together to create a coherent style of theatre. Designers will undertake independent research into past productions performed in the chosen style and come to devising sessions armed with drawings, sketches, images and illustrations. These will help to extend the performers' understanding of the chosen style and help them to think about how they are going to accommodate the designs, enhancing their own exploration of that style.

Design styles

In the previous chapter we suggested that while the group's chosen theatrical style might be very specific – commedia, verbatim theatre, absurdist theatre, for example, the *design* for the devised piece might fall into one of six broad styles:

- naturalism
- selective realism
- representation
- symbolism
- expressionism
- minimalism.

You are unlikely to be successful as a set or costume designer if you align yourself to a group that wishes to adopt a minimalist approach to design or that is devising a physical piece of theatre where the actors' bodies create the setting for the piece. However, if your design skill is mask design or lighting/sound design you could probably make a significant contribution to enhancing the effectiveness of this style of theatre.

Each of the other categories has its own design requirements although it might be helpful to divide the list into those design styles that aim to reproduce or approximate 'reality' (naturalism, selective realism, representation) and design styles that aim to heighten or distort reality (symbolism, expressionism, minimalism) where the designer's brief is to create an atmosphere or tonal quality rather than to provide a recognisable location or period for the action.

Naturalism, selective realism, representation

Set and costume design

During the gathering and creating phase, set and costume designers need to accumulate authentic costumes, furnishings and props.

The set designer will want to establish the use of the staging form, and create working parameters for the setting, so that performers understand the boundaries of their acting space and where their entrances/exits are going to be. If the piece is to be fully naturalistic, the sooner the cast get used to working within an approximation of the finished design the better, even if you are just using a bench to represent the upholstered chaise longue or an upturned box to suggest where the wardrobe will be.

Even where the design style is selective realism or **representation**, the performers need to know which aspects are to be selected and where they will be. Basic design decisions, like decisions made about the contents of the piece and its final shape, are unlikely to be finalised until the second half of the process, but it is helpful to performers to have a broad idea of what will be where, during their early experiments with material. Designers need to be flexible and responsive to the needs of the developing piece and be prepared to make adaptations to support the work in progress.

The costume designer will need to establish an over-arching costume design concept for all the performers fairly early on in the gathering and creating phase, although it will be many weeks before the final costume is finished.

Depending upon the period setting of the piece, the designer may be able to find approximations of the final design for the group to rehearse in. Long rehearsal skirts for the women and structured jackets for the men can make a difference to the way the actors move, sit and stand. If naturalism is the chosen style, the sooner the actors become accustomed to their costumes the better. Using the right accessories can also transform an improvisation or rehearsal of a scene, so make sure that these aspects are given attention early in the devising process.

Technical design

Technical designers can also make a huge contribution to the devising process in the early stages. Experimentation with lighting states and with soundtracks, special effects or music can actually act as a stimulus to the performers' creative work. You can suggest the time of day and year for a mainly naturalistic piece through lighting and sound or evoke a particular period through the selection of appropriate music, even if this is only used to create the right ambience in the rehearsal room.

It is unlikely that mask designers will be involved in groups where the broad categories of naturalism, selective realism or representational styles are being employed.

AQA Examiner's tip

There is a difference between being flexible and being ignored! Do not allow yourself to be coerced into abandoning your ideas late in the process. When designers are involved throughout the devising process it is unusual for them to have to change direction in the assessing and discarding phase.

Symbolism, expressionism, minimalism

Set design

Although set designers for these broad styles will not need to be concerned with the authenticity of the materials that they use, they will have to create designs that provide an appropriate environment for the devised piece which is likely to rely on distinctive aspects of setting to achieve its overall effect.

It might be that the set designer is called upon to provide little more than what amounts to a series of surfaces, levels, steps and galleries for a physical piece of theatre, where the actors intend to leap, climb and swing from different parts of the stage. Alternatively, the designer for a piece of absurdist or surrealist theatre might need to create an extremely intricate and detailed, yet distorted, version of reality, for example with outsized objects like huge chairs, or warped clock faces, furniture made to resemble enormous pieces of fruit, or doors that open into an alternative bizarre landscape.

Set designers need to provide a basic ground plan for where the action takes place, but in the early stages of the process, their ideas, drawings, pictures and design sketches should be as plentiful as the performers' and should be aimed at developing and stimulating the devising process rather than merely complementing the style of the piece.

Some groups may devise in a style which demands multi-functional settings or furnishings. In which case the designer may want to experiment with different configurations of doorframes, picture-frames, windows, mirrors, hoops, buckets, boxes, crates, ropes, stools, umbrellas in varying sizes and proportions.

Costume design

Costume designers will also need to be inventive and experimental in the early stages of the process and consider how the use of colour, fabric and shape can contribute to the particular needs of the piece whether symbolic or expressionistic. They should also be thinking about the effects created by hats, cloaks, footwear and ornamentation on their costumes and bring in plenty of samples, drawings and photographs to help them capture the appropriate style of the piece.

Mask design

Mask designers are likely to be involved in these broad styles of theatre and, again, their role is to stimulate the devisers and to participate in the creative process. Mask designers need to bring in pictures of a variety of styles and types of mask to help the group decide which are most appropriate to their style of theatre and dramatic purpose. They also need to provide working masks for the performers to get used to.

Performing in masks is a specialist skill, and actors who have no experience in mask work need to begin to wear practice masks almost as soon as the devising begins.

The mask designer's job does not stop with the manufacture of the masks but involves coaching the actors to exploit them in performance. When an actor is wearing a mask on stage, the audience's attention focuses immediately upon the way the actor uses his body and gestures. The actor's movements have to be heightened and highly disciplined to allow the actor to communicate both through the mask, with the use of his head and neck, and in spite of the mask, through the use of his body and hands.

Depending upon the style of masks adopted, the actors may also need to be trained to be heard.

Technical design

Technical designers are very important within these styles and their experimentation with lighting and with sound can form an essential part of the gathering of stimulus for a symbolist or expressionist piece. The amplification and distortion of sound; the use of reverb (a sound effect which creates the impression of a slight echo); lighting from unnatural angles in abnormal colours; the creation of looming shadows: these are just some of the methods by which the technical designer might enhance the symbolic or impressionistic style for the performers.

Structuring and rehearsal

For all of the broad styles of theatre and all design skills, the structuring and rehearsal phase of the process is a very busy one. Designers need to be working on the designs that the group have approved. Set designers, costume designers and mask designers will all be engaged in the construction process of their designs. By the time the group have established a pattern of rehearsing their more-or-less completely devised piece, the designers should aim to provide them with their more-or-less completed designs. Technical designers will be overseeing the rigging of their lighting plots and/or compiling their soundscape or technical effects, finalising their cue sheets and there should be a sense of nearing completion in every department.

Designers should also be on hand to offer advice about the performers' best use of the individual features of the designs that they have produced, so that the effects of the production as a whole are fully integrated. Their work is not yet over!

Assessing, discarding, polishing

This is an activity which involves every member of the group. Designers should not merely be concerned with their own designs at this point but all group members should be looking at the whole piece with objective eyes. You will be using the guidelines in Chapter 22 to help you appraise the success of the finished piece, but in particular you will need to ask the critical question: do all aspects of this production reflect the chosen style of theatre? If there is anything on stage that fails to do that or which detracts from the nominated style, it must be addressed, whether it is a performance or a design issue. That is why you need to leave ample time for this final phase of the work.

If there is no designer in the group

Go through all the advice offered in the previous paragraphs to help you to make corporate design decisions throughout the devising process.

25 Performers in the devising process

Most professional companies of devisers are made up of performers. Sometimes one or more of the group assumes a directorial role; sometimes an individual member assumes a management role which involves contracting specialised designers or scriptwriters. However, the core of most devising ensembles consists of a band of inventive performers.

As a performer, you need to be an active member of the devising company, originating ideas, contributing to discussions and working relentlessly on your own performance skills.

The purpose of the task is not merely to tell a story to an audience, to convey a theme or message or to replicate a particular style of theatre, but to *demonstrate your skill of acting* within a devised framework. You will be assessed both on the originality and effectiveness of the piece that you have devised and on your mastery of your chosen skill.

The specification outlines the aspects of an actor's skills that are assessed during the presentation of the devised piece:

Creation of a role or role(s), interpretation of character and/or communication of meaning through, for example:

Vocal techniques: the appropriate use of vocal expression, regional or national accent, clarity of diction, pace, pitch, pause, projection, intonation, inflexion and rhythm; verse speaking

Physical techniques: the appropriate use of movement, body language, gesture and space; agility, ensemble playing, synchronisation, fluency

Facial expression: eye contact, listening and response, expression of mood; actor/audience relationship

As at AS Level, you must develop your own acting skills during the devising process in order to demonstrate your abilities as a performer, as well as your strengths as a deviser.

Acting styles

In Chapter 23 we suggested that whatever theatrical style you select, you should ensure that you have the relevant performance skills to pull it off.

We identified four broad categories of performance skills that might be appropriate to your chosen style:

- naturalistic acting skills
- caricatured acting skills
- physical movement-based performance skills
- specialist theatre skills, for example, singing, dancing, mask work.

Performing well, in any of these skill areas, demands a high level of preparation. Naturalistic acting skills are no easier to acquire than physical movement-based skills. Each presents a significant challenge.

All the categories offer actors the opportunity to display excellent technical accomplishment, whether the *emphasis* of the particular skills is upon control of the body, the voice or the face. Remember to think about each of these three aspects of a performer when you are devising, rehearsing and polishing your work.

Devising with or without a director

With or without a specific director in the group, performer-devisers must go through the phases of:

- gathering and creating
- structuring and rehearsing
- assessing, discarding and polishing.

Depending on the chosen theatrical style, performer-devisers are likely to begin their work in the 'gathering and creating' phase thinking more about characters than about plot.

If you are working in a naturalistic style, characterisation will be critical to the success of your piece. Similarly, if you are working in a style that requires stock characters, such as **commedia** or **farce**, you will need to develop exaggerated characters that are consistently realised.

Each of these styles demands attention to detail in relation to vocal, physical and facial expression.

Sometimes, from a very simple starting point, you can create and enlarge upon an idea until you have devised a credible family, community or virtual world, simply through skilful characterisation.

Depending upon group size and on your chosen style of theatre, you may be **multi-roling** within your piece. If so, differentiation between roles is absolutely essential.

One useful method of generating material in the initial stages is to write down, on separate bits of paper or card, a series of different period settings. For example:

- wild west
- the court of Henry VIII
- First World War – in Britain or Germany
- Victorian England
- medieval village
- Britain in 2050.

These go into a hat and you pick out one of them at random. If you have a director, he or she can choose one.

In another hat you have bits of paper indicating different roles, for example:

- young, single female
- young, single male
- powerful, rich, high status character
- law enforcer
- criminal
- victim
- idiot
- wife and mother
- father
- counsellor/confidante

> **AQA** Examiner's tip
>
> Only adopt multi-roling if it is appropriate to the theatrical style you have chosen. Never do it within a naturalistic piece simply to fit your plot line. Devise a different plot!

■ poor person, desperate

■ boastful person, detested

■ wicked person, feared

■ good person, respected.

Each of the performers in the group picks one at random and you then improvise and/or script a scenario using the setting and the characters. The permutations are endless. If you have a particular setting in mind from the outset, you can be more specific with your characters.

The aim is to create – in your chosen style of theatre – as detailed and precise a realisation of the setting and characters as you can. Generality is the enemy of successful devised work. You should always be aiming for detailed work that communicates a sense of place, period and character as precisely as you can.

If you have a directing candidate in your group he or she can be instrumental in helping you to develop or discard improvisations based around your characters. Your director can help you to **storyboard** your ideas.

The director may be a powerhouse of ideas and have all kinds of suggestions for the direction that your piece might take. Remember though, that devising is a collaborative art and that you need to take control of your skill development for yourself.

If you do not have a director, you need to share the responsibility between you. One useful strategy is to record the work in progress and view it critically, together.

26 The director in the devising process

In this chapter you will learn about:

- the director's role in the devising process.

Link

Remind yourself of what is expected of the director by looking back over Chapters 3, 13, 14 and 24 in your AS coursebook as well as at Chapters 3 and 4 in this book.

If you have chosen directing as your skill, you will have a very important role. Unlike a director of a published play, you and the actors and designers come together initially on a completely equal footing and with a blank page!

The rest of the group will look to you for ideas as well as for direction and objectivity as they generate, discard and polish their work.

Your role might be a combination of director, note-taker and note-giver. You will need to have plenty of energy to keep the group enthusiastic and interested in what they are doing. You need to develop an instinct for when things are working and when they are not. You will need to be tactful when you feel the need to cut a scene or halt a particular line of devising.

It will be your role to help the performers to structure the devising/rehearsal process; you may be asking individuals to write up scenes or scenarios to 'fix' them; or you may take on the task of some informal scripting yourself. You should ensure that the group keep to the rehearsal schedule as far as possible and leave enough time after the devising stages to rehearse and refine their work thoroughly.

Always remember that devising is collaborative. Avoid being dictatorial, but retain a firm grasp of the theatrical style that you have chosen. You are in the best position to ensure that both the performance and design elements are consonant with that style.

Remember that even directors with professional devising companies have little idea how a piece will turn out when they arrive at the first rehearsal. It is your job to:

- help the cast come to a full understanding of the style that you are striving to achieve
- lead their research into it
- provide stimuli when they reach a dead end or feel despondent
- help them shape their work to realise the intentions for the audience that you have agreed upon, as a group.

Case study: devising a piece in physical theatre style

- how one group of students created their devised piece using physical theatre as their chosen style.

AQA Examiner's tip

Hannah's description of the devising process contains details about the decision-making processes of the group as well as her own input.

To construct her supporting notes out of this account, Hannah would have had to cut and tailor her material to the precise demands, and word limit, of the three separate sections.

Introduction

This chapter consists of one student's personal account of the devising process that she and her group experienced. It is written by Hannah, who was one of six acting candidates in a group of eight students which included a lighting designer and a costume designer.

Hannah begins by describing the initial ideas of the group, and she traces the development of the piece as the students gathered and generated their material, as they structured and rehearsed their piece and, finally, as they assessed and polished their piece for presentation.

Choosing a style – physical theatre

One of the reasons that the group included the members that it did was that we all wanted to work in a physical theatre style.

Our first task was to ensure that we all shared an understanding of the demands of the style and we did this by gathering and sifting many sources of information including:

- various definitions of the style made by practitioners and contemporary critics
- books, articles and websites devoted to physical theatre
- live productions in the style and DVDs of work in the style.

Definitions

As a result of our research we identified the following fundamental features of the physical theatre style that we wanted to incorporate into our work:

- the use of physical skills such as dance, mime, clowning and other circus skills; use of masks and/or puppetry or a combination of such skills used to tell a story
- the importance of visual elements
- the idea that text is only one component of the work, not necessarily the most important
- the intention to appeal to the instinctive, emotional side of the audience – to their hearts rather than their heads.

Books, articles and websites

We all read as much as we could find on the physical theatre style (see Further reading section). We also read a number of playscripts as produced by Kneehigh and Complicité to widen our understanding of how devised pieces become working scripts.

We also found the magazine *Total Theatre* to be a source of inspiration, with many articles devoted to different physical theatre pieces.

It was also very helpful to revisit the WebQuest on physical theatre from our AS studies.

Examples seen

We have seen the extreme physicality of groups such as DV8 (live and on DVD) and Stan Won't Dance (*Revelations* live). However, although we admired their work we were realistic enough to know that we did not have the physical skills to emulate their amazing flexibility.

Other physical theatre companies showed us a form that we felt we could work in, these were:

■ Kneehigh – *Brief Encounter, Rapunzel*
■ Complicité – *Disappearing Numbers*
■ Stan's Café – *The Cleansing of Constance Brown*.

We are not dancers or gymnasts but we can convey ideas through movement, ensemble work, use of levels and carefully rehearsed and choreographed lifts, and we certainly hoped to move the emotions of the audience.

Fig. 27.1 *A scene from* **The Cleansing of Constance Brown** *by Stan's Café in 2007*

■ Physical theatre techniques that we have seen

We made a list of some of the physical features/ideas that we had seen in physical theatre productions.

Seen	Possible variation
Actors using a toy scooter (*Brief Encounter*)	Roller skates Skateboard
Flying (love scene in *Brief Encounter*)	not feasible
Use of different levels (in *Revelations*, where the whole set was a climbing frame)	Health and safety may need care, but rostra frames might work
Crowd scenes, synchronised movement used to create sense of bustle (India in *Disappearing Numbers*)	Swarming/shoal exercises to suggest a crowd
Lifts (ability of groups to support weight of members; demanding in DV8; some simpler examples by Push on YouTube website.)	Related to trust exercises we have done in practical sessions. Again, helps to create different levels and visual interest

We decided to focus on the use of space, and ensemble movement could help us create an effective group identity.

The inspiration for our 'story'

Our inspiration for the story of our physical theatre piece came from a visit that we made to a local care home for the elderly. One of the residents told us that she had been a former ballroom-dancing champion. However, she now suffers from arthritis in her knees that prevents her from walking more than a few painful steps.

We were genuinely affected when she told us that most nights she dreamt that she was dancing but that every morning she had to wake up to the reality of her very limited movement.

This conversation gave us the idea for our piece. The theme would be old age, and our focus would be on both the changes that it brings us physically and the memories that sustain us emotionally.

Our group aims

We now needed to create a story with:

- a clear shape
- significant opportunities to create physical images
- the potential to have a powerful effect on an audience.

Because we wanted a highly physical piece, we decided to concentrate on memory and flashback rather than on the lack of mobility of the central character's present-day reality. We decided to base the piece around the day when a once-energetic woman (whom we called Margaret) has to move into residential care; we decided that the piece would include flashback sequences of her memories.

This would provide the opportunities we wanted for physical action for the acting candidates as well as for our lighting candidate, Martin, who could really go to town on the 'flashback' and 'memory' sequences and our costume candidate, Katrina, who wanted the challenge of creating different, specific period costume.

The devising process

The first stage of our devising process was spent generating and gathering ideas.

So, in our first practical session, we adopted an approach used by Kneehigh and we started by reminiscing about our own early memories. We listed memorable events in our lives. Birthdays, holidays, Christmases, visits to the pantomime, zoo or circus: these were the positive memories that we considered.

Then we thought about sadder, more negative, experiences: the illness or death of someone dear to us; the separation of parents; fear. We then divided into two separate groups and each took twenty minutes to improvise a short scene based on a happy memory.

We chose to develop the scene set in a fairground, which allowed us to create a recognizable location for the action and one which lent itself to inventive lighting and sound; it also offered opportunities for very physical acting methods.

We then repeated the process with sadder memories and created two useful scenarios. The first explored the day of Margaret's husband's funeral, while the second looked at the moment when Margaret leaves her own home to go into a care home.

My group looked at the old lady's departure, suggested her moving around, picking up items, such as photos, packing the last objects and then sitting, dejectedly waiting. However when we performed this idea, the other group quite rightly pointed out that, although it was moving, it was not exactly physical theatre. Their idea for the funeral was far better; the whole group could be included, representing Margaret's family and friends. They suggested using masks, and also wearing masks on our hands, to suggest a larger number of people. (One person + two masks = three people!) This idea was so effective that we used it more than once in our piece.

By repeating this process of generating material we eventually arrived at a sequence of events, from Margaret's life that would be the basis of our devising work.

▪ Structuring a timeline

These are the scenes that we decided to include:

▪ Margaret alone, ready to leave her house for the care home, surrounded by cardboard boxes
▪ her first day at school
▪ her sixth birthday party
▪ the fairground scene
▪ meeting with her future husband or her wedding
▪ a seaside holiday with her three children
▪ her husband's funeral
▪ today.

With six actors in our group we were working to create about 30 minutes' worth of material. We wanted to create short, well-shaped scenes with seamless transitions, achieved through physical theatre skills.

▪ Research

We created a mini-biography for Margaret: for example, we decided that she had been born in 1924. This allowed us to determine a date for each episode and helped Katrina in her research into costume.

We each undertook a specific aspect of the piece to research into. For example, I researched into fairgrounds in the 1930s, looking into sideshows and the types of fairground 'rides' that would have been available. I discovered that carousels, swing boats, cakewalks and dodgems would have been included in the fairground, but that ferris wheels and octopus-style rides had not reached England.

There was plenty of material, on the internet, in books, and most usefully in the local museum, which had an enormous collection of photos of everyday life in our area going back to the 1890s. This was research that we could all use, and the group soon realised that our own elderly relatives could help as well. Richard had made a trip back to the elderly lady whose dream was our starting point and found she was very excited by the idea and extremely helpful, with memories and photos!

■ Making decisions

Once we had gathered our material we needed to make decisions about staging our piece.

We had always visualised using a variety of levels, but now were faced with the problem of how to create these safely. Health and safety should always be a consideration when you are devising and rehearsing, and as devisers in a physical style we knew we needed sturdy and reliable ways of creating the levels that we wanted.

Our first experiment was to make a frame of rostra blocks and to form a tower. This worked quite well because the blocks formed a firm base and stayed secure. We could build them three or four units high, which offered the flexibility we needed. We briefly considered doing the performance in the gym and using the wall bars, but as we experimented we found that 'audience' focus was lost if we went too high; the venue also presented difficulties to Martin, who found the gym difficult to light with any degree of subtlety.

We finally decided to integrate enormous cardboard boxes into our setting. These were ideal to suggest Margaret's packing-up of her old life and were also big enough to contain *us* for our surprise opening. By attaching cardboard around the rostra blocks, we achieved sturdy platforms for our more physical work while keeping them looking identical to the cardboard containers.

■ The process of structuring, devising and rehearsing

The table below shows how we shaped some of our ideas into practical, physical theatre.

Scene	Physical theatre ideas used and intended effects
The opening scene – Margaret and her memories	We used huge cardboard boxes which contained Margaret's 'memories' in the form of the rest of the cast, creating a surprise for the audience when we jumped or crawled out of them.
First day at school	We presented this as quite a scary memory. We used masks on our hands to suggest 15 students crowding around the new girl.
	Lucy appearing on Richard's shoulders became the frightening, enormous teacher. The audience should share Margaret's memory of being small.
6th Birthday	1930s party with typical party food – we created the 'jelly' by physically wobbling. This is a humorous scene in which party games are played frenetically, for example, pass the parcel where we mimed the contents of the parcels to make the audience laugh.
Fairground	Swing boats, carousel horses, dodgems, all presented through physical theatre skills. We used appropriate fairground style music to excite the audience.
	Hoopla: Margaret throws a hoop, and the prize she wins is her husband-to-be. They enter the 'tunnel of love'. This is quite a sentimental scene for the audience.

AQA Examiner's tip

Although you may be used to working in one particular space, site-specific theatre is a popular development, encouraging companies to view unusual spaces as potential theatre venues.

The Wedding	Margaret's journey down the aisle is accomplished on a skateboard – so she can glide in, pushed by the bridesmaids; Frank, her husband is on roller skates; both spin as they meet. We hope to capture the excitement of this wedding for the audience.
Seaside holiday	Swimming, lying on boxes; miming water activities; then the tide comes in; sound/lighting FX
	The children build sandcastles; the scene ends with a note of foreboding as Frank begins coughing.
Frank's Funeral	Frank is carried in at shoulder height; he then stands behind Margaret, almost touching her; he observes his own funeral and also watches over his wife. The family are hidden under many black umbrellas. The audience are saddened but also reassured that Frank is still spiritually present.
Today	Returns to the opening tableau with Margaret alone. We used a voice-over: 'Are you ready, Mrs Grant?'
	Everyone rushed to Margaret and created an upright lift, as high as possible.
	In our first version, Margaret said 'No', but we changed that to 'Yes' as she clutched the photo album, to represent her more positive attitude; she still had her memories.

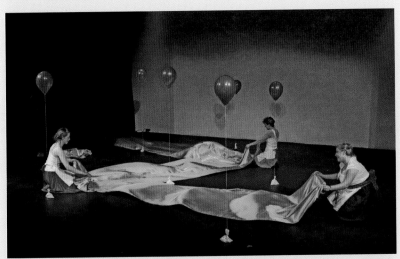

Fig. 27.2 *Students using simple but colourful props in a devised drama*

One problem facing all devisers is how to link episodes together smoothly. We found a solution for this by using projections of photographs taken from 'Margaret's album' which appeared on the cyclorama as one scene segued into the next. It provided a cover for the changes as well as a strong link.

We also integrated a moment in each scene where we involved the audience: for example, we offered them sweets during the first day at school scene, party balloons during the sixth-party scene and confetti to throw for the wedding scene.

We felt that this really helped the audience to feel involved and to share the emotions of the scene.

We also checked that everyone had sufficient to do. We all had principal characters, I played Margaret throughout and did not multi-role. The rest of the actors each had a main role and many other roles as part of the ensemble. For example, Richard played Frank; Kirstie created an irritating child in the seaside scene; Lucy was the teacher; Emma was the main Bridesmaid. Neil was a stallholder in the fairground.

Katrina's costumes were brilliant. She kept changes to a minimum and focused on the different stages of Margaret's life. The long, drab coat that Margaret wears in the first scene is taken off to reveal a child's gymslip, and the blouse under that is actually a dress – tucked up – that she then wears for the party. For the fairground she just adds a pretty hat. Her Bride's outfit is an enormous skirt fixed on by the Bridesmaids. The rest of the actors wear neutral costumes each in a block of one colour, but then add items like a ribbon or a tie for each change of scene.

Martin's lighting has one distinct state for the first and last scenes, but also an array of different specials; for example, coloured gobos at the fair, birdies to cast shadows of the teacher.

The visual aspect of physical theatre was well represented.

■ Late rehearsals – assessing/discarding/polishing

In the final two weeks of our allotted time we started to perform to 'trial' audiences. First, to the other Drama and Theatre Studies groups, then to the rest of the sixth form, and then to parents for an evening performance. Each time we invited feedback and acted upon suggestions or criticism where we felt they were appropriate.

We re-worked sections of the birthday party scene, where we had been a little self-indulgent with the number of games we included. For example, we were told that a sequence spent in 'blind man's bluff' did not capture any of the excitement of the game, so we added more 'obstacles' and shrieks to inject some more energy into it.

We also cut a Punch and Judy section from the seaside scene as the piece was bordering on being too long and this was one of the least effective moments.

Most importantly we viewed a recording of our piece which helped us to identify moments that needed to be more fully synchronised, or moments where the pace was flagging. We were honest with one another and the piece benefited from our honesty through some judicious cutting and additional rehearsal of 'problem' scenes.

It was a worthwhile and rewarding process which resulted in a piece of physical theatre that we were proud to have created.

■ Further reading

Simon Murray, *Physical Theatres: A Critical Introduction*, Routledge, 2007

Dymphna Callery, *Through the Body: A Practical Guide to Physical Theatre*, Routledge, 2002

Simon Murray, *Jacques Lecoq*, Routledge, 2003

Michael Wilson, *Storytelling and Theatre: Contemporary Professional Storytellers and their Art*, Palgrave Macmillan, 2005

John Wright, *Why is that so Funny? A Practical Exploration of Physical Comedy*, Nick Hern Books, 2006.

Total Theatre magazine: see www.totaltheatre.org.uk/magazine/

28 Supporting notes

This chapter focuses on the supporting notes that you need to produce to supplement your practical work. At the end of the chapter you will find a set of sample notes that show the sort of material that you might include.

Your supporting notes should show your understanding of your chosen theatrical style and demonstrate how it has helped you to shape your devised work. They should provide evidence of the research that you have undertaken, including reference to productions that you have seen in the style of your choice. You should document your practical exploration of the style during the devising process.

Your notes should include clear details about the devising process and your practical exploration and experiment in the style, as well as your personal assessment of the potential effectiveness of your devised piece for an audience. You should also reflect upon the development of your selected skill in relation to your chosen style.

AQA Examiner's tip

Do not be tempted to write more than you need to. The exam board recommends a certain length. If your notes are over the limit, edit them down. The highest marks go to notes that are concise.

Link

Look back at Chapter 24 in your AS coursebook for the precise requirements of the notes for each of the available skills.

How should the supporting notes be presented?

The notes should be clearly presented, ideally word-processed, and written as concise but *full* sentences. You may use bullet points (sparingly) within the notes where you are summarising features of style or exercises that you have completed. Use specialist theatre terminology wherever necessary. The notes should be divided into three sections, as explained below, and should be, *in total*, between 1,500 and 2,000 words in length.

You need to provide evidence of the exploration that you have made into your chosen style, so you will have to include a bibliography and/or a webliography, and acknowledge the sources and resources you have used. This information does not count towards your word allowance.

You may include sketches and diagrams, whatever skill you are being assessed in, but make sure that if you are offering a design skill, you know exactly what the exam requirements are.

Organising your supporting notes

Divide your notes into three separate sections, each being between about 500 and 700 words long. The divisions should be as follows:

Section one

In 500–700 words, outline the key features of your chosen style and justify your choice in terms of how the style will help you to realise clear dramatic intentions to your audience.

Provide evidence of research undertaken into your chosen style, including reference to plays seen in production, or on DVD as well as those read. (Bibliographies are not included in your word limit.)

Section two

In 500–700 words, outline your devising strategies and explain how you have used the skills of the group to create drama which fulfils your shared aims. Include your assessment of the devising process and the emerging piece, looking especially at its refinement and development and the way in which it has been improved as a result of both practical and theoretical research and feedback.

Section three

In 500–700 words, offer a personal evaluation of the piece and its potential effectiveness for an audience. Evaluate the development of your own skill in relation both to the piece and to the chosen style. Reflect upon your contribution to the development of the piece. You should also refer to health and safety factors that you have considered.

Preparing your supporting notes

You should begin to prepare your supporting notes as soon as you start work on your devised drama. Keep track of your exploration of your chosen style, of the plays that you read, and those that you go to see. The more notes you make along the way, the easier it will be for you to construct your final set of supporting notes that will be seen by the moderator on the day of your practical exam.

Sample notes

Look carefully at the sample support notes below. The student is a member of a group who have devised drama in the distinctive style of **commedia dell'arte**.

These notes should give you an idea of how much material to include in each section, as well as the type of aspects to be covered. The student is offering acting as a skill.

Section one

Key features of our chosen style: dramatic intentions for our audience. Research and exploration of the style of commedia, including plays read and productions seen.

Having studied Goldoni's ***The Servant of Two Masters*** last term for DRAM 3, my group decided that it would be both challenging and fun to devise our drama in the style of commedia dell'arte.

We have seen a live production of ***The Servant of Two Masters***, directed by Michael Bogdanov and starring Les Dennis, and we have also read and explored, in practical workshops, one of Goldoni's other popular plays, *The Venetian Twins*. We have also read numerous commedia scenarios from a range of sources (see bibliography) and from different periods of the development of commedia in Italy and wider Europe.

What these plays and scenarios have in common is a distinctive form of devised comedy, based on simple but exaggerated physical actions and predictable running gags. What attracted us to the style was the fact that we wanted to make our audience laugh and, in commedia, we had a style that, if performed properly, seems to be almost guaranteed to deliver laughter.

We also visited the Victoria and Albert Museum where we were able to view a recording of a piece of drama called *Arlecchino and Zanni*, devised by Marcello Magni (of Complicité) with Kathryn Hunter and Jos Houben. This devised piece, originally produced at the Battersea

Arts Centre in 2002, explored the anarchic figure of Arlecchino through the ages. This gave us inspiration to devise our own piece taking the bare bones of a scenario – in true commedia fashion – and developing it into a complete short drama.

One of the scenarios that we worked on practically is called *The False Turk – in Twelve Minutes* and this scenario taught us that, using commedia methods, it is possible to reduce even the most complicated plot into the sort of time frame that we have, which is about 30 minutes.

We have researched commedia dell'arte extensively as background to our study of **The Servant of Two Masters**.

The key features of commedia that we are going to incorporate into our devised piece are as follows:

▪ stock characters, including, for example, masters and servants, old men and young lovers, a bragging captain, a pedantic doctor, a wily and a stupid servant

▪ flimsy plot-lines revolving around standard themes, for example, lovers prevented from marrying by a disapproving father; money/miserliness/mercenary marriages; greed – both for food and money

▪ lazzi – pieces of physical comic business or comical routines

▪ fast-paced dialogue – often including set pieces such as, tirades, laments, disquisitions and hilarious exchanges of insults

▪ interaction with the audience

▪ masks and traditional costumes (we have a mask designer in the group)

▪ simple settings – possibly cartoon style

▪ a limited number of props.

Based on our own experience of watching a live production of **The Servant of Two Masters** we identified certain commedia 'ingredients' that we wanted to use as they had made us laugh the most. These were:

▪ an energetic fight scene between **Beatrice** and **Silvio**, 'his' rival in love. This was a 'no holds barred' comic routine which included a swordfight conducted across the length of the stage and also involving action with **Beatrice** standing on a bridge duelling with **Silvio**, who was standing in a gondola below – as the gondola moved under the bridge they swapped sides! This fight eventually moved into the auditorium where a 'member of the audience' was 'accidentally' stabbed!

▪ lazzi of fainting – where **Clarice** was staggering around the stage waiting to be caught by **Silvio**

▪ lazzi of the 'dance of glee' which both **Pantalone** and **Dr Lombardi** did at various points in the action – when things appeared to be going their way

▪ the whole idea of disguise – a staple of commedia

▪ frantic pace and comic invention

Word Count: approx 600 words

Bibliography

Plays read:

The Servant of Two Masters by Goldoni

The Venetian Twins by Goldoni

The King Stag by Carlo Gozzi

Commedia Plays in a collection by Barry Grantham (Nick Hern 2006)

Tartuffe by Moliére

Plays seen live:

The Comedy of Errors by Shakespeare (RSC on tour)

The Servant of Two Masters by Goldoni (directed by Michael Bogdanov)

Plays seen (recordings):

Arlecchino and Zanni a devised piece by Marcello Magni, Kathryn Hunter and Jos Houben

Mistero Buffo by Dario Fo

Critical Work on commedia:

John Rudlin, *Commedia dell'Arte: An Actor's Handbook*, Routledge, 1994

Bari Rolfe, *Commedia dell'Arte: A Scene-Study Book*, Persona Books, 1977

Barry Grantham, *Playing Commedia: A Training Guide to Commedia Techniques*, Nick Hern Books, 2000

Mel Gordon, *Lazzi: Comic Routines of the Commedia dell'Arte*, Johns Hopkins University Press, 1983

Thurston James, *The Prop Builder's Mask-Making Handbook*, Betterway Books, 1990

Henry F. Salerno, trans, ed, *Scenarios of the Commedia dell'Arte, Flaminio Scala's Il Teatro delle Favole Rappresentative*, New York University Press, 1967

Websites used:

www.commedia-dell-arte.com/index.shtml

www.davidclaudon.com/arte/commedia.html

www.italian.about.com/library/weekly/aa110800a.htm

www.shane-arts.com/commedia-stock-characters.htm

www.webarchive.org

www.mcauley.acu.edu.au/staff/delyse/commedia.html

Section two

Devising strategies: using the skills of the group to achieve shared aims. Assessment of the emerging piece: the place of research and feedback in shaping the devised work.

Subject matter

Having read thirty commedia scenarios we chose *The Path of True Love* for our cast of five boys and two girls plus mask designer. This scenario revolves around lovers – the Innamorati – prevented from marriage by Pantalone, the father of the prospective bride. The cheeky servants, the zanni, help the lovers to achieve their goal.

Obviously, as this is a devising project, although we have researched versions of this scenario, we are devising it fully, ourselves.

Devising

Devising for this commedia piece has been fun, but highly disciplined. We have produced six five-minute scenes telling the story of Pantalone's attempt to marry his daughter, against her wishes, to the middle-aged braggart, the Captain (Spavento).

We all researched commedia characters and I discovered that the Captain figure is always an outsider to the town which allows him to invent his own 'pedigree' and history of bravery in action without being challenged. The Captain always has an ironic name – spavento means 'fright' in Italian. I decided to call myself Captain Scaredy Pants and invented a list of battles that I had, naturally, won 'single handed'.

Using the descriptions of various lazzi from Barry Grantham's book, *Commedia Plays*, we created an outline structure. We spent every rehearsal in the first four weeks of preparation, improvising scenes and lazzi using the simple sequence of events from the scenario. We recorded everything so we were able to look back at what was funny and what was not!

When we were running out of steam, one of us would produce something ridiculous like a carrot or a large saucepan and chuck it into the mix and we had to improvise a silly scene using that object. Nine times out of 10 these objects stimulated our invention. Only the hat-stand that we tried working with, failed to spark our imagination.

Examples of scenes

In Scene 1, Zanni introduces Lelio, Isabella, Pantalone and Franceschina directly to the audience as they run around the stage in two different chase sequences. Isabella clearly wants to be caught by her lover, Lelio, while Franceschina wants to avoid the clutches of old (limping) Pantalone at all costs. We improvised using obstacles such as a single real painted flat and a variety of mimed objects – doors and cupboards for the actors to run around, through or over; to hide behind or in. Josh wrote his own introduction to the play, as Zanni, drawing inspiration from *Mistero Buffo* using rhyming couplets and he accompanies the chase with frantically paced music on his banjo.

(Lazzo of chasing and of Emperor's props – meaning invisible props!)

In Scene 2 Captain Scaredy Pants strides on in full military regalia (somewhat dishevelled) and bribes Zanni for information about the financial status of Pantalone, the availability of his daughter and the likely size of her … dowry. The Captain approaches Pantalone and gains his consent to woo Isabella; Pantalone is convinced he has landed a 'catch' for his daughter and dances with glee.

As Captain, I hold up and jingle a huge bag of coins to Zanni to get information out of him but when he approaches to claim his bribe, I open it and give him a tiny copper coin.

Tim's dance of glee took ages to perfect with its high knees-up action and simultaneous swishing of the arms from side to side.

(Lazzo of money and dance of glee)

In Scene 4, to foil the Captain, Isabella and Franceschina swap clothes in a comic routine simply exchanging their head-dresses and the maid's apron, as they pretend to be each other. Isabella adopts a coarse voice and Franceschina a haughty one. When Pantalone arrives and points out the Captain's mistake, I swiftly change knees and propose to the correct mistress. Before exiting the scene, a 'mouse' frightens me and I leap into the arms of an astonished Pantalone.

(Lazzo of exchanging clothes, listing – all my assets and conquests prior to the actual proposal – also in rhyme, proposal and the surprise embrace)

Feedback from invited audiences was very positive, however it did persuade us that in some instances, for example Becky's fainting lazzo, we needed to make our actions more exaggerated.

Word count = 680 words

■ Section three

The development of my skill of acting in commedia style. Assessment of the potential effectiveness for the audience. Health and safety.

Acting in commedia style

In developing the Captain, I have drawn on my research to establish his braggart characteristics.

Vocally I have created a loud 'basso profundo' which changes rapidly to a feminine squeak when frightened. I have also adopted a ridiculous exaggerated Spanish accent both (much spitting on H sounds) to distinguish me from the other townsfolk and to stress my 'Latin lover' type.

I have experimented with a variety of stances and walks. When stationary, I puff out my chest and try to occupy as much space as possible, my feet are planted firmly on the ground.

My research suggested a variety of different approaches to walking, such as military marching and the 'Mountain walk' in which the heels of my high boots come down first, then the foot rolls on to the ball. This actually looks very effective. When I am frightened I run on the spot, head thrown back, arms in the air, kicking my feet forward and howling pathetically before leaping into Pantalone's arms.

Although the Captain is a stock character there is variety in the scenario as I am a bully to Zanni, I am obsequious to Pantalone and insufferably lecherous to the ladies. I achieve this vocally as I am wearing a mask. Fortunately it is so well made that it does not impede either vision or audibility.

The mask is flesh-coloured with a huge menacing nose. I am wearing a scarlet doublet over a jerkin and breeches of light yellow with scarlet stripes; I look truly ridiculous and I have a huge sword strapped to my side which keeps getting in the way, especially as I try to kneel to propose to the girls.

My lazzo of proposal consists of me lowering myself awkwardly on to one knee (I am playing the role as a slightly out of condition forty-five year old). As Franceschina shifts her ground, I naturally have to shuffle after her with my sword banging along the floor as I go. When I realise I have proposed to the wrong woman I do an elaborate swivel, whip my sword round to the other side and shuffle after Isabella.

I am fairly satisfied that I have achieved the necessary pace of delivery – the proposal is fast and full of tongue twisters as well as being in rhyme. I punctuate my delivery with out-of breath wheezes as I pursue first one and then the other 'object of my affections' around the space.

Fig. 28.1 *The Captain character*

Assessment of the potential effectiveness of the piece

Judging by the reactions of our invited audiences we have succeeded in creating a comic piece in the style of commedia with the potential to be very effective. We have worked hard to make the set pieces, such as the sword fight in Scene 4, as slick as possible. It is both funny and a bit awe-inspiring, as Rob is an accomplished fencer and has coached me to be a reasonable one (for a novice). I am mainly parrying his attacks and Rob has taught me a series of dodges and, in true commedia style, I am continually trying to ward off his attack – I use a chamber pot as a shield at one point – and pulling Pantalone in front of me to deflect Lelio's strikes.

Stephen's masks are impressive and pictures and prints of all the commedia stock characters have helped us to assemble costumes that are both appropriate and authentic looking. The set, in keeping with the commedia style, is simplicity itself, consisting of a single reversible flat depicting first a tree and then Isabella's boudoir.

Health and Safety

There are health and safety issues surrounding the sword fight, but we are using wooden swords with rounded 'points'; the sound of clashing steel is supplied by Zanni and a set of cymbals!

Any form of physical theatre demands regular warm-ups, constant practice and accuracy to avoid injury and we have been meticulous in our rehearsals to achieve this.

The reversible flat is on castors and is also attached to a bar by a rope above the acting area to prevent it falling over as it is occasionally spun during action.

(690 words)

Supporting notes word total = 1,900 words

29 Clear intentions for the audience

- ensuring that you communicate clear intentions for the audience.

Link

Look again at page 117 in Chapter 22 Devising strategies (under the heading: Finding a style/Intentions for the audience).

When you are devising your own work, it is vital that you consider how it will affect your audience. You need to establish clear intentions for your audience from the outset and evaluate your achievement at the end of the process, in terms of these intentions.

Your choice of style will largely determine what effect you are likely to achieve with your devised piece. A piece presented in a **naturalistic** style will demand that your audience experiences a different level of engagement with the dialogue, for example, than a piece presented in a physical style. However, your choice of subject matter will also qualify your audience's experience.

When you are devising your own material, as opposed to interpreting the work of a published playwright, you have a unique corporate insight into the dramatic meaning of your piece. Although some pieces of devised drama, presented in a physical or non-naturalistic style, depend for their effect on a certain obscurity of concrete meaning, it is always counterproductive to put before an audience a piece of drama that the devisers themselves find obscure.

Even if you have devised, for example, a piece of 'Theatre of Cruelty', composed mainly of movement and incoherent sounds, groans and cries, you must ensure that it *means* something to you as a group. Otherwise, you will struggle to communicate anything of value to your audience. Maybe you only want to disturb your audience, to disorientate them or shock them. These intentions can be channelled into creating a coherent theatrical experience for your audience.

So, know what you want to achieve; strive to find theatrical expression for your intentions and subject your finished piece to rigorous scrutiny in terms of what you have achieved. Perform your piece to an objective critical audience in advance of the exam and listen to the honest responses that you receive.

Try not to be too defensive. If more than one member of your audience is bewildered by what you have presented, do not dismiss their comments. Try to address them and to ensure that areas of confusion or uncertainty are made clearer. On the other hand, if you have devised a 'murder-mystery' piece and members of the audience have solved the mystery in the first five minutes, you will have to introduce more elements of uncertainty to stay true to your chosen style.

In short, you need to ensure that your audience's reaction to your piece matches your expectations. If it does not, remedial action is required.

30   Assessing the finished piece

In this chapter you will learn about:

■ the importance of assessing and refining your finished piece

■ some potential solutions to last-minute problems.

This chapter emphasises the importance of assessing your finished piece. Throughout Unit 4 we have referred to 'assessing, discarding and polishing' as the third and final phase in the devising process. But what can you actually *do*, if, with three weeks to go before your practical exam, you decide that you are not happy with what you have produced?

The table below offers some possible solutions.

Problem	Potential solutions
The piece lacks an interesting plot line	Ask yourself if plot is an important aspect of your chosen style. If it is, go back through your original notes and check if you have discarded any revivable plot-lines.
	Remind yourself of one or two of the plays that you have seen/read in your chosen style. What made their plots more interesting? Use improvisation to develop your own plot or to introduce aspects from your source.
	Use improvisations to develop the critical moments of your plot.
	Use improvisations to develop one or more of the relationships within the piece.
	Ask a critical outsider which aspect of the plot he or she would have liked to learn more about – then develop it.
A naturalistic piece lacks believable characters	Use some of the strategies suggested in Chapter 6 to add substance to the characters for the actors to build upon.
	Look at the relationships within the piece. How can you use these to develop your characters?
The piece lacks an authentic/suitable setting for the action	Go back to your research if you are missing authenticity or, if your setting is simply too bland to be effective, try transposing your piece to a different specific setting/time: the Russian Revolution; the Spanish Civil War; New York during the Wall Street Crash; Britain during the First World War. Use research and authentic design elements to help create a completely different atmosphere – make sure you get it right!
The piece lacks dramatic tension	This is a problem often associated with pace and structure. Are all your sections approximately the same length? Is the pace varied or constant? Try re-structuring some of your sections. Vary the pace and increase energy levels.
	Try to use pause/silence effectively at critical moments.
	Cut out any repetition in the dialogue or movement sequences.
The dialogue is implausible or the language is clumsy	Go back to your research. Ensure that your characters are speaking dialogue that is appropriate both to the period setting and to their individual roles in life.
	Consider how age, class, status, family relationships and occupations modify the way people interact with one another.
	If you are presenting a period piece, cut out all modern colloquialisms.
	Try substituting or complementing some of the dialogue with meaningful body language and eye contact.
The piece is in a physical theatre style but the execution of it is uneven.	Practise, practise, practise!
	Alternatively, replace the less successful physical routines with still moments and choric speech.
In a piece of physical theatre one member of the group is letting the whole piece down.	Find a less physical way of integrating your fellow group member into the work – could s/he be a still point at the heart of the action? Or placed above or behind the more physical parts? Is there scope for a narrator figure?

The piece is hampered by over-long transitions and blackouts	Transitions are crucial to the success of devised work, and blackouts should be avoided at all costs. If you must use lighting to effect scene changes, try using different colour washes so the actors are seen changing the set or exiting/entering but they continue to *act*.
	Spend an entire rehearsal session simply rehearsing the transitions. Scenery can be changed in a balletic or physical style; music can be used to 'cover' the transitions, or, depending on the style of the piece, one scene can begin while the other is being removed.
	Avoid unnecessary costume changes or modification to the set.
	In physical theatre fluid transitions really matter because they are the hallmark of the seamless physical style.
The piece does not have a suitable ending	This is a major problem. Your dramatic structure is crucial in achieving a sense of completion. Possible solutions, depending upon your chosen style, include:
	Direct address to the audience/narrative summing up
	A well-crafted final tableaux or freeze frame
	A return to the opening sequence with variations
	A birth, marriage or a death
	A significant sound effect or music
	(Avoid the 'waking up-it was all a dream' solution!)
There are some suitable props but the actors mime others	Make sure you either have all the props you need (and that you are rehearsing with them for at least the last 2 weeks of the preparation process) or you mime *all* the props (in a precise and disciplined way).
	Your selected style should guide you here. Never mime props in a naturalistic or realistic piece.
	You are the devisers – do not devise a section where the characters drink tea and eat scones unless you are sure to be able to acquire tea and scones and to rehearse with them well in advance of the exam!
The style is secure but the content has little meaning	Go back to the plays and productions that inspired your choice in the first place. Try to define the 'meaning' behind each one. Remember that dramatic meaning is not always communicated through the dialogue alone. The juxtaposition of a well-dressed character and a beggar dressed in rags can make meaning; a physical sequence that leaves one character isolated can make meaning; the reactions of a crowd – indifferent or ecstatic as they listen to a speaker – can make meaning.
	Try to identify all the points in your piece where there is meaning and find a way of highlighting each moment and/or linking them together for the audience.
	If that fails … add another short scene full of meaning.
The piece is fine, but it is hard to say what style it is in.	This is the biggest problem of all and the most difficult to solve with three weeks to go. Go back to the plays and productions that inspired your choice; rekindle your focus. Make a list of the following aspects that typify your chosen style, for example:
	the intended effects for the audience – laughter/tears/enlightenment/horror/desire for change
	choice of venue
	style of setting
	style of costume
	use of design elements
	number of performers
	dramatic structure
	political viewpoint
	period setting/context
	ratio of dialogue to movement
	degree of physical agility/dexterity
	use of verse/prose/song/narrative/monologue/duologue
	story-telling elements
	relationship with the audience.
	Try to identify as many of these aspects as you can in the work you have produced. Make any necessary adjustments to strengthen stylistic links, either through scripting, movement or design elements. Make sure that you emphasise these in your supporting notes.
It is not ready!	Plan additional rehearsals; work for longer periods; banish diversions. Keep at it! You will be amazed by how much you can accomplish with a corporate will to succeed.

31   Summary of Unit 4

Further reading

Alison Oddey, *Devising: A Practical and Theoretical Handbook*, Routledge, 1996

Anne Bogart, *A Director Prepares*, Routledge, 2001

Viola Spolin, *Improvisation for the Theatre*, North Western University Press, 2004

Litz Pisk, *The Actor and His Body*, Methuen, 2003

Chris Johnstone, *House of Games: Making Theatre for Everyday Life*, Nick Hern Books, 1998

Goat Island, *Schoolbook 2*, Goat Island and The School of the Art Institute of Chicago, 2000: see www.goatislandperformance.org/publication.htm

Tim Etchells, *Certain Fragments: Text and Writings on Performance*, Routledge, 2000.

In this unit you have learned about:

- the need to choose a theatrical style for your devised work
- how to choose a suitable style
- devising strategies
  - gathering and creating material
  - structuring and rehearsal
  - assessing, discarding, polishing
- devising methods for different styles of drama
- the available skills for assessment
- choosing your skill
- creating an ensemble of devisers: drawing up a contract between group members
- the role of the designer within the devising process
- devising as a group of performers
- the director's role within the devising process
- how one group devised a piece of drama from concept to finished piece
- how to prepare and present your supporting notes
- the importance of having clear intentions for your audience
- how to assess the finished piece and to refine it where necessary.

Glossary

A

absurdist theatre: a theatrical genre of the 1950s and 60s in which traditional theatrical conventions were abandoned in favour of a style of presentation which emphasised the meaninglessness of human existence.

adaptation: 1) a play created by adapting work created in a another medium (such as a novel or a film) for the theatre.
2) a translation or a rewriting of an existing play which makes significant changes to the original version.

anachronistic: placed in the wrong historical period.

aphorism: a short, witty saying.

apron: the part of the stage in front of the **proscenium arch**.

aside: words spoken that apparently only the audience can hear.

B

blank verse: a form of unrhymed poetry that has a regular rhythm and line length.

blueprint: a highly detailed plan.

bourgeois: the conventional, respectable middle-classes.

box set: a naturalistic setting, depicting a room consisting of three continuous walls with workable windows and doors.

business (or **biz**): a piece of action or interplay between characters that is not scripted but added for dramatic or comic effect.

C

cante jondo (deep song): traditional Spanish poems with simple form but highly emotional content, generally dealing with love, pain and death.

cartoon style: a highly exaggerated performance style, usually reserved for comic and villainous characters.

Code of honour: in Spain, the code of honour insisted upon honourable behaviour at all times and placed extreme importance on the idea of upholding and defending family honour – even to the death.

comedy: a humorous play, usually with a happy ending.

comedy of manners: a form of sophisticated comedy which satirises the lives of the upper classes.

commedia dell'arte: a form of comic theatre which originated in Italy and is based on improvisation.

commissioning: employing a writer to write a new script, usually to a specific brief or for a particular company.

cyclorama: a cloth or screen stretched tight in an arc around the back of a stage set.

D

design concept: an over-arching view of how a production will look and sound. It includes all aspects of theatrical design.

deus ex machina: the Classical Greek stage machinery that made a god appear to 'descend from Mount Olympus' to solve problems that the humans could not. The term describes any convenient, yet implausible, conclusion to a play involving divine or regal intervention in the lives of ordinary mortals.

dialectic: designed to stimulate consideration of both sides of an argument.

docu-theatre: documentary material presented in dramatic form.

dramatised novel: a play adapted from a novel.

duologue: a play or part of a play with speaking roles for only two actors.

E

ensemble: a group of actors working together and taking equal responsibility for the performance.

epic theatre: political theatre appealing more to the intellect than the emotions; a threatre from which Brecht adopted.

exposition: usually the first scene of a play, which gives the audience much of the information they need to make sense of the unfolding plot.

expressionism: a form of theatre that originated in Germany in the early twentieth century in which characters' inner feelings and/or thoughts are expressed outwardly in a form of physical expression.

F

farce: a form of popular comedy which presents characters in an increasingly improbable series of situations.

Fates: in Greek mythology there were three Fates – Clotho who spun the thread of a person's life, Lachesis who influenced the luck which that life received and Atropos who dictated the inescapable fate. When the thread was cut, this meant death.

flats: pieces of stage scenery used to create the impression of walls. A wooden frame is covered with stretched canvas or hardboard and painted or papered. They are usually about 6m high and 2–3m wide. When placed behind a 'window' on stage they are called 'backing flats'.

fourth wall: a term used by Stanislavski to describe how an audience in a proscenium arch theatre viewed the play as though through an invisible wall; the other three walls comprise the set.

G

gel: a coloured filter, placed into a lantern to cast either a strong or subtle light; short for gelatine, hence the spelling, from which they were originally made.

genre: a particular style of theatrical piece.

gestic acting: communicating the social attitude of a role in performance, through a combination of gesture and attitude involving deportment, intonation, facial expression and handling of props.

gobos: a cut-out stencil device used to create special lighting effects when placed within a profile spotlight – the beam is shaped to suggest, for example, prison bars, a dappled woodland or light pouring through a window.

H

Historical dramatisation: a popular style since Shakespeare wrote his history plays in the 16th century. Modern history plays include Peter Shaffer's *The Royal Hunt of the Sun* (1964) which explores the spanish conquistadors' expedition to Peru, and *Speaking like Magpies*, by Frank McGuinness, (2005) about the Gunpowder Plot.

I

imagery: figurative speech, including metaphors, similes and allusion used to stimulate images in the mind of the reader/audience.

impersonation: the imitation of the voice and mannerisms of a real-life person who is famous or notorious.

in-yer-face-theatre: shocking and violent theatrical presentation of disturbing and challenging subject matter.

J

Jacobean: the period of the reign of James I in England (1603–25). Jacobean comedy is notable for its satirical tone, while Jacobean tragedy is famous for being a very dark form of drama, depicting moral corruption and extreme violence.

jargon: specialist words and vocabulary used by a particular group or profession.

L

lazzi: improvised comic action within a piece of commedia dell'arte.

M

melodrama: sensational, sentimental plays, based on exaggerated and often incredible plot lines.

minimalism: an approach to staging which adopts a bare or nearly bare stage with limited use of visual design elements.

montage: a method of juxtaposing different images and/or theatrical elements to produce certain effects.

motif: a theme or idea in a play which recurs and which is elaborated upon.

multi-role: when actors play more than one part in the same play they are said to be 'multi-roling'.

N

naturalism: a type of drama which began in the late nineteenth century as an offshoot of **realism** which presented human character as being formed by heredity and environment.

O

oracle: in Ancient Greek times, people believed that the 'oracle' was the fount of all knowledge; the word oracle can be used to describe both a prophet and a piece of prophecy.

P

parable play: a play which is intended to teach a moral or social lesson.

performance score: the written directions of a piece of theatre that has few words in it and/or is based on physical skills.

period: the span of time within which a play is written and/or set – often linked to the reign of individual monarchs.

physical theatre: a style of performance which places most emphasis on the movement of the actor rather than the delivery of lines.

pietà: a picture or sculpture of the Virgin Mary holding the dead body of Christ on her lap or in her arms.

poetic drama: plays written in verse or in a heightened, poetic form of prose.

political theatre: theatre which promotes a specific political message or discusses a specific social issue.

pratfalls: comical falls and slapstick horseplay.

proscenium arch: the framed opening that separates the stage from the audience in traditional theatres.

prose: speeches that are written in continuous form without the aural features of rhyme or the visual structure of poetry.

R

realism: the faithful representation of life in literature and theatre.

representational: a setting that represents a location on stage rather than attempting to create the impression of reality on stage.

Restoration comedy: a rumbustious and often bawdy style of comedy that emerged after the restoration of the monarchy in 1660.

revenge tragedy: Elizabethan/Jacobean popular drama in which the main character seeks bloody revenge for the murder of a close friend or relative.

revolve: a stage with a large circular area that can be rotated either as part of the action or to reveal new sets.

rhyme: the similarity in the sound of word-endings, especially at the ends of lines.

running gag: a comic action, expression or routine which is repeated throughout a scene or play.

S

satire: using humour or exaggeration to expose and criticise people's stupidity or vices.

scenarios: imagined series of events or set of circumstances.

selective realism: a form of realism which presents a naturalistic acting role within a setting which contains a selection of authentic, realistic furnishings but which does not attempt to recreate a completely realistic set.

set-piece: a carefully crafted piece of stage action that depicts a situation that is typical within the genre of the play.

slapstick: originally two pieces of wood used by one character to hit another, making an exaggerated sound: generally now used to refer to any boisterous physical comic activity.

social milieu: the social world which individual or groups of characters inhabit.

spass: the German word for 'fun', used by Brecht in particular for social satire.

specials: a type of lighting effect designed to create specific illusions, for example, a bubble machine.

Stanislavkian: pertaining to the ideas or methods of Stanislavski.

storyboard: create a series of scenarios or images to make up the sequence of a plot.

subtext: the meaning behind the lines; what a character is thinking rather than saying.

surrealism: an artistic movement which started in the 1920s and creates its effects by juxtaposing incongruous images.

symbolism: an artistic/literary movement in which symbols represent aspects of characters' inner lives and ordinary objects are associated with deeper meanings.

synoptic assessment: the type of exam that tests your knowledge and understanding of the connections between different aspects of your course.

T

Theatre of Cruelty: a theory of drama proposed by Antonin Artaud in his book *The Theatre and Its Double*. The theory had many advocates in the twentieth century, including Peter Brook. Productions in this style tend to present a violent and ritualistic form of theatre.

theatrical censorship: British theatre has periodically been subject to political, religious or moral censorship. All theatre censorship in the UK was abolished in 1968 by the Theatre Act.

total theatre: a term applied to work which involves many varied aspects of performance styles, strongly visual and often devised and/or experimental.

traffic: in theatre terms, the comings and goings on stage, the stage business and action.

tragedy: a style of theatre which tracks the downfall of someone from security and happiness to abject misery and, usually, death.

tragi-comedy: a genre that blends elements of tragedy and comedy; it can take one of two forms, either a potentially tragic series of events is resolved happily, or a comic situation is presented with dark or bitter overtones.

transitions: the movement and changes between scenes in a play

transitive verb: a verb used with a direct object after it, e.g. she gave him an apple (from the *Latin transitivus*, meaning 'passing over').

V

verbatim theatre: a form of documentary theatre constructed from the actual words spoken by or written testimony of real people talking about real events.

verfremdungseffekte: alienation effects – devices which make the familiar seem strange to an audience.

W

well-made play: type of play with a formulaic structure which originated in France in the early 1800s.

workshops: rehearsals that explore the themes, issues, characters of the play in preparation, often including improvisations to explore and experiment with different aspects of the play.

Z

zanni: cheeky employees or servants.

Index